Postmemories of Terror

Palgrave Studies in Oral History

Series Editors: Linda Shopes and Bruce M. Stave

Postmemories of Terror

A New Generation Copes with the Legacy of the "Dirty War"

Susana Kaiser

POSTMEMORIES OF TERROR

First published in 2005 by
PALGRAVE MACMILLAN™
175 Fifth Avenue, New York, N.Y. 10010 and
Houndmills, Basingstoke, Hampshire, England RG21 6XS
Companies and representatives throughout the world.

PALGRAVE MACMILLAN is the global academic imprint of the Palgrave Macmillan division of St. Martin's Press, LLC and of Palgrave Macmillan Ltd. Macmillan® is a registered trademark in the United States, United Kingdom and other countries. Palgrave is a registered trademark in the European Union and other countries.

ISBN 1–4039–6464–5
ISBN 1–4039–6465–3

Library of Congress Cataloging-in-Publication Data

Kaiser, Susana, 1945–
    Postmemories of terror : a new generation copes with the legacy of the "Dirty War" / by Susana Kaiser.
        p. cm.—(Palgrave studies in oral history)
    Includes bibliographical references and index.
    ISBN 1–4039–6464–5—ISBN 1–4039–6465–3 (pbk.)
        1. Argentina—History—Dirty War, 1976–1983—Influence.
    2. Argentina—History—Dirty War, 1976–1983—Public Opinion.
    3. State—sponsored terrorism—Argentina—Psychological aspects.
    4. Memory—Social aspects—Argentina—Buenos Aires Metropolitan Area—History—20th century. 5. Youth—Argentina—Buenos Aires Metropolitan Area—Attitudes. 6. Youth—Argentina—Buenos Aires Metropolitan Area—Interviews. 7. Public opinion—Argentina—Buenos Aires Metropolitan Area. I. Title. II. Series.

F2849.2.K34 2005
982'.024—dc22   2005047561

A catalogue record for this book is available from the British Library.

Design by Newgen Imaging Systems (P) Ltd., Chennai, India.

First edition: December 2005

10 9 8 7 6 5 4 3 2 1

Printed in the United States of America.

A los desaparecidos

Contents

Series Editors' Foreword

Susana Kaiser's *Postmemories of Terror* extends the geographic reach of the Palgrave Studies in Oral History series to Latin America. More significantly, in a contemporary world invaded by terror, confronted by torture, and concerned with human rights, her work is particularly relevant.

Argentina's military dictatorship between 1976 and 1983 earned an infamous reputation for torture and terror. Thousands joined the ranks of the *desaparecidos*, "the disappeared," who were taken into custody by the dictatorship, never to be seen again. Their fate left an indelible mark on Argentine society. For many years after the events, groups such as the Mothers and Grandmothers of the Plaza de Mayo gathered on a weekly basis in Buenos Aires to keep alive the memory of those lost and the shame of the nation resulting from "the Dirty War." This volume explores how a younger Argentinean generation attempts to make sense of an era of which they have little or no direct memory.

While oral history ordinarily involves firsthand memory recalled years after events have occurred, Susana Kaiser employs the theory of "postmemories," which has been used to understand how the children of Holocaust survivors cope with the traumatic experience of their parents. What do young Argentineans know about what happened during the dictatorship? How did they find out about it? What sense do they make of these events? The volume is based upon sixty-three interviews undertaken by the author, who focuses upon themes such as justice, human rights, societal silence and fear, the imposition of terror, accountability, and just plain indifference in the face of dramatic events. Kaiser's analysis is probing and her insights should contribute to our understanding of how future generations may comprehend traumatic events in a post-9/11 world. Hence, her work transcends the focus on Argentina and has the promise of wide application.

We are pleased to include this volume as part of the Palgrave Studies in Oral History series, which is designed to make oral history accessible to the general reader as well as to students and scholars. As the series grows, it is our intent to demonstrate oral history's diverse substantive and methodological contributions. *Postmemories of Terror* moves us toward achieving that goal.

Bruce M. Stave
University of Connecticut

Linda Shopes
Pennsylvania Historical and Museum Commission

Acknowledgments

Writing this book has been a difficult, challenging, and rewarding experience. Researching how young Argentineans remember the traumatic events of the dictatorship is a project that I could have not envisioned, planned, and completed without the participation and collaboration of many people.

This is definitely a joint project. The coauthors of this study are the sixty-three young people who enthusiastically shared with me what they had been told about the dictatorship, their understanding of these events, and their thoughts about the present and the future of Argentina. While I looked back into my own experiences during those years, they taught me how my generation was transmitting this past and how it was being remembered. I learned a lot from them and I hope that I have not betrayed their trust in this project.

There are many people with whom I had long conversations in Buenos Aires that helped me to analyze and contextualize my findings: the *Madres de Plaza de Mayo* (mothers of the disappeared), members of HIJOS (children of the disappeared), and professors Alfredo Ghezzi, Aída Rotbart, Beatriz Castillejo, Felipe Pigna, and Alicia Sierra. And I am extremely grateful to the teachers, professors, and friends who introduced me to their students, relatives, and acquaintances.

This research was originally conducted for my dissertation. I was very fortunate to work with a very supportive committee. John Downing was its chair, my professor, and my advisor. Most important, he is a very dear friend. I have worked with him since I went back to graduate school and I thank him for his support and encouragement throughout each phase of this quest, up to the publication of this book. I also thank Henry Selby, America Rodriguez, Virginia Garrard-Burnett, and Charles Hale. I am grateful to the Institute of Latin American Studies at the University of Texas at Austin, particularly to its director Nicolas Shumway and to Anne Dibble.

My year at the University of California, Berkeley, as a Rockefeller postdoctoral fellow offered me the perfect environment to start working on this book manuscript. I am indebted to Michael Watts, who directed the project Communities in Crisis, the Human Rights Center and its director Eric Stover, the Townsend Center for the Humanities; Joe Nevins, with whom I shared many conversations about our projects; the graduate students at the seminar on Mass Violence, Accountability, Memory; and the participants at the dissertation writing workshop on Reconstructing Communities in Crisis.

I completed this project while teaching at the University of San Francisco. I cannot envision a better environment to pursue research related to human rights and social justice. My thanks to Father Stephen Privett, president of the university, Dean Jennifer Turpin, my colleagues in the Department of Media Studies and the Latin American Studies program, and to Kathy Nasstrom for her feedback on some drafts. I also thank my colleagues with whom I shared the many "ethnic minority" faculty-writing retreats organized by Pamela Balls Organista and where significant portions of this manuscript were completed.

I am indebted to Linda Shopes and Bruce M. Stave, editors of the Palgrave Studies in Oral History, for their support and enthusiasm for this project and their invaluable feedback throughout its different phases. The final version, however, is my sole responsibility. I also thank Palgrave Macmillan personnel involved in the production process.

I appreciate Mildred Burton's generosity for allowing me to reproduce in the cover of this book the image of her painting "The Mother of the Torturer."

I cannot name all my friends and colleagues whose support was invaluable. There are those who are far away and with whom I had long telephone or e-mail talks; some are part of my family of friends (which includes my cats): Maria Ester Barbieri, Armando Dugour, Jim Isenhath, Judith Ghinger, Vicky Sianja, Diana Morales, Claudia Boschiglia in memoriam, Liz Ruiz, Yeidy Rivero, Nidia Ojeda, Fernanda Hoekstra, Carlos Galli, César Buedo, Becky Lentz, Clemencia Rodriguez, and many, many more. Liz Ruiz also provided much needed copyediting, in particular for the lengthy quotes translated from the vernacular subculture of young Argentineans. These people are just a few of all those who helped me through this journey.

From the bottom of my heart, *gracias* to all of you!

Introduction

Introduction

The year is 1998. Twenty-two years after the military coup that unleashed one of the bloodiest repressions that Argentina has ever experienced, I am in Buenos Aires, my hometown, researching memories of the horror I once witnessed firsthand. I walk into the National Museum of Fine Arts to see the exhibit of works by Mildred Burton, a renowned Argentine painter. Ten minutes later, I am practically frozen contemplating a painting. It's the portrait of a woman who reminds me of Mona Lisa. Around her neck, a thin chain holds a quite unusual charm: a piece of a human finger. Who is she? Why is she wearing such a morbid necklace? The name of the painting answers my question: "The torturer's mother." I am transported back to the years of terror. While the generals and their accomplices orchestrated state terrorism and thousands of people were systematically and brutally kidnapped, disappeared, tortured, and killed, other Argentineans enjoyed an economic bonanza and traveled around the world. Like the mother in the painting, thousands of Argentineans adorned themselves with trophies without ever asking where they came from. They did not ask who was paying for their pleasures—the trips to Miami, the vacations in South Africa's apartheid society (indeed an appropriate spot to take a break from the repression), and the endless shopping that gained them the nickname "I'll take two." Whether it was for condominiums in Brazil or Ray Ban sunglasses, the affluent upper middle class went on mad shopping sprees because they had more expendable income than ever, thanks to the economic policies implemented during the terror.

I think about different mothers in the Argentina of the 1970s. Some had children who tortured and killed and others had children who suffered these abuses. How does the mother of the painting compare with our Mothers of the Plaza de Mayo, the Mothers of the *desaparecidos* (disappeared people)? How does her wanton ignorance contrast with the Mothers' courageous search for information about their missing children? Is she as proud of her son the torturer as the Mothers of the *desaparecidos* are of their daughters' and sons' political activism? Did she ever ask her son where he got that "precious stone"? Whether out of fear, ignorance, complacency, or an ideology born of greed and hatred, the mother in the painting, like many in Argentine society, is an accomplice to the terror.

Still looking at the painting, I am reminded of a ring I once had: three braided bands in pink, white, and yellow gold that my dear friend Marta Borrero borrowed from me the last time I saw her, twenty-two years earlier.[1] Was she wearing this ring when she disappeared? Did it become a trophy for her torturer and assassin? A ring on the finger of the friend I lost. A finger without a ring in the painting I am contemplating. Where is my ring now? Is it adorning the finger of a torturer's mother, wife, lover, or daughter? Was it melted to augment the pile of gold amid the spoils of war? Is it inside a jewelry box or maybe in a pawn shop window? We know that memory attaches itself to objects and places. A painting of a surreal necklace brings a memory of a simple gold ring and I am suddenly plunged into the past, into the terror of the 30,000 *desaparecidos*.

Memory is a subject permeating my stay in Buenos Aires. I explore memories of terror while digging into my past, cleaning out my family's home, and discovering old photos, letters, notebooks, and toys from my childhood. My memories keep coming back. It is time to close that place. I am "editing" my past, carefully deciding what stays and what goes.

My personal memories are intertwined with the collective memories of the terror. At the Cultural Center of the City of Buenos Aires, there is an exhibit titled "Memory's Restitution" (Restitución de la Memoria).[2] I then walk into the retrospective of Ricardo Carpani, whose drawing of Victor Jara—the famous Chilean musician assassinated by Pinochet—I found in my parents' home. It now decorates my office in San Francisco. Carpani's voice comes out from the video being screened. He talks of the need to reclaim our collective memory in order to recover the hope we need. If we do not have our own memory, he warns, the borrowed memory is colonization. One week later, I watch a play about a young woman coming to terms with her father's disappearance. She hugs her father's jacket, the only thing from him left to her. As I watch the play, a friend sitting next to me, whose husband was taken away when their daughter was three months old, whispers to me about her daughter's special attachment to her disappeared father's leather jacket. The playwright is correct. Memory attaches itself to objects.

How many stories and memories keep coming back to those of us who witnessed the horror? What are our own memories of the terror? Which are the experiences and stories that have been silenced? Which ones forgotten? How are we transmitting these events to the post-dictatorship generation? How are young people remembering terror?

This book focuses on how young Argentineans remember the traumatic events of the military dictatorship (1976–1983), their "postmemories." Marianne Hirsch defines "postmemory" as a second-generation memory characterized by displacement and belatedness, which is the memory of the children of survivors of cultural or collective trauma (the Holocaust in her case).[3] Descendants remember their parents' experiences through images they have seen and stories they were told. Postmemory, thus, implies intergenerational interconnections by which people adopt their elders' memories as their own. It is the process of reconstruction of memories by the descendants of the witness generation. We are talking of "memories of memories," to borrow an expression from Luisa Passerini, who also talks of layers of memory, of a chain of representations by which you receive a representation and you create new ones.[4] Although more mediated and less connected to the past, postmemory is in itself a powerful and highly significant form of memory.

Based on oral histories with young people from Buenos Aires who were neither direct victims nor political activists, but who were born during the terror or afterward, and who had an entirely mediated knowledge of it, I explore how the post-dictatorship generation was reconstructing this past from three main sources available to it: inter- and intragenerational dialogue (including the extended family, friends, neighborhood, and community), education, and the communication media—the media broadly defined to include television, popular music, film, and street demonstrations.[5]

By incorporating the voices of the average person, beyond victims and victimizers, this work empirically explores the impact of state terrorism on millions of Argentineans. Research on societies that have recently undergone mass human rights abuses has disregarded the "second-generation/non-victim" perspective. Young people's stories shed light on how the memory construction process works by revealing how those who lived through the dictatorship were reconstructing and transmitting this experience to their descendants. These are key issues for assessing the legacy of terror and the roles that this new generation of citizens might play in the consolidation of democracy.[6] These conversations with young Argentineans discuss selected and recurrent themes such as societal fears and silences, patterns of remembering and forgetting, historical explanations, impunity, indifference, and justice. They also provide much needed examples of key but often abstract concepts such as the meaning of accountability, a culture of impunity, and the legacy of fear.

Historical Background

Let us now focus on the events whose postmemories we explore here. On March 24, 1976, a military coup installed a bloody and repressive dictatorship in Argentina. During the seven years that followed (1976–1983), the dictatorship implemented a program of state terrorism aimed at eliminating political dissent that left an estimated 30,000 *desaparecidos*.[7] The systematic abduction, torture, and killing of activists, as well as the kidnapping of babies born in the torture chambers, characterized the reign of terror imposed by the military juntas. Human rights violations ranged from torments of pregnant women that included the torture of the fetus to torturing individuals in the presence of their relatives to make them speak, including mutilations, torture, and killing of children, and impalements.

How can we begin to understand why these crimes happened? How was it possible for the perpetrators to commit such atrocities? Who allowed this to happen?

Were there any precedents? Indeed, a few insights into Argentina's history tell us that massive human rights violations did not start with the last dictatorship.

During the years as a Spanish colony, following the "discovery" and brutal conquest of America, Buenos Aires was the port where African slaves were brought to work in the silver mines of Potosí (Bolivia). This key role in the slave trade, certainly less visible than the sugar or cotton plantations in other regions of the continent, contributed to the chronicles of the horror.[8] In 1816, Argentina declared its independence from Spain. This was followed by postindependence wars and the ascendance to power of an oligarchy that continued to annihilate indigenous populations while taking over their lands—a genocidal campaign that is another bloody chapter of the country's history.

During the twentieth century, two political parties emerged that continue to have a presence in Argentine politics. One was the Radical Party of Hipólito Irigoyen, which challenged the hegemony of the elite Conservative Party. His government ended with a military coup in 1930. This initiated a cycle that lasted more than fifty years and could be defined as "military dictatorships interrupted by civilian governments." The other was the Peronist Party, named after Juan Domingo Perón, who, with his wife Evita, was massively supported by the workers' movement. Perón, elected president in 1946, was overthrown by a military coup in 1955 before completing his second term. Evita had died, he went into exile, and the Peronist Party was banned for almost two decades. During this period, several guerrilla organizations emerged. Most were inspired by the Cuban Revolution and some had close ties to the Peronist Left. Furthermore, many movements for social change, not involved in armed struggle, were extremely active on several fronts. The dominant classes perceived them as a threat.[9]

In 1973, Perón returned and became president for a third term, with his wife Isabel Martínez ("Isabelita") as vice president. At that time, the two main guerrilla groups were ERP (Ejército Revolucionario del Pueblo) and Montoneros, a Peronist organization with whom Perón would soon cut ties. Perón died in 1974 and Isabelita took over. Her government issued a decree to combat and annihilate "subversion." Repression and killings at the hands of paramilitary groups increased. Violence was accompanied by economic turmoil. Although the guerrillas did not pose any significant threat, they were the excuse for the military to take power in 1976.

But to analyze the dictatorship isolated from the regional political context would result in a partial vision of it. During the 1970s, military regimes were a widespread form of government in the Americas. The militarized continent was, in part, the result of events that developed in the post–World War II period. The U.S. fear of communism gave rise to the encouragement of a new role for the Latin American military. The Doctrine of National Security, an ideology developed with the endorsement of Washington and by the joint armies of the Americas, aimed at presenting a common front to prevent the spread of communism. A strong army, prepared to fight subversion, became essential to supplement or even replace those civil governments unable to fulfill the role demanded of them.[10] The School of the Americas in Panamá (later relocated to Ft. Benning, Georgia, and in 2001 reincarnated as the Western Hemisphere Institute for Security Cooperation) was the institution where Latin American soldiers were trained for these tasks.[11] Operación Cóndor was an "enterprise" promoted by the CIA through the DINA (Chilean dictatorship's intelligence agency) and with the governments of Argentina, Brazil, Bolivia, Chile, Uruguay, Paraguay, and Peru. It coordinated intelligence and repression throughout the region: Uruguayan police tortured people in Argentina, paramilitary groups kidnapped Argentine exiles in Brazil, and Chilean death squads carried out assassinations in Buenos Aires.[12]

As a precedent, and in preparation for a potential communist insurgency, in the late 1950s, the Argentine military had hired French specialists in fighting "communism" in Indochina and Algiers. Thus, the dictatorship was guided by French and U.S. counterinsurgency techniques (notably the French *doctrine de guerre revolutionnaire*," founded on the premise that subversive warfare is a war to conquer the population's soul and needs to be fought on all fronts), which the military adopted in implementing a state of terror to impede any support for what they considered the enemy.[13]

Many factors weakened military rule: escalating international criticism for its human rights record, a disproportionate increase in foreign debt (from 8 to 45 billion dollars), an economic plan detrimental to national industries—with the consequent rise in unemployment and criticism from sectors that had previously supported the dictatorship—and the defeat in the war against England over the Malvinas/Falkland Islands in 1982. It was time to leave. In preparation for handling power, the military issued the "Final Document on the Struggle against Subversion and Terrorism" (dated April 28, 1983), a self-amnesty in which pride for the "mission accomplished" scantily referred to certain "mistakes" that might have been committed.[14]

Raúl Alfonsín, from the Radical Party and the first civilian president after the terror, took office in December 1983. He ran and won on the basis of a human rights agenda, promising thorough investigations into the crimes and punishment of the culprits. The Truth Commission to investigate disappearances (1983–1984) and the military juntas' trials (1985), which resulted in the top commanders being sent to jail, were without precedent in a region devastated by violence and terror.[15] The Comisión Nacional para la Desaparición de Personas (CONADEP) issued its report, *Nunca Más,* which became an overnight bestseller. CONADEP was the second truth commission in a Latin American country making the transition to civilian rule. The first was in Bolivia and others followed in Uruguay, Chile, El Salvador, Ecuador, Guatemala, Honduras, and Perú.[16] It would also influence the design of the South African Truth and Reconciliation Commission (TRC).[17] A key difference is that the much publicized inquiries of the TRC sought truth and reconciliation, while the Argentine commission aimed at truth and justice and its report played a major role in the prosecution of high-ranking officers.

Unfortunately, the process of bringing torturers to justice was short-lived. The legalization of impunity through amnesty laws and presidential pardons revealed the civilian governments' partial commitment to justice and the military's power to set limits. "Full Stop" and "Due Obedience" were impunity laws approved by Alfonsín's government in 1986 and 1987, respectively.[18] "Full Stop" applied the statute of limitations to the prosecution of torturers and assassins, and "Due Obedience" acquitted them on the basis that they were obeying orders, even though the Nuremberg Trials established that this was in violation of international law and refused defenses based on superior orders. The Argentine trials had sentenced the top commanders, but when it was time to prosecute their subordinates, the government sanctioned "Due Obedience" in response to an uprising led by younger officers who demanded a stop to attacks against the military.[19]

The process of legalizing impunity was completed when Carlos Menem, from the Peronist Party and the second civilian president, pardoned the few *represores* who were in prison (1989–1990).[20] (*Represores* is a generic term for torturers, assassins, "disappearers" [of people] and their accomplices). This radically altered the moment of great expectations that had characterized the commencement of civilian rule.

Competing Memories

But how are these events remembered? We know that nations are political constructs, imagined, contested, and shaped through political processes, marked by the creation of myths and heroes that can unite people into groups sharing identities and memories.[21] Moreover, as Ernest Renan noted a long time ago, "The essence of a nation is that all individuals have many things in common, and also that they have forgotten many things."[22] In post-dictatorship Argentina, as in other societies that underwent repression such as Franco's Spain or Pinochet's Chile, we can talk of a process of reconstructing a common history and memory, of which what is to be remembered and what is to be forgotten are essential components.[23]

Memory has political value and power. Historical accounts that are reshaped to fit and legitimize a present social order are based on the perception that the past influences actions in the present and the future, that people's memories affect their beliefs and choices. The importance of the past and the political value of memories are precisely their active existence in the present.[24] Oral history presents us the "way in which popular memories are constructed and reconstructed as part of a contemporary consciousness."[25]

Different mnemonic groups battle for the acceptance of their versions of the past; a society's memories are subject to manipulation and challenges, and are negotiated and defined within a context of debate.[26] Conflicting positions toward the dictatorship characterized the post-1983 Argentine democratic transition. Who the victims are, who is responsible, why things happened the way they did, what could have been avoided, and what is to be done now are some of the issues engaging—and dividing—society. Since there are many memories competing for hegemony, the interaction between dominant/official and alternative/popular memories is key to understanding these battles to control the past. We can talk of three major "memories" of the dictatorship as represented in public discourses, each one corresponding to a different ideological position toward this past. Each of them can be explored following Peter Burke's useful advice: "Who wants whom to remember what and why? Who wants whom to forget what and why?"[27]

One can be labeled as the "Military" version. Certain sectors of the armed forces and their supporters want to be honored for winning their "war against subversion." The dictatorship presented the previous period as a total chaos—which it was—where society was "endangered" by subversive terrorists—which was not true. In fact, estimates of the size of guerrilla organizations combining ERP and Montoneros range from 800 to 1,300.[28] During the terror, authorities denied that anything wrong was going on, often claiming ignorance about the brutal and obvious state-orchestrated repression—that is, there were no prisoners; the *desaparecidos* were vacationing in Europe. The dictatorship defined its reign of terror as the "Process of National Reconstruction"—popularly referred to as *proceso*. Labeling a conflict is one way of assigning meaning to it. Human rights abusers often use terms that conceal the brutality of their actions and that may shape future interpretations. At the beginning of civilian rule, and during their trials, military leaders continued to deny their crimes in spite of the evidence incriminating them.[29]

But there have been changes. In 1995, a *mea culpa* by Army Commander General Martín Balza was the most significant official acknowledgment of their crimes. However, extremely conservative sectors within the armed forces continue to vindicate or deny crimes. Outrageous declarations are combined with ludicrous claims by military officers—for instance, they do not "remember" where they were at that time, had no idea of the existence of tortures and disappearances, or insist that there was no systematic stealing of babies.[30] But only a few publicly voice their support for this position. This silence may show how critical society is of the terror but also how the unpopularity of this ideology restrains its supporters from expressing overtly what they think—a "politically correct" silence that might hide a different reality.[31]

In sharp contrast is the human rights movement's historical explanation, the second major frame of memory. For them, atrocious crimes against humanity were committed, a genocide that should be fully investigated and followed by punishment of those found guilty. They won't settle for less than full disclosure of truth and justice. Through their activism on many fronts, different organizations continue to investigate what happened in order to reconstruct the truth of the horror that took place. They continue collecting information, denouncing those responsible, and demanding accountability under the provisions of national and international law. They are committed to campaigns aimed to ensure that society won't forget this past and to reminding the public at large that impunity is not an option they are willing to accept. The three most visible groups are those dominated by relatives of *desaparecidos*: the Mothers of the Plaza de Mayo (mothers of *desaparecidos*), Grandmothers of the Plaza de Mayo (grandmothers in search of their grandchildren), and HIJOS (an organization formed by the adult daughters and sons of *desaparecidos*, murdered political activists, or activists forced into exile). The acronym HIJOS stands for Hijos Por la Identidad y la Justicia Contra el Olvido y el Silencio (Daughters and Sons for Identity and Justice against Forgetting and Silence).

Between these two polarized positions is the third major category of memory, this wide arena of many intermediate and negotiated explanations that seek to construct a past with a history that many groups can share. This intermediate position includes analyses of the events that recognize the crimes but often question their magnitude, admit that "excesses" were committed, try to rationally "explain" them, divide responsibilities in ways that encourage a discourse that usually favors forgiving and forgetting. Quite often, it assigns society to the position of a passive spectator. Within this version, the dictatorship is also known as the "dirty war," another labeling that shapes interpretations and connotes images of a fight between two armies rather than the massacre that took place.[32] This position can be recognized in the discourses of political parties and politicians willing to negotiate assignment of guilt and punishment. The most popular ideological explanation here is what is known as "the theory of the Two Devils"—the violence of the state as a response to the violence of the guerrilla forces, the two devils that terrorized society.[33]

Thus, these were the main events, ideas, and actors that characterized the process of democratization. As for the political environment at the time of this fieldwork, the conversations presented in the chapters that follow took place in 1998, at a very special juncture in the country's history, a time when the past had decisively intensified its presence in the public sphere. Local initiatives and major developments in the globalization of justice had reinvigorated the challenges to impunity. Former dictator Videla was jailed for kidnapping babies born in captivity, a crime not contemplated by the impunity laws. HIJOS were very active with their *escraches* (public demonstrations against *represores*).[34] New "Truth Trials" emerged to reconstruct the truth of what had happened to disappeared people.[35] Impunity laws were revoked, thereby allowing the initiation of trials against those *represores* not previously put on trial.[36] Campaigns to bring human rights abusers to trial in foreign forums increased at this time, as well.[37] Public outrage defeated Menem's initiative to turn a former torture center (ESMA) into a monument to "national unity." The Soccer World Cup (el Mundial) was taking place in France and discussions about it often prompted comparisons with the 1978 Mundial that took place in, and was won by, Argentina at the peak of the repression. Media coverage of all these events was extensive and it was almost impossible for a person who watched television, listened to the radio, or read a newspaper to be unaware of the human rights violations committed or the issues of legal retribution and impunity.

Memory Matters

Why explore memory? Why are we so interested in what we call, often rather vaguely, collective, cultural, social, public, historical, or popular memory to refer to those shared memories that are socially and culturally influenced? Why are we so concerned about how societies remember if we know that memory is uncertain, inconsistent, and deceiving?

During this fieldwork, an incident occurred that attests to the fragility and unreliability of memories. I was with friends who were back in Argentina after living many years in exile. We had not seen each other for over two decades. There were emotions, embraces, the joy of being reunited, and the sadness for those who were no longer with us.

One of my friends reminded me of a day when, twenty-two years earlier, during the year of the military coup, in the midst of the repression and the terror, I ventured into her apartment, where a Montonero activist was in hiding for a couple of days. The activist was depressed, fearful of the dangerous circumstances in which he found himself, and apprehensive about what the future held. So, two of my friends decided to "cheer the guy up." He'd been talking about all the things he had not yet done, one of which was flying in an airplane, and my two friends wanted to help him fulfill his dream of flying. I was a flight attendant at the time, so they called me up for help. Apparently, I went to my friend's place at the crack of dawn, carrying my airline uniform in a bag. Military presence in the neighborhood was intense because a high-ranking officer lived next door. Once in the apartment, I expeditiously put on my uniform as they finished preparing breakfast. We woke the activist up with a "show," a tongue-in-cheek simulation of a flight takeoff: my bilingual welcome speech, instructions for mask and life jacket, and as finale breakfast on a tray. The activist was doubled over with laughter. For half an hour, the surrounding horror had faded and we laughed in spite of the fear. When the laughter subsided, I apparently changed back into my civilian clothing and left without a word.

As my friend told the story, I was perplexed. The tricks of memory hit my own recollections. I didn't remember a thing; I had completely edited this episode out of my memories; it had been totally forgotten. As I write these lines, I still cannot remember that this happened, despite confirmation from other old friends, not present, who had heard about the incident later on. I have only a vague recollection, jarred by the story told me, of walking very quickly toward a building, very early one morning, carrying a bag and frightened. I am convinced that the fear I felt at that time acted as the big eraser. What other reason could there be for this memory gap? Of the other three witnesses, besides myself, only one is still around to remind me of this episode. We do not know what happened to the activist who hid at my friend's house for three nights. We do know that our other friend is one of the 30,000 *desaparecidos*.

As I explored the reconstruction of this past by the post-dictatorship generation, I kept reminding myself not only of the unreliability of memories but also of their importance. For memory is more about what we believe happened than about what actually took place. Indeed, the value of actual facts is relative if they are not perceived as truth. Hence, memories of the dictatorship may be subject to distortion but, ultimately, they constitute Argentineans' perceptions of the past terror and reveal what this historical period meant for them. As Portelli notes, memory is a "process of creation of meanings."[38] What these young Argentineans believed happened, their postmemories, may prove more important that what actually happened. For what we think took place in the past informs and shapes our way of thinking and acting in the present, or how we insert ourselves within a historical process. That is why in the pursuit of truth and justice we must be relentless in uncovering the facts within the haze of our selective and sometimes contradictory "memories."

By looking at how societies remember, we want to learn about many things.[39] There is the process of collective remembering, how different groups and communities construct particular representations of a historical event. We can identify diverse "memory communities"[40] within the post-dictatorship generation, such as the already mentioned major memories.

We are concerned with the mechanisms of historical memory and amnesia, and with how and by whom those mechanisms are influenced. Since we cannot remember everything, memory is highly selective, registering some data and discarding others.[41] Because memory and amnesia are "different sides of the same coin,"[42] what is remembered or forgotten about the dictatorship are both "memories" of it.[43]

We want to identify the modes by which public memories are transmitted and the ways in which historians, the mass media, or other official records shape the memory of communities—that is, the truth commission's report, investigations by human rights groups, textbooks, or television programs. Oral histories present an inventory of different forms of transmission and provide insights into how young Argentineans assign meanings to these messages.[44]

We are interested in the uses of memory and of oblivion, the political questions that arise when a nation selects what to remember, and the effects of governments' attempts to manipulate memory. The ultimate fantasy in controlling individuals' memories is found in Ridley Scott's film *Blade Runner*, where the "replicants" (fabricated "human beings") were given a memory chip determining their past and remembrances. But imposing memories is not that simple in real life. As in Argentina, countless examples worldwide reveal that the promotion of mass amnesia and selective remembering is not always effective.[45]

In this work, I am also concerned with how memories are shaping the way in which young people are inserting themselves in the historical process initiated by the dictatorship. I rely on Tzvetan Todorov's concept of exemplary memory, when the past becomes a principle for action in the present and the lessons learned are used to struggle against current injustices.[46] Memory at the service of justice is a central issue for human rights activists, whose insistence on remembering the past is aimed at challenging impunity. I am particularly focused on this way of remembering, on an active memory firmly grounded in the present and looking at the future. Since memories are the representations we have of the past, our knowledge of it—I am interested in the link between knowledge and political activism and in whether or not silences result in ignorance and ignorance in a lack of participation; that is, if I do not talk, I do not know; therefore it is really simple to take no action.

We need to consider, as well, that young Argentineans' postmemories are influenced and filtered by terror. Survivors of political violence, ranging from Holocaust victims to Southeast Asian refugees, present syndromes that are consequences of prolonged and repeated trauma.[47] But the direct victims are not the only ones affected. Martín-Baró studied the collective nature of post-traumatic stress disorder (PTSD), proposing the concept of "psychosocial trauma" to define the damage produced by state terrorism on individuals and society in general. He theorized that we can identify a traumatized Palestinian society or a disturbed Nazi German society capable of aberrant institutional behavior. He further argued that climates of fear and terror might cause a collective political apathy.[48] In Argentina, research conducted during the terror revealed that people accepted otherwise unacceptable conditions out of fear.[49] Adapting to fear or ignoring the surrounding horror—issues discussed by participants—show how a traumatized or disturbed society behaved during the repression and how this process works over the years.

The case of Argentina merits special attention to the generational component of memories. Pierre Nora suggests that a generation is a realm of memory, a product of memory, and an effect of remembering.[50] Generations align themselves around historical markers. Its members share what stands behind them and are fabricators of mnemonic sites that are revived by narratives, documents, or firsthand accounts. But what does it mean and where lies the relevance of a generation becoming a *lieu de mémoire* (site or realm of memory)?[51] Moreover, Nora argues that generational memory grows out of social interaction and finds expression in public places and centers for collective participation such as demonstrations or coffee shops, noting that the starting point for exploring generational memory is an inventory of these sites.[52]

We are faced here with two main generations shaping memories of the terror. The members of the generation that witnessed the events are playing a main role in constructing representations of them, in interpreting what happened, in explaining its genesis. It is in this process, and in the transmission of this past to their descendants, that they are creating the *lieux de mémoire* of this past. As a member of this generation, I am aware that our stories and silences are characterizing "the generation of the dictatorship." This is done by our looking back at where we were, what we did and why, and by looking at how, why, where, and with whom we share our recollections. I am referring to all the witnesses, irrespective of their ideology or political participation during those years. Exploring the witness generation, thus, contextualizes historical events and contributes to the understanding of contemporary politics.[53]

There are certain historical markers of the generation of the dictatorship, specifically of those politically active during the early 1970s, which were times of struggle for social change, of intense participation on a variety of fronts by large segments of the younger population, leading to the military coup of 1976 and the subsequent repression. These markers consist of major marches and public demonstrations, certain cafés in Buenos Aires, bookstores, books, magazines, and songs. They include the café "La Paz" on Corrientes Avenue, the music of Intillimani, Quilapayún, and Huerque Mapu, the magazine *Crisis,* and books such as Eduardo Galeano's *The Open Veins of Latin America* and Frantz Fanon's *The Wretched of the Earth.* Moreover, because *lieux de mémoire* often have a geographical component, we can rely on the notion of the topography of memory as a useful framework to "read" the city of Buenos Aires and identify those sites that embody society's memories. We can mention the Plaza de Mayo, a legacy of colonial times surrounded by an embodiment of three big powers (the Government Palace, the cathedral, and major banks) and a physical space that also lies at the heart of Buenos Aires' political activism—and repression; we can also name former torture centers or buildings shattered by the violence of "counterinsurgency" operations, as military authorities labeled their raids to seize their victims.

But what about the post-dictatorship generation? What is the meaning that those historical markers have for the young Argentineans whose stories we discuss here? How are they adopting their elders' memories and reconstructing their postmemories of terror? Nora notes that each generation rewrites its generational history.[54] He further argues that subsequent generations "hold what they supplant in reserve for possible revival toward new ends."[55] Thus, young people are also involved in a memory construction process, in writing their generation's history, in aligning themselves around historical markers, in defining the relevance and weight that the dictatorship has for them, in creating *lieux de mémoire* of this past. Their attitudes toward this historical period illustrate how they reinterpret those events and the particular goals that this past is serving. Their postmemories also have specific contents and particular media for their transmission. They too have their gathering sites, their events, and their own forms of cultural production ranging from videos to popular songs. As we will see, hip-hop can be turned into a cry against torture and disappearance.

The generational transmission and elaboration of traumatic pasts points to the importance of post-conflict generations as political actors in present and future times. This past is not over and young people have roles to play in either remembering or forgetting this past. Young Argentineans' postmemories are necessarily shaped by their elders' experiences during the terror. But memory also "sidesteps"; there is a "horizontal or lateral passage of memory."[56] This intragenerational sharing among young people reaffirms or challenges their elders' stories.

However, the memories of those who lived under the dictatorship might be constantly reshaped by what is discussed—or silenced—at home, in the work place, or with friends. Our memories undergo constant changes and the events we witnessed are transformed by the stories we tell. As Gabriel García Márquez warns in the introduction of his autobiography, "Life is not what one lived, but what one remembers and how one remembers it in order to recount it."[57] The post-dictatorship generation, thus, has been listening to diverse, and changeable, stories about the years of terror.

Whose Histories?

Whose life stories are we talking about? The sixty-three young people with whom I had the conversations in this study were members of the post-dictatorship generation who lived within the metropolitan area of the city of Buenos Aires, capital of the country, where the repression had been particularly severe. Approximately 35 percent of the country's population lives in this area and people from other provinces or neighboring countries have migrated there. There is an interaction of communities and young people are often in contact with peers from different cultures and backgrounds, including families who brought with them the experiences of other Latin American dictatorships.

The selection of participants was based on two criteria: one generational, the other relating to their families' experiences during the dictatorship. With a few exceptions, at the time of fieldwork (1998) their ages ranged between fifteen and twenty-two. Fifteen years had passed since the return to civilian rule and twenty-two since the military coup, hence the reason for the selection of this age bracket was to secure a group of varying ages who were all born after the coup and thus were "children of the dictatorship."

My subjects were "gray zoners," meaning that they were not "direct victims" of the repression—as is the case with children of the *desaparecidos*—and were neither human rights activists nor advocates of military rule—all of whom know well where they stand regarding the past.[58] My decision to talk to those who could be situated in this middle zone was intended to facilitate a deeper understanding of the processes of memory construction in wider sectors of society, necessarily shaped by how those sectors were affected or touched by the dictatorship. However, working with gray zoners had its surprises. There were interviewees with police and military officers in their families, with disappeared relatives, with stories of exile and persecution—signs of the pervasiveness of the repression and of how blurry a gray zone is. Hence, I found several links with "direct victims" and "victimizers" among participants.

There were similarities and differences among participants. They may have been comparable in age or may have studied from the same textbooks, but they were from different social, cultural, or ideological backgrounds. All of them grew up during civilian rule. The older ones, who were very small during the dictatorship, were the only ones who had some remembrances of life under terror or the Alfonsín years. For most participants, "Menemismo" (President Menem's policies) and neoliberalism were their main referents of democracy. I refer specifically to a glorification of the market economy, the dismantling of state institutions, the privatization of basic services, an economic growth with high social costs, including unemployment and underemployment, a widening gap between the "haves" and the "have nots," the obscene ostentation of overnight millionaires, rampant corruption at all levels, and impunity for the dictatorship's crimes.

Participants were representative of a wide spectrum of social classes, ranging from those who were born and lived in shantytowns to those belonging to an upper class and residing in exclusive neighborhoods. Few belonged to these two extremes and most of them were from different sections of the middle class. This variety is reflected by the occupations of their parents, which are usually indicators of income—for example, a lawyer, a building superintendent, a small business owner, a police officer, a professor, a housekeeper. Some lived in single-parent households supported by women. In many cases both parents worked, in others the mother worked at home. Most of them studied, either attending high school or college. Many of them also worked in a variety of occupations.

Participants

Each participant is listed by code name, participant number, age, and occupation at the time of the interviews (May–August 1998). I have indicated whether it was an individual interview or group session, the audio tape(s) where the interview was recorded, and any available and/or relevant details about the participants or their families. Information about each participant is uneven due to the variations in the time I spent with each one or the type of information they were willing to share.

I conducted eleven in-depth interviews that lasted from one to three hours and seventeen discussion groups including fifty-two participants. Discussion groups with high school students usually included four participants and lasted one hour. Other groups were usually limited to two participants and lasted from two to three hours. Transcripts of the interviews number 450 single-spaced pages. Tapes and transcripts are located at the Gleeson Library, University of San Francisco. All interviews were conducted in Spanish and translated by me. This didn't pose major difficulties but added another level of translation to the one that, as Bourdieu reminds us, starts with the process of transcribing, where in addition to the many things that are lost (tone of voice, silences, emphasis, gestures, body language) the punctuation chosen can change the whole meaning of a sentence.[59] I have tried to convey participants' voices with as little editing as possible. Edits were mainly the removal of word and sentence repetitions or reordering of the sentences to convey more accurately the meaning given by interviewees.[60]

I have quoted most participants, but some more than others because their personalities, ways of thinking, or family experiences during the dictatorship made their opinions especially illustrative of this study's findings—for instance, if they had relatives in the military, parents who had been political activists, or if they played certain roles in the group discussions we had that shaped the interchange of ideas among their peers and myself. Quotes were selected considering the following criteria: those that in my judgment best represented a particular trend or pattern; those that provided a wide spectrum of the accounts circulating. Since the aim was to identify memories of the dictatorship, I made sure to include as much variety as possible, even if an opinion was expressed by only a couple of participants.

I have not included the specific questions that prompted the answers or comments quoted, in order to maintain uniformity between quotes from participants interviewed individually and those in group discussions where statements were often responses to other participants' words. (See appendix with sample questions.) Similarities and exceptions are indicated with such statements as "the majority," "some," or "none." Unless otherwise specified, when I say "most of," "many of," or "few of" the young people, I refer to the sixty-three participants in this study or to the peers they referred to and am not generalizing about Argentinean youth.

Alberto (#23), 21. Studying for teacher's certification. Discussion group. (Tapes #15–16).

Alicia (#25), 19. Parents and uncles are police officers. Studying for teacher's certification. Went to a Catholic nun's high school. She is a catechist at a parish in a working-class neighborhood. Discussion group. (Tapes #16–17).

Analía, (#1), 20. College student at public university, communication major. Lives in a high-class neighborhood. Individual interview. (Tape #1).

Andrea (#52), 15. High school student at public school. Has a disappeared aunt. Discussion group. (Tape #31).

Andrés (#41), 18. High school student at public school. Coproduces a community radio program. His father was a Peronist activist, at times in hiding during the terror. Discussion group. (Tapes #27–28).

Antonio (#37), 20. Studies Law at private university. Works at the administration office of a hotel. Individual interview. (Tapes #26–27).

Ariel (#50), 15. High school student at public school. Discussion group. (Tapes #30–31).

Beatriz (#44), 15. High school student at public school. Discussion group. (Tape #30).

Carlos (#2), 21. Works as clerical employee at an advertising agency. He is interested in studying computer graphics but dropped his studies for financial reasons. He would also like to become an instructor in gymnastics/exercise. Individual interview. (Tapes #1–2).

Carmen (#30), 22. Student at public university, education major. Works at shopping mall. Discussion group. (Tapes #20–21).

Clara (#60), 17. High school student at public school. Discussion group. (Tape #31).

Claudia (#8), 15. High school student at one of the two top public schools of Buenos Aires. Her parents are medical doctors and she lived in the United States since she was three years old until she was nine. Discussion group. (Tape #6).

Cristina (#58), 17. High school student at public school. Discussion group. (Tape #31).

Diego (#28), 21. Studying for teacher's certification. Very active in religious organizations. Many family members were Peronist militants. Discussion group. (Tapes #19–20).

Elena (#19), 15. High school student at public school. Discussion group (Tape #11).

Elsa (#62), 17. High school student at public school. Her uncle was exiled; her aunt had many friends who disappeared. Discussion group. (Tape #31).

Elvira (#40), 22. High school student at public school. Coproduces a community radio program. Discussion group. (Tapes #27–28).

Ester (#54), 15. High school student at public school. Discussion group. (Tape #31).

Eugenia (#34), 22. Studies medicine at public university. Works at an export/import firm. Attended high school at Catholic nun's school. Her father worked at a government office and lost his job during the dictatorship. Individual interview. (Tape #24).

Fabiana (#46), 15. High school student at public school. Discussion group. (Tape #30).

Fernando (#33), 20. He is a musician and studies music. Works at computer firm. Discussion group. (Tape #23).

Flor (#4), 16. High school student at an elite public school. She is active at the student center and very critical of the dictatorship. She is the only participant who has no television at home. She loves to read and reads a lot. Individual interview. (Tape #4).

Gloria (#17), 17. High school student at public school. Discussion group. (Tape #11).

Graciela (#45), 15. High school student at public school. Discussion group. (Tape #30).

Guillermo (#32), 20. Student at a private university, computer science major. Works at computer firm. His father retired from the military. Lived his childhood in military bases. Discussion group. (Tape #23).

Héctor (#13), 16. High school student at public school. His parents are from Paraguay. He participated in two discussion groups. (Tapes #7–8).

Hugo (#48), 15. High school student at public school. Discussion group. (Tapes #30–31).

Inés (#63), 16. High school student at an exclusive private religious school. Discussion group. Her mother's cousin was a guerrilla and was killed. (Tape #32).

Irma (#38), 19. High school student at public school. Coproduces a community radio program. Her family has lived in a *villa* (shantytown) for three generations. Discussion group. (Tapes #27–28).

Jorge (#42), 18. High school student at public school. Works in a newsstand. Coproduces a community radio program. Discussion group. (Tapes #27–28).

Josefina (#64), 16. High school student at an exclusive private religious school. Discussion group. (Tape #32).

Juan (#35), 23. Student at public university, communication major. Works as journalist in a newspaper. Individual interview. (Tape #25).

Laura (#26), 19. Studying for teacher's certification. Was pregnant from Ricardo (#27) and they were planning to move together after the baby was born. "Red diaper baby," both parents were political activists, mother was in the Communist Party. (Tapes #19–20).

Leo (#47), 15. High school student at public school. Discussion group. (Tapes #30–31).

Leonardo (#16), 22. Studying for teacher's certification. He works at a "clandestine" quiniela agency (gambling comparable to lotto). Discussion group. (Tape #9).

Liliana (#18), 15. High school student at public school. Discussion group. (Tape #11).

Lucía (#6), 15. High school student at one of the two top public schools of Buenos Aires. Her mother teaches literature. The only confessed "Menemista" among the interviewees. Her family includes an "adopted" grandmother who is a Mother of the Plaza de Mayo. Individual interview and discussion group. (Tapes #5–6).

Luciana (#56), 15. High school student at public school. Discussion group. (Tape #31).

Luis (#20), 18. High school student at public school. Discussion group. (Tape #11).

Mabel (#57), 17. High school student at public school. Discussion group. (Tape #31).

Marcelo (#3), 21. Works as clerical employee at an advertising agency. College student at private university, public relations major. Went to a parochial primary school and to a public high school. His girlfriend's uncle disappeared. Individual interview. (Tape #2).

Mariana (#5), 16. High school student at an elite public school. Her late maternal grandfather was in the military. Individual interview. (Tape #4).

Mario (#61), 17. High school student at public school. Discussion group. (Tape #31).

Marta (#31), 22. Student at public university, history major. Individual interview. (Tapes #22–23).

Mercedes (#36), 24. Studying at public university to be a professor of English. Individual interview. (Tapes #25–26).

Miguel (#51), 15. High school student at public school. Discussion group. (Tapes #30–31).

Mónica (#15), 20. Studying for teacher's certification. Wants to teach in rural areas. Discussion group. (Tape #9).

Nelson (#14), 15. High school student at public school. His family is from Uruguay, where his aunt disappeared. He participated in two discussion groups. (Tapes #7–8).

Noemí (#55), 15. High school student at public school. Discussion group. (Tape #31).

Nora (#29), 18. Studying for teacher's certification. Discussion group. (Tapes #20–21).

Omar (#49), 15. High school student at public school. Discussion group. (Tapes #30–31).

Pablo (#21), 16. Student at a technical school. Discussion group. (Tapes #11–12).

Patricia (#43), 15. High school student at public school. Her aunt was exiled during the dictatorship. Discussion group. (Tape #30).

Pedro (#12), 18. High school student at public school. He participated in two discussion groups. (Tapes #7–8).

Ricardo (#27), 18. Laura's (#26) *compañero*, father of the baby she is expecting. High school student at public school. "Red diaper baby," both parents were political activists. Discussion group. (Tapes #19–20).

Roberto (#22), 26. He is from the province of Tucumán. Studying for teacher's certification. Works at the administration of an educational institution. Discussion group. (Tapes #15–16).

Sandra (#59), 17. High school student at public school. Her uncle went into exile during the repression and still lives in Israel. Discussion group. (Tape #31).

Sara (#7), 15. High school student at one of the two top public schools of Buenos Aires. Her parents are very critical of the dictatorship and know many people who disappeared. Discussion group. (Tapes #5–6).

Silvia (#24), 20. Studying for teacher's certification. Discussion group. (Tapes #16–17).

Susana (#11), 16. High school student at public school. Discussion group. (Tape #7).

Teresa (#53), 15. High school student at public school. Has a distant relative who disappeared. Discussion group. (Tape #31).

Verónica (#65), 16. High school student at an exclusive private religious school. Her late paternal grandfather was in the military. Her mother's cousin was a guerrilla and was killed. Discussion group. (Tape #32).

Víctor (#39), 21. High school student at public school. Coproduces a community radio program. Discussion group. (Tapes #27–28).

My Own Memory Journey

As an Argentinean who lived in Buenos Aires during the years of terror and a member of the witness generation, I have a very clear stance toward this historical period. I am extremely critical of the human rights violations committed, their perpetrators, and the collaboration or indifference of those who allowed these atrocities to happen. I align myself with the human rights movement. I admire and support the Mothers, the Grandmothers, and the HIJOS. I reject the legalization of impunity and think that the whole society should be active in the pursuit of accountability. I refuse any attempt to address this past that does not consider truth and justice. My conviction is rooted in my personal experiences, in the events I witnessed, in rational and informed analysis of what went on. My knowledge is not secondhand; I lived through it.

In the midst of the repression, I worked for the national airlines and my travels back and forth allowed me to witness the terror as both an insider and an outsider. I knew people who disappeared. I have friends who went into exile and whom my job allowed me to visit in the cities to which they escaped. I compared the silences of the national media with the information available in other countries. I remember people disappearing, telephone calls warning "Don't go to visit 'Pedro,' he's in the hospital" or " 'Cristina' is out of town"—unmistakable warnings that those people had been taken away, and of the risks in calling them or visiting their homes. I also remember well the return to civilian rule. I was already living in the United States and had left Argentina during the final phase of the dictatorship, worn out by the horror and in need of "fresh air." I remember the conflicting emotions I felt, two years later while visiting Buenos Aires, seeing familiar faces at a café, the joyful feeling of "You are alive!" the fear of asking, "What happened to 'Juan'?" or of listening to what followed the question "Do you remember 'Marta'?" A generation devastated by the terror was reconstructing the pieces of this past—the dead, the disappeared, the exiles who settled abroad, those who returned, and the ones who had retreated into internal exile. There was also the fear of asking, "Where do you stand in relation to this horror?" Do you condemn or condone?" It was a moment when people had to define themselves publicly, when fissures became visible.

Hence, when I landed in Buenos Aires in 1998, sixteen years after I had left, I was going home to research a period that I had lived, involving issues very important to me and with which I have a strong ideological and emotional involvement. In addition to my own experience, I was loaded with information gained over many years of closely following the events taking place in the aftermath of the dictatorship.

So I went to research other people's accounts of this past so well known to me, aware of the diversity of memory, conscious that my memories of the dictatorship were quite different from those of many who were around me during that period. What we were doing at that time, with whom we associated, or how much we dared to open our eyes and uncover the details of the horror that was taking place are factors that have marked all Argentineans who are part of the witness generation, and those factors affect the many ways we remember those historical events and, consequently, the historical explanations we have given to the next generation.

While I was conducting these interviews, I was transported to the years of the dictatorship and every discussion stirred up my own recollections. I kept asking myself how my memories had been shaped and how I had processed the information received over the years. What participants were telling me inspired many conversations with friends and colleagues with whom I shared the different phases of my fieldwork. These conversations brought back memories of old friends and acquaintances, anecdotes of moments we had shared under terror, and, in my case at least, stories that had been forgotten and had remained hidden in some little corner, blocked from my conscience, maybe as a direct consequence of my own fears during those years. And, by exploring how participants' elders had transmitted this past, I could not avoid thinking about my own role and responsibility as a member of the witness generation. Writing this book, thus, is also a personal commitment to remember what happened during those years, an act of memory.

Dynamics of the Interviews

During this fieldwork, there were three main questions guiding my conversations: What did young people know about the dictatorship? How did they learn what they knew? How were they processing their knowledge about this past?

To ask young people about historical facts made them quite nervous about the amount and the quality of what they knew, often revealing an evident self-perception that they know very little about anything. I constantly perceived an implicit anxiety of the kind students feel when they are concerned with passing or failing an examination. "How will you grade me?" was a question that I read in many faces. Several participants were very candid in stating their concerns. Some told me that they had wanted to read something and be more prepared for the interview. Others were worried about not knowing the information I was looking for and commented that the interview had made them think of how little they knew about this past.

Hence, one of the first things I explained was that I was not interested in who knew more but in the process by which past events had been transmitted to them, that I was looking for how they knew about certain things and not for how much they knew. It became important to reassure them that I had lived the historical period to be discussed, knew about it, and had no intention of comparing their knowledge to mine. Rather, I was looking for information that only they could give me, such as with whom they had talked about this past, when, and where, or what they had read and seen about it. In other words, this was not a test; I was learning from them, using their experiences and opinions to fill the gaps in my knowledge. This clarification usually paved the way for lively talks and discussions.

There were various ways by which we created a friendly and familiar rapport between us. Except for a few group sessions at schools, many meetings were at my family's home, at coffee shops, restaurants, and even in public squares. Whenever possible, these conversations took place around a table with coffee, refreshments, and food on it, providing a relaxing atmosphere. We discussed the dictatorship while eating croissants, pastries, or pizza. We joked and laughed, and some participants even sang songs that spoke of this past.

Group discussions were often so intense that participants forgot that I was there while they engaged in passionate debates where all talked at the same time. As a result, many words are lost, but it shows how controversial the issue is and the emotions it generates. Some participants expressed enjoyment at discussing this topic and noted that they felt comfortable talking in an informal environment, as compared to a classroom with an authoritative figure standing before them. The dynamics of the encounters varied depending on the particulars of each interview or discussion group. At times I let them talk with little interruption, at others I took an active role leading the discussion.

Many of the comments that I heard were not easy to digest. I was often surprised, shocked, and extremely worried by the things I was listening to. Certain stories made me shudder and I would not have hesitated to challenge them in any other circumstance. When asked, I told them about my life under terror. But I was especially careful not to alienate participants or pressure them into fashioning their comments to please me and avoid confrontation. I believe that it worked well, that I was not an intimidating interlocutor, and that, in general, participants felt free to say whatever they wanted. They told me many stories demonstrating their trust in my intended use of the information they were sharing. Furthermore, our talks seemed to have prompted conversations at home or with friends, and even encouraged some to read a book or watch a particular film.

Before Turning the Page

Exploring postmemories of terror leads us into a labyrinth where topics, causes, effects, assumptions, facts, or myths constantly move in different directions, only to merge and overlap. The book is organized as a series of conversations about different themes. But those dividing lines are blurred and, like memory, float back and forth.

After this introduction, the book is divided into ten chapters and an afterword. Chapter one focuses on the historical explanations circulating by seeking answers to the question "Why did it happen?" It discusses how knowledge about the dictatorship had been conveyed in a fragmented mode, with few details about its genesis or major players. It analyzes the acceptance of ideological justifications that overlook how many sectors tolerated, condoned, or benefited from the terror.

Chapter two analyzes societal fears, past and present. It provides answers to the question "What was it like to live under terror?" It focuses on how these experiences have been transmitted to young people, analyzes the legacy of fear, and discusses its current and future implications for the post-dictatorship generation.

Chapter three discusses generalized social silences within families and at school, which I link to the intergenerational transmission of the paralyzing effects of terror. It focuses on the lack of talk about the dictatorship, on the recurrence of the comment "we don't talk about that." It identifies young people's perceptions of the reasons behind those silences and what they made of such a lack of talk about this past.

Chapter four analyzes the paradox of knowing but not knowing. It is about stories of threats, exiles, killings, or disappearances. It discusses misinformation and self-deception. It explores society's awareness and denial of what was going on during the terror and the process by which information about human rights abuses became then widely available, or the switch between "nobody knew [at that time]" and "everybody knows [now]."

Chapter five explores the cultural scenario of legalized impunity. It discusses participants' impotence and anger at the absence of justice and their experiences living in an environment where killers and torturers were benefiting from amnesties. It examines what I describe as the "normalization" of living with *represores*, meaning how they circulate in public places, run for office, or are licensed as kind parents of the children they seized after disappearing their biological parents.

Chapter six addresses indifference through the value that this past has in young people's lives. It analyzes answers to the questions "Why bother?" and "So what?" It discusses an apparent generalized indifference and how the pervasiveness of impunity was influencing feelings of impotence, apathy, and cynicism. It looks at the younger generation's interest—or lack of it—in learning about the dictatorship and participating in struggles for accountability.

Chapter seven explores young people's perceptions on the value and need for justice. It is about answers to the question "What would you do if you were Minister of Justice?" It analyzes opinions about who are responsible for the crimes committed, who should be punished, and how.

Chapter eight looks at the communication media's role(s) in transmitting and reconstructing this past. It discusses the various texts that constitute the dictatorship's "textbook," such as television programs, films, popular songs, demonstrations, or sites that symbolize terror. It analyzes how the media provided historical referents, set up agendas, and reinforced or challenged societal silences.

Chapter nine explores the problems of representing and transmitting horror. It is about answers to the questions: "How do we convey the magnitude of the atrocities committed without 'saturating' the public with its details?" and "How graphic should the portrayal of violence be?" It looks at how particular representations of this violent past had been interpreted and their impact on people.

Chapter ten looks at human rights activism from two angles. One focuses on interviewees' opinions on the role that mothers and children of *desaparecidos* play in society as "memory keepers" and "justice seekers." The other incorporates opinions from the activist children of the disappeared, whose different experiences and memories help to contextualize and compare the content and perspectives of postmemories of the "gray zoners."

Before turning the page, let me remind readers that memories are like snapshots that capture remembrances at a specific moment and that when the moment changes, these memories can also change. Consequently, exploring postmemories of terror is like freezing certain individuals' perceptions of the past within a certain social-political-cultural environment, at a particular point in time. Since a society's memories are constantly being reconstructed, these conversations are just a glimpse into a particular group of people, at a particular historical moment, at a particular moment of their individual lives: sixty-three young people from Buenos Aires in the year 1998. Referring to the voices of survivors and witnesses of the terror, poet Juan Gelman has said that we should listen to them, that what they have to say will help us weave the quilt of the nation's collective memory.[61] I trust that what the voices of the post-dictatorship generation say in the following pages will make for another patch in this quilt.

ONE

Conversations about Knowledge: Why Did It Happen?

Introduction

To discuss knowledge about the dictatorship we should acknowledge that fear, silence, and knowledge are categories without rigid divisions. They are interconnected alternately as cause and effect of each other, configuring a cycle whereby fear provokes silences and silences limit the scope of historical explanations. This chapter starts the exploration of this cycle by focusing on what is known about this past. It identifies the different historical explanations for the repression that were being circulated by examining answers to the question "Why did it happen?" It looks at how the post-dictatorship generation was accepting or challenging these accounts.

There are significant differences between the "what happened" and the "why it happened." Exploring the "why" is to look into the historical explanations articulated by the different memory communities coexisting in the aftermath of terror. It is to enter into this wide arena where conflicting versions of the past compete for hegemony. It is about recognizing the different players, discussing guilt and responsibility, and situating the events within a larger political and historical context. We go beyond the stories that my mother told me and look at the stories that politicians, opinion leaders, textbooks, and the communication media were telling.

Historical Explanations Given to the Younger Generation

In answering the question of what led to the military coup in 1976, why those events took place, and why people were persecuted, tortured, and disappeared, many participants brought up the need for order. According to Josefina, a sixteen-year-old student at a very exclusive private high school: "There was no order. Something was needed to reorganize everything. Maybe the medicine was worse than the disease but there was need to search for a way of reorganizing." The fact that the social chaos accompanying Isabel Perón's presidency was repeatedly mentioned as a reason for the coup suggests that this may be the only explanation many participants had received.

Some interviewees had been told that there were actually no reasons for the repression. As Luis, a fifteen-year-old high school student, candidly stated: "I was told that there was no reason, no excuse, nothing. People were taken away and tortured for nothing." Now, undoubtedly, there is no justification for human rights violations. But the campaign of extermination of dissidents was part of a political project and the comment shows how information about the details of the terror, which seem to be well known to all, has been separated from any contextual content.

I also heard remarks that the reasons why the terror happened are a "secret" known by a few. "I think that there must be an explanation but they don't want to make it public. It won't come out. It must be some place, in an office, a file folder, I don't know" (Miguel). There were indeed rumors of secrets files kept by the military and dusted boxes sometimes appear with some information inside.[1] However, we don't know whether "the big archive" of centralized information ever existed and, if it does, where it is. But the belief that the perpetrators must open their files for society to understand what happened is a perception of a society lacking the knowledge and experience to analyze historical processes and the power to demand the truth. Human rights activists teach us a lesson with their ongoing struggle for the disclosure of any available information.

Other comments simplify the crushing of a broad political movement, the actors involved, and how the process took place. According to Ariel, a fifteen-year-old student:

> I'm now remembering that the other day we were with a classmate who told us that the military kidnapped and all that because there were efforts to impose communism and, apparently, the military didn't want that. Well, neither [the military nor communism] is good. Then democracy arrived.

There were interviewees who blamed their ignorance on the limited talk about this past: "We didn't know anything. If we'd have talked about this before, we'd now be able to tell you a lot of things" (Elena). "We don't know a lot because no one tells us anything. If they'd give me books, if we could talk once a week in school" (Héctor). This was not the only criticism of the educational system and the way history is taught. According to Gloria, a seventeen-year-old high school student:

> They never told me the reasons why. Nor did I ever hear any talk about the reasons. Always [talk about] the history but never "why" [it happened]. Also, there are times

that if you ask no one knows the answer. They tell you all the history but they never tell you "It was for this reason."

Hence, participants were very explicit in pointing to the main consequences of persistent silence and made specific links between silences and knowledge. They highlighted the little information that has been transmitted to them, their elders' incapacity to answer their questions, and their generation's limited knowledge about this historical period. The lack of information does not mean that participants could not articulate explanations for the dictatorship or identify causes and responsibilities, but it may be the reason why certain historical accounts had been widely accepted.

Dichotomies: of "Two Devils," the Guilty, and the Innocent

The foreword to *Nunca Más*, the report of the commission to investigate disappearances, begins with the words "During the 1970s, Argentina was shaken by a terror, which originated from both the extreme right and the extreme left." This statement gave an official stamp to what is known as "the theory of the Two Devils." With few exceptions, this emerged as the keystone in what has passed as a historical explanation for the "dirty war." The explanation reaffirms the concept of "war against subversion" claimed by the dictatorship when the atrocities became evident and identifies the transition as a "postwar" period. It separates from the whole of society an apparently insulated conflict between the military and the "extreme left terror." In this view, this society "convulsed" by terror neither had any participation or responsibility, nor has any role to play in the present in demanding accountability. Moreover, this explanation does not call for an evaluation of the role played by large sectors of society that, either from fear, ignorance, or convenience, remained witting bystanders but not protagonists.

Furthermore, the "postwar" scenario emerging from this explanation calls for the reconciliation between two armed adversaries. We know that the higher estimates of guerrilla forces barely amount to 5 percent of the estimated 30,000 *desaparecidos*. The figure for victims murdered by the guerrillas in the period prior to and during the dictatorship is 687, most of them military or security forces personnel, and a few civilians.[2] Which are the two armies? Where does society in general fit into this equation?

"Two Devils" has had different, well-defined phases over the years. This has contributed to frame under it several significant steps of the historical process initiated with the dictatorship. The first phase of the "war" was followed by the second phase of blaming both sides and jailing military junta members and some guerrilla leaders at the commencement of civilian rule.[3] The third step was marked by the presidential pardons to both "devils."[4] The fourth step was the *mea culpas* of army chief General Balza and Firmenich (leader of the Montoneros) who in 1995 broadcast their confessions in the same television program within one week of each other.[5] Ciancaglini and Granowsky refer to this as a version of the theory that could be called the "Two Angels," where both sides metaphorically shake hands, while Firmenich's statement implies that all the dictatorship's victims were Montoneros—or *montoneriza* the *desaparecidos*.[6]

Participants seldom explicitly invoked "Two Devils" as the cause of what happened, but many interpretations of the repression supported it. References to war, enemy armies, and opposite ideologies were constant, with "bad guys" and victims from "both" sides. The notion of two "guilty parties" was rarely questioned. The variations were in the type of analysis or the facts considered—"both were wrong," "both suffered," "both lied."

According to Alicia, a nineteen-year-old student at the Normal School:

> For me, both sides were responsible, the military as well as the subversives. There was one who was the head of the Montoneros, someone who was responsible. There are guilty people in both bands. What happens is that there's more talk about the military because they were the legal forces. But I believe that there are guilty parties in both sides. Although I don't know if it will ever be discovered who was really the brain within the Montoneros or the ERP, the one who organized everything.

Later in our conversation, and during a discussion on how to teach about this historical period, Alicia, a future teacher, further referred to the "two sides" in arguing for the objective teaching of history. She recommended that explanations should detail:

> How it started, why, not setting any side as bad or good but showing the things that both did. [Details of torture and horror] are useful to see the bad things done by the military. Now, we should show that Montoneros or ERP also wreaked havoc. There were innocent people who died and people who were not innocent, or not so innocent. I think we should try to reach a balance between both sides, without portraying the military as bad or the subversives as bad. But it's very difficult.

The "two sides" were also used to explain suffering. Mario, a seventeen-year-old student, was one of the few participants who took great care in stressing the losses suffered by the military and civilians at the hands of the guerrillas. He aimed to present a balanced appraisal of the period and brought in information given to him by children of military personnel and friends in the police:

> I think that both sides, the two bands, suffered. There were always two groups, the people and the military. People died. Some people will tell you that there was much security during those times. Some people will tell you that the military were a piece of shit and others that communism is also a piece of shit. They died from all sides. I have a friend who was a cop and didn't go to work because her friend was sick.

And she saved herself because a bomb exploded at a place where a meeting was taking place and all her [police] co-workers died. People who say that there was always only one band bothers me. This isn't the case. I think that, in history, you have to be neutral. This is my point of view. But it was badly mishandled, both the theme of the *desaparecidos* and the bombs. The kids who were doing the military service, because it was mandatory, kids of eighteen years old, five and eight-year old girls who were playing ball; they all died. Because a bomb has an expansive wave. [They] planted a bomb in the middle of downtown Córdoba; all kinds of people died. Were they guilty? No one was guilty.

Mario's account ignores the fact that there were few casualties among civilians as a result of guerrilla activity and that, on the other hand, many young men doing military service disappeared at the hands and as victims of the military for being considered "subversives" or dangerous witnesses.[7] Mario's stories might be popular within circles linked to the armed forces, where he seemed to have several friends, but they are not accurate.

Verónica, a sixteen-year-old high school student at an exclusive private school, used the two "evil" camps to express differences of opinion within her family:

I know a lot about the coup through my parents. Because my grandfather, who died when my father was very little, was in the military. So my dad is a supporter of the military and my mom is a supporter of the guerrilla forces. But they didn't participate in anything because they're extremely pacifist. And they're not truly supporters because they believe that both sides were wrong, because both sides used violence and both tortured. But my dad supports the military and my mom the guerillas. I believe they think the way they do because of their families' background. Their ideas conflict. [My parents] agree that the coup was necessary and that the military had to do something. But what [the military] did wasn't the way because they paid with the same token.

The idea of the two confronting armies was also present in accounts of participants whose relatives were political activists. We need to remember that public statements by Montonero leader Firmenich promoted the notion of "popular war" and implied that all the *desaparecidos* were armed combatants, therefore reinforcing the notion of two armies. Andrea, a fifteen-year-old high school student, talked about her disappeared aunt:

I don't justify killing anybody, be it a military or a subversive as it was said then. My aunt was a Montonera. [My parents] were also activists but not Montoneros. I believe they stopped when my brother was a kid. My dad told me, "In those times, you either killed or were killed."

The "Two Devils" theory was included in explanations that incorporated other actors, beyond the military and guerrilla forces. Juan, a twenty-three-year-old communications major, who was aware that repression was not only directed toward armed combatants, had accepted that state terrorism was a response to violence of the "left":

> There was a guerrilla force called Montoneros that planted bombs. Those who occupied the state at that time, who were the military, aimed at exterminating it, paying back with the same token, or worse, by killing those who planted the bombs. And then tried to destroy from its roots any idea close to communism, or the left, or what at that time was called extremism.

In some comments, blaming the two sides included speculation on the motives that each had to become involved in this conflict. According to Leonardo, who was twenty-two and was studying for his teacher's certification:

> There are the two extremes. The authoritarian military and the famous subversive who also had its interests and wanted to revolutionize and change everything. Let's say that no one is a saint. They all had their agenda. I don't believe there's only one side.

"Saint" would prove to be a common expression for defining innocence and guilt, a dichotomy that is the result of framing the dictatorship under two polarized evil sides.

Guilty or Innocent?

Military authorities campaigned to convince the population that society was divided into friends and foes and that while there were consequences of being on the wrong side, those who behaved according to what was expected of them had nothing to be afraid of. Nothing was more explicit than the warning by General Ibérico Saint-Jean, de facto governor of the province of Buenos Aires at the peak of the repression: "First we will kill all the subversives; then we will kill their collaborators; then . . . their sympathizers; then . . . those who remain indifferent; and finally we will kill those who are timid."[8] There is no doubt about what their campaign entailed; indeed this was a candid way to publicly identify the enemy and define the rules of the game. Dictator Videla was a little more cautious. He did not target the timid but explained that a terrorist was "not just someone with a gun or a bomb, but also someone who spreads ideas that are contrary to Western and Christian civilization."[9] It should not be surprising that one of the memories transmitted is that anybody could disappear. This is true, mostly because many qualified for the label of "terrorist."

When a person was taken away, it was common to hear comments that were variations of "[She/he] was involved in something" or "[She/he] must have done something." Notice the use of words that are simultaneously all-inclusive yet undefined. But these vague statements summarized the idea that abductions, tortures, killings, or disappearances were the victims' responsibility. This is one effect of the repression on what Martín-Baró calls the "spectators of the terror," meaning those who are "aware of the repression, whether by direct or indirect knowledge."[10] He argues that when spectators can distance themselves emotionally from the victims of the repression, they convert them into scapegoats and justify their punishment. Distancing happens when it is possible to identify the victim with punishable attributes such as "subversive" or "guerrilla" and see oneself as a "good person."[11]

Blaming the victim for her disappearance is a belief that was apparently engraved in society and, as its recurrence throughout our conversations indicates, transmitted to the younger generation.[12] As Nora's mother told her: "The military weren't so bad. If you were not a 'crazy one' and were not involved in anything strange, nothing strange happened to you." According to Mario: "I have military friends. If you talk to a military officer's son, he'd tell you that kids at that time were hell raisers; they asked for [the repression]." Or, as Leonardo said when discussing justifications for the repression: "I found people who told me, 'Well they must have done something.' That's a typical phrase."

One form in which this belief manifests itself is as comments implying that the fact that nothing happened to a person is proof that those not involved in "subversive" activities were safe. Carmen was twenty-two and studying education at a public university. She shared what she learned from her mother, someone who saw many positive angles of the dictatorship:

> According to what my mother tells me, those were very revolutionary times. She says, "You were of two bands, the guerrilla forces or the military. But if you were not in any of those two, nobody would do anything to you. It's as if you were clean." What I've always heard is that "[they] were taken away for something; [they] must have been involved in something because, otherwise, they wouldn't have been taken away." My mother tells me, "I wasn't involved in anything, and I was never taken away." And I say, "But why mom, because they said something?" "No," she says, "Remember that many planted bombs and [did] this and that; they weren't saints. They were not going to the university to study. No, they gathered to plot, to see where they'd plant the bomb."

That the victims were guilty is often explained by arguments implying that they had committed bad actions, that they were "no saints." However, these ambiguous allegations seldom specify what the "sins" were that caused the fall of that person from a state of holiness into the inferno of the torture chambers.

Acceptance of the clash between two armies suggests that those victims who were not military or guerrillas were the "innocent" ones. Moreover, since 30,000 people cannot be guerrillas or terrorists (they would not have disappeared so easily), the conclusion seems to be that the remainder were "innocent" people taken out of the blue.

But, what is the meaning of "innocence," and what made a victim innocent or guilty? Judging human rights abuses based on the culpability of the victims implies that the "guilty" had received a too harsh but maybe deserved punishment. It also opens the possibility that outrage for the atrocities can be limited to the fate of the "innocents," those who "weren't involved in anything." Yet, I should point out that most participants thought that whatever crimes had been committed, nothing justified what was done to thousands of people. Moreover, some comments reveal an awareness of the arbitrariness of defining guilt and innocence. As Víctor argued: "It would be important to clarify that everybody was innocent but [the repression] was so well-planned that [the military] knew whom they'd take away and whom they wouldn't." Indeed, the great majority of the *desaparecidos* were taken away because they wanted to change the system, "for being involved in something."[13]

"Something" was political participation in a variety of capacities, tasks, and environments, be it the neighborhood, the workplace, or the school—struggles that have often been smeared with the labels of terrorism, anarchism, or communism.[14]

Rival Historical Explanations

The prevalence of "Two Devils" does not exclude the circulation, albeit limited, of equally powerful rival explanations. A few participants were well informed about several political, social, and economic reasons for the coup and revealed awareness of the broader scope of the repression, either replacing the dichotomy military/guerrilla or broadening it to include other players. The alternative historical accounts that I heard confirm that information challenging simplified dichotomies was circulating. The issue is who had access to or interest in it. Most of the participants who voiced these views had been exposed, usually through their families, to more information about the period. Thus, silences do limit knowledge and ignorance influences the unquestioned acceptance of simplistic explanations.

Destroying a Political Movement

The primary argument against the war between two armies explanation is that the dictatorship aimed to destroy a broad political movement. In those accounts, the basis for the repression is ideological. Participants made references to activists on many fronts and all those whom the dictatorship saw as its enemies replace the guerrilla forces as the targets of repression. Irma, a nineteen-year-old student, chose the word "innocent" to refer to those who were involved in a political project and were a potential obstacle for the dictatorship's plans:

> I think that, at that moment, those who wanted to govern were not interested in "thinking" people. Because when you think you develop ideas, you can have a democratic government and do better things. At that time, [people in power] had no

interest in allowing this. They wanted to take power and manage everybody by using force and killing. They didn't care about the methods. In reality, that's what they did, they killed all those innocent thinking people who wanted the best for the country. They called them subversives or gave them any label, so these people wouldn't think and raise the consciousness of other people. It wasn't convenient for them. Like nowadays, it's not convenient for them that there are people who think and study.

Andrés, an eighteen-year-old high school student who situated the coup within a larger historical background, had a comparable explanation and argued that the dictatorship aimed to exterminate a generation of activists:

> There were times of many struggles on many fronts, following other bad [military] governments. And it's as if everybody was involved in the struggle. If you wanted something you could not remain passive. Those were times when people struggled, especially young people. That is why they took away so many young people. [Authorities] didn't want that. [They needed] to eliminate those who had struggled or were struggling, so they could not tell or teach anything to the rest.

For Leonardo, the dictatorship was an inevitable clash between political and cultural forces, an account that broadens the arena of ideological battles and incorporates other actors. He also evaluated how military campaigns, such as the elimination of thousands of people, imposed a way of living:

> It seems to me that there were two very different projects. One was that of the military, this whole concept of nationalism and rigidity. And they saw that the country was leaning into another direction due to cultural forces from abroad, like flower power. So there were two different sectors, very difficult to reconcile. Apparently, the stronger one won because there were 30,000 *desaparecidos* and they weren't military personnel. I think that that's what happened, two sides trying to lead the country toward their ideals, in opposite directions, never able to agree because of their huge differences. They clashed, as they were meant to clash, and the stronger one at that moment won. But I believe that people continued to do what they wanted, as it always happens when power is in some hands and many things happen underground. I found young people who, influenced I believe by elders who told them that what [those eliminated] were doing wasn't good, that they were all drug addicts, hippies that needed to be stopped, or something like that. There are people who still justify [the military]. I don't know if they justify the deaths but yes the *proceso* and the dictatorship.

To Restructure Economic Priorities Toward a Neoliberal Policy

Very few historical explanations considered economic factors. I talked, however, to one group of classmates from a working-class neighborhood who produced a community radio program and had researched the period for a school assignment.[15] For them, the dictatorship was linked to the imposition of neoliberal economic policies similar to those being implemented in the 1990s. They were also critical of narrow definitions of democracy. Víctor, a twenty-one-year-old student, explained neoliberalism's trajectory, comparing Martinez de Hoz and Cavallo (ministers of economy of the dictatorship and Menem's first term respectively):[16]

> The assassins, the ones who made the coup, were the military, police, army, navy, etc. But I think that the planners were, as always, those who run the country, the ones who pull the puppet's strings, the economic powers, and the big corporations. That period was the beginning of privatization, something that was not achieved but was initiated by Martinez de Hoz and continued until Cavallo, his best student. When you research Martinez de Hoz's economic plan you realize that it wasn't only at that time that this happened, and that we now have Menem and everything is fine. This is the same but under what is called democracy.

Along the same lines, Elvira argued that repression was the tool to crush opposition to a major restructuring of the economy:

> The difference is that, before, people were more nationalistic; they defended what was theirs. If someone would have said at that time "Let's privatize everything" it might not have been accepted. People would have resisted. Thus, I suppose that they had to do all this [repression] to start privatizing everything and that the people would say nothing. We now vote, we have democracy, but people are starving.

Regional and International Influences

Some explanations focused on the regional and international context of the dictatorship and the perception that there was either an external cause or a careful coordination among many countries, including the United States, in orchestrating the repression to deter communism. Silvia, who was twenty years old and was studying for her teacher's certification, expressed this position:

> Let's say that the army was the formal power but the real power was in the hands of another person who, obviously, was from abroad. Because if you compute all the military coups across the Americas you realize that, obviously, someone was coordinating this or there was agreement for this to happen. I remember discussing it with someone that it wasn't a coincidence that this had happened in all the countries; they were all ruled by the military.

Ricardo was an eighteen-year-old high school student and his parents had been members of the Communist Party. During my conversation with him and his partner

Laura, a nineteen-year-old who was studying for her teacher's certification and was the daughter of political activists, they discussed a backlash against revolutionary struggles throughout the continent. In Ricardo's words:

> There was a time where the typical thing in Latin America was to see coups d'état in all countries. If you think about it, there were coups all over. And it was logical that it would also happen in Argentina because it was one of the countries with revolutionary movements. It was general. No one can explain this to me, but thinking and looking at how history evolved in all the countries, the coups were not isolated; they were all very similar. Some [dictatorships] ended because societies are different, like Argentina, or Chile where they ended only recently. But there are countries that continue that way. I don't think they were isolated coups d'état, it was something very precise. Besides, there were many Argentine military in Central America.

Laura added to these observations: "It was all part of the United States' plan of national security. They sent brigades from the CIA. The Americans had anti-guerrilla schools for young officers in Central America." Their knowledge about the School of the Americas, the U.S. institution training Latin American soldiers, and their awareness of how the Argentine military collaborated with other dictatorships was rare among the young people with whom I talked.

In explaining the reasons for the coup, Marta, a twenty-two-year-old student of history at a public university, also commented on dictatorships throughout the Americas and pointed to U.S. responsibility for the repression:

> Due to Isabel Perón's bad administration and to communist currents, revolutionary movements. It was also a process that took place in all Latin America and not only in Argentina because of Isabel Perón. I incorporate this within a process suffered by the American continent. I don't know, this is a new hypothesis that I'm recently thinking about. That everything was under the control of the United States to repress all the communist currents, part of a global policy.

By advancing other alternative historical explanations of the terror, a few participants incorporated other key players into the events and broadened the framework for its analysis. For another outcome of the knowledge that had been transmitted is reflected in young people's appraisal of the roles played by different actors and institutions.

Roles Attributed to Different Actors and Institutions

What happened in Argentina was not the product of an isolated group of cruel military. State terrorism and mass human rights violations do not happen without the support of large sectors of the population, be it by direct support or complicit indifference. This was the case in Nazi Germany as well as in Argentina, where large sectors functioned as a "large acritical social mattress."[17] Pilar Calveiro, who survived her disappearance, argues, and convincingly demonstrates, that the camps of torture and extermination cannot be seen as rare aberrations isolated from society.[18] This relationship is further articulated by Habermas's claim that "there is such a thing as collective responsibility for the mental and cultural context in which mass crimes become possible."[19]

But what did young people know about all this? I always made sure to ask who supported the dictatorship. One institution became a recurrent topic of our conversations: the Catholic Church. So let us start this discussion about society's support of the repression by looking into the Catholic hierarchy's position during the terror and its aftermath.

Catholic Hierarchy

The Catholic hierarchy has always been a leading actor in the country's political life. Most of it either condoned repression or remained silent while the military annihilated people, including nuns, priests, or lay Christian activists. Only four bishops, of eighty, publicly denounced the dictatorship. One of them, Angelelli, was then assassinated in a fake car accident.[20] There are even reports of some priests witnessing torture sessions to encourage confessions to guilt of political crimes or give away information about other activists.[21]

Several interviewees were or had been students at Catholic institutions and others participated in many activities within the Church, mainly as catechists (lay educational workers). Thus, their level of knowledge about what the Church did during the terror allows assessing how this past was being transmitted in Church circles. In most of the religious high schools participants attended, the Church's role during the dictatorship was never discussed. As Inés, a sixteen-year-old student, said: "In spite of all the religious instruction, we don't talk about [the dictatorship]". But many young people were aware of the Church's political power and that its position during the terror is subject to debate.

Although the Church could have saved many lives, some participants had accepted the idea that it had no power to stop human rights abuses.[22] According to Carmen:

> They say that the Church knew of all the moves at that time but couldn't do anything because its hands were tied. They even say that the Mothers [of the Plaza de Mayo] approached the Church and the Church did nothing. It washed its hands.

Nora, an eighteen-year-old future teacher, was a catechist who hinted that the Church's actions were based on what was more beneficial to the institution:

> During the dictatorship, the Church remained in the margins. I think that it did so because it couldn't [intervene]. But you have to separate the Church from religion.

I think that if it spoke out about . . . the military had the power . . . and the Church has been always very powerful. It wasn't very convenient for the Church to speak.

Eugenia, a twenty-two-year-old student of medicine, discussed complicity by remembering the silences in the classroom at the convent school she had attended:

The nuns never talked about politics, about any political topic, less about this one. I imagine that this is due to the relationship between the Church and the military at that time. We never discussed this topic. It's a cover-up by the Church to see in the news that they [military leaders] were receiving communion—these are well known images—and afterward they sit behind a desk and give orders to kill.

Bishops and generals together were widely documented in media images throughout Argentina and the world and, as Eugenia accurately pointed out, it suffices to decode the meaning of some images to understand the level of the Catholic hierarchy's support.

A few participants talked about the nuns and priests who were eliminated while the Church's hierarchy remained silent. I also heard of more explicit collaborations: priests visiting concentration camps, bishops and priests who kept lists of prisoners, even speculations that priests may have tortured and killed. As Nelson explained: "There was a priest involved in this, a priest who blessed them [the prisoners] and then killed them and tossed them away, something like that."

Alicia was a catechist and there had been discussions about what went on within her Church, where Father Mugica, a prominent activist from the Peronist Left, was assassinated in 1974, two years before the coup. According to her:

The Church was involved. Some disappeared because, like father Mugica, [they] challenged the government. Father Mugica was from my parish; he was killed at the door, after giving his sermon. It's true that Mugica was very Peronist. He helped the poor from "Villa 31" [a shantytown]. And in his sermons he opposed the government. That wasn't convenient for the government so he was killed there at the door. Even now people from Villa 31 keep on coming. They come from all over for the anniversary of his death. Yes, the Church had much to do and [monsignor] Quarrachino took to his grave thousands and thousands of [names of] dead people. Because the guy knew. I don't know how much of this is true but they say that he had the lists with the names of the *desaparecidos*. I believe that the Church was much involved because it has a lot of weight and much power, and it will always have it, all over, not only in Argentina.

The files kept by certain priests have been the focus of investigations by human rights activists. Relatives remember well when they unsuccessfully knocked on doors and met with religious authorities looking for help to find the *desaparecidos*. One of these priests was Graselli, a former Navy chaplain who, at the time I had these conversations, was chaplain and confessor at a private religious school for young women.[23]

The harsher criticism, and the most complete level of knowledge of the Church's collaboration with the dictatorship, came from a few very religious participants. Diego was a twenty-one-year-old future teacher. In his religious circles, the political role of the Church, past and present, had been a topic of discussion. For him, the institution is guilty beyond any doubt:

> I'm Catholic but it's an institution whose members are human beings and many of those wearing the purple stuff were worse sons of bitches than I could ever be. There's no doubt about it. I think that many approved and supported that regime. But we should salvage guys like [bishops] Angelelli or Nevares, who wasn't killed but always struggled [for human rights] until he recently died. And then Mugica and all those. We discuss [those differences]. We discuss the role of the Church during those times and in the present. This is a constant discussion. You arrive at a position of power where, one or the other, either you know what happens and are an accomplice of what's happening, or you're stupid and holding a position that you don't deserve. Whether they did it or allowed it to happen, in my opinion, carries the same responsibility as the one who pulled the trigger.

Hence, awareness of the Church's specific roles during the terror was quite limited. Although few participants doubted that the Church knew what was going on, there were different opinions about the nature of its actions, ranging from open collaboration to indifference, to an inability to act.

Society at Large

So who else are the guilty? Who are to blame? Which levels of responsibility can we identify in society at large? Several participants were aware that large sectors of society had supported or tolerated the military regime since what went on could not have been solely the military's venture. Verbitsky has analyzed how, in Argentina, all military coups are civilian-military and civilians participate even when the main actors and visible power are the military.[24] However, who these civilians were and why they plotted with the military was not always very clear.[25] Contributing to this ignorance is the fact that it was hard to find people openly defending the dictatorship. But this should not be taken as a sign that all its supporters later became critical of it and would not allow or call for a similar repression in the future. For the lack of current public support might include not only those who are truly critical of what went on but also those who would not now dare to publicly admit their approval of the dictatorship. Only time will tell whether these "shy voices" decide to speak out.[26]

We can divide society's support between calls for a coup and approval of the dictatorship that followed. Research on attitudes toward the coup indicates that Isabel

Perón administration's chaos was one reason why the coup was perceived as something inevitable.[27] I heard comments suggesting that wider sectors of society called for a reinstallation of order and wanted the change promised by military authorities. There had been so many coups before that this seemed like a logical and inevitable next step. Another recurrent opinion—that only the powerful benefited from the repression—reveals the belief that social class or economic power determined attitudes toward the dictatorship.

According to Eugenia:

> I think that there were people who called for [the dictatorship] as something necessary to bring some order. Also, [they] created an environment so people would want [the military], an atmosphere of social, economic and political disorganization. During the dictatorship, the most powerful people were, of course, making profitable businesses. They received huge loans that they never paid back. So they were very pleased with it. Yes, I think that these people supported the military government.

Some participants mentioned people's individualistic nature and the lack of concern for what does not affect them. As Juan, raised within an apathetic family, summarized:

> I think that people gave power [to the military]. I never understood how, if [the military] is one group, they can [dominate] a whole nation, do whatever they want against the people. People also supported them during the Malvinas/Falkland War. "Let's go to war" and everybody, "Great, we're going to win," as if it were a soccer match. People were all in agreement. [The military] shouldn't be able [to prevail]. But I think it's like at my house, "It's OK, they didn't hassle me, as long as they don't hassle me they can do whatever they want." I think that the majority of the people, 80%, are like that.

Other explanations argued that, rather than being indifferent, the population took sides—another facet of the "Two Devils" rationale. According to Alicia: "The people were also divided into two [bands]. Let's be honest. Those who were doing well and were benefiting from the military coup sided with the military, and those who didn't sided with the so-called subversives."

Mariana, a fifteen-year-old student and the granddaughter of a military officer, was one of the very few participants who included the political leadership among the dictatorship's supporters:

> I think that, in part, people allowed this to happen, to reach those levels. For me, there were many politicians involved who tolerated this. Although many people involved in politics became targets of the military, for that [repression] to happen there were also many of them who sided with the military.

How Does Society Feel about What Happened?

If sectors of society called for the coup or supported the repression, is there any feeling of guilt and responsibility? How does society feel now that the details of the atrocities committed are well known by all? In the televised *mea culpa* mentioned earlier, General Balza stated that almost everybody was guilty of causing the clash between Argentineans, either by action, omission, consent, absence, or excess; that the guilt was in the collective unconscious of the whole nation although it was easy to blame a few in order to avoid this responsibility.[28] This institutional endorsement of collective blame can only benefit the perpetrators and their collaborators. Why transmit a generalized statement when there are concrete cases of guilt and levels of responsibility? There were those who orchestrated the terror, those who tortured and killed, those who benefited under it, those who collaborated on various fronts, those who were terrified and did not offer any form of resistance.

However, the notion of collective guilt was almost nonexistent among interviewees, indicating that society was not willing to accept blame for these crimes and that people were not ready to explore levels of responsibility. Jorge, an eighteen-year-old student, was one of the few exceptions:

> Everybody was responsible. There wasn't only one group of people responsible. The military and the people, all of us are always responsible, for whatever happens. Ones for accepting, others for doing, we're all responsible.

But I had access to some short essays written by fourteen-year-old students at a public high school. The essays were responses to the screening of a documentary about the dictatorship and a couple of excerpts reveal how some young people perceived society's responsibility. In answering the question "Do you think that what happened in the period portrayed in the video is the responsibility of the military, or is civil society also responsible for it?" One student wrote:

> I consider that the period portrayed is not only the responsibility of the military but of the whole society that, faced with those unpunished acts, closed their eyes and didn't confront the reality, either from fear or because they didn't believe what was happening. I believe that all Argentineans have a level of responsibility for that situation.

In discussing society's reactions to the possibility of new legal proceedings against *represores*, another student wrote:

> [One sector of society] is very upset at the possibility of reopening legal proceedings. It might be because to awaken the memory means to assume the portion of responsibility that corresponds to each one of those who remained silent, looked the other way, or chose not to hear.

The risk and burden of awakening memories have a double edge. For some people, it may imply confronting issues of guilt and responsibility, but, for others, it seemed not at all problematic. Analía, a twenty-year-old communications major, explained support for the dictatorship by making connections to present times:

I know that there were many people who agreed with what was done. I understand that at the time of the military coup the people, in some way, approved of it. They expected a military coup because they were fed up with the chaos of the previous government. I know that many people supported them. I know it through [available] information, not because someone told me that. A while ago there was the party of Aldo Rico [military officer].[29] Evidently, there are people who still agree with having the military in power. But this is really insane. It's like saying that there are people who still condone what the Nazis did, which has been proven as a historical genocide, and there are people who still support it. So, it wouldn't be surprising that there are people who still think that what was done was well done. I wouldn't be surprised.

This comment linking past and present support for human rights abusers is an intelligent observation about Argentinean society. Some military and police officers with a proven record of human rights violations have been elected to office.[30] The fact that people are willing to vote democratically for recognized torturers and assassins challenges the notion that people do not remember what the candidates did and suggests that people might remember, approve, and want them back.

The comparison with the Nazis calls for some attention to Nazism in Argentina. We should remember that after World War II several Nazi criminals such as Eichman, Mengele, and Priebke found a safe haven there.[31] Examining tolerance for this ideology is helpful for understanding the support for the repression and contemporary attitudes toward human rights abusers. Acceptance of extreme amorality does not start overnight. Although none of the participants mentioned anti-Semitism as a reason for special repression, Nazism did emerge in a few interviews.[32]

Marcelo was twenty years old, studied public relations at a private university, and talked about Nazism as a "feeling": "My grandfather would often say 'Yes, because Hitler, the Jews.' I believe [he says] that without knowing. Because I don't think he ever read a book [about it]. It's more a feeling than an ideology from knowledge."

Mónica, a twenty-year-old student at a normal school, spoke of her boyfriend, the son of a high-ranking police officer:

Look, I have a boyfriend and we have big and constant fights. Maybe we don't argue as a couple but we do fight a lot because of this issue. He has the idea that Arian races are superior because of their blood and ideology. [He says] "Hitler for me was great because he repressed and killed, and sent everybody to the gas chamber." I think this guy isn't well informed. [My boyfriend] is a cutie but there are certain issues that you wonder, "How is this possible?" You listen to him talking, and he always talks and reads his little books and stuff about that period. And you think, "Is this guy really aware of what happened, of how many people died?" There are many people like my boyfriend who speak without really knowing and they commit themselves to an ideology or ideas they grabbed from anywhere. This reflects what happens in society. You play it by ear without going deeper into the subject.

Because Mónica was extremely critical of the dictatorship's crimes, I asked how her boyfriend reacted to her way of thinking. This was her answer:

What does he say because I think differently? For example, that it was OK that they killed so many people [in Argentina]. That it was necessary to discard all those people that were going to. . . . Let's say that [he] wanted to remove the rotten apple from the bag to avoid spoiling the rest. Indeed, I believe that that's what he tells me.

Silvia described a comparable situation. She first told me that she had not heard young people around her defending the dictatorship because "I've socialized with what I consider intelligent people and they don't think that way. I don't know what I'd do with such a person, what I could tell her." So then I asked, "Would you date someone who thinks that way? How does your boyfriend think?" To my surprise, this is what she said:

No, he doesn't [think that way]. He regards [the dictatorship] as wrong, detestable, although he thinks that Hitler is an idol. He doesn't agree with the fact that he killed the Jews, of course he doesn't agree with that. But in the sense that he was able to dominate the whole world by himself, a genius regarding the power he had. I fight [with him] when we talk about that.

At times, it seemed that Silvia and Mónica were discussing their boyfriends' Nazism as if it were a particular taste for certain kinds of television programming, as if saying, "He likes sports but I prefer soap-operas." These comments reveal either little knowledge of what Nazism is or a belief that it is possible to be both an admirer of Hitler and a sensitive soul who respects human rights. This admiration for Hitler by members of the post-dictatorship generation cannot be overlooked if we want to comprehend society's attitudes toward the *represores*.

Conclusions

Every single one of the young people with whom I talked knew something of what had happened during the dictatorship, but few knew why it happened. Although participants were conscious of the level of human rights violations committed they were not very clear about either their genesis or their full impact. This is the weakest area of knowledge transmitted to the younger generations. The ideological, political, or economic causes of the terror had been largely ignored. It is in participants' assessment of why the repression happened that a fragmented and decontextualized knowledge becomes evident. The memories transmitted favor historical explanations that distort and simplify the events.

There was a generalized acceptance that the violence of the state was a response to the violence of the guerrilla forces. The military/guerrilla dichotomy continued to frame debates about the past. References to the "two devils" were innumerable, at times very explicit, often hidden in accounts presenting deeper and more informed explanations. Among the implications of focusing on two main actors is the minimization of the role played by those sectors that collaborated in the implementation of state terrorism or profited under it—the Church hierarchy, politicians who were their ambassadors or mayors, corporations, journalists, and intellectuals. Knowledge of the degree of collaboration of civilian sectors was very limited, even when several participants implied that the dictatorship could not have happened without society's support or tolerance.

Ignorance of the political activism of most of the *desaparecidos* shows how little had been transmitted of the social struggles of those times. Popular discourse labeled all political activists as "subversive terrorists" and failed to recognize that the *desaparecidos* were active on many political fronts, as workers, students, artists and within churches or community organizations, and included those who gave them shelter or medical assistance. State terrorism massacred all its enemies, whether they were involved or not in armed struggle.

Notions of guilt and responsibility were simplified by contrasting "Two Devils" with "innocent" victims. There was a manifest confusion of the meaning of key concepts such as "guilt" and "innocence." The belief had been transmitted that the danger of disappearing was based on "being involved in something" and the possibility of survival on "not being involved in anything," implying that the victims were to be blamed for their suffering. This is a triumph of the dictatorship's discourse that needs to be seen in relation to discourses assigning collective guilt. Blaming either a few or the whole society is in either case a sign that the truth is yet to be disclosed. Undoubtedly, it would be highly beneficial for society if all Argentineans asked themselves what they did during those years, and why. It will help in the process of disclosing the truth and determine levels of responsibility, assigning guilt. But it seems that the witness generation was not ready to offer a comprehensive explanation of why the horror happened and what society's role in it was.

A few interviewees drew attention to the complexity of the interests that were at stake during that period. In challenging the dominant explanation, they articulated competing and equally powerful discourses and talked about a number of factors that led to the dictatorship such as efforts to destroy a political movement, the imposition of an economic plan, or the regional and international context of the repression.

In those cases, participants invariably had had access to more information, which illustrates the link between silence and lack of knowledge.

We now move on to analyze fear, another element of the cycle and a key determinant of the knowledge about the dictatorship that we have explored here. Fear produces silences, which are shapers of limited knowledge. Hence, we aim at tracing the chronology of why participants had such an incomplete and fragmented knowledge about this past.

TWO

Conversations about Fear

Introduction

It was a cold morning in the Buenos Aires winter of 1998. I was sitting in the video room of a public school with five fifteen-year-old boys. We were talking about the dictatorship that ended the year they were born, specifically about stories of those years that their families had told them. One of them interrupted me:

> I have a story to tell. Once upon those times . . . I live in a building where, on the fourth floor, a guerrilla used to live. And the military came. My dad was, and still is, the building's superintendent. So the military came and aimed their machine guns at my parents. I don't know the questions they asked; they were looking for my sister. My parents were held at gunpoint, sitting against the wall, while they were being questioned about my sister. Maybe this was to scare [my parents]. My sister was at the kindergarten. She was four or five years old. And [the military] killed the [guerrilla] who lived there. He was killed in that building. (Miguel)

This story conveys, probably better than any other that I heard, how memories of terror, filtered by fears and silences, were being transmitted to the younger generation: in a distorted, edited, and decontextualized form. Miguel's father was the superintendent of a building where a guerrilla lived and was killed by a military counterinsurgency operation. Based on what we now know about how those squads operated, it is logical to assume that the military had been watching their target for a while and that his father was aware of this surveillance and forced to collaborate, at least with his silence and pretense of normality.[1] Obviously, he and his wife were terrified by the military presence, a probable consequence of the recurrent threats they might have suffered, the many times they were held at gunpoint. It is also evident that they needed to share this past, but more than twenty years later they still had problems dealing with the event. Whatever the reason—fear, guilt, or denial— the only way they could tell the story to their son was through a version of events that had probably suffered many edits. A commando searching for a guerrilla would not be looking for a four-year-old girl who fortunately "saved herself" by being at the kindergarten. There are probably layers of distortions in the story they told their son and in how the son made sense of different accounts of that period that he might have heard from his parents, all of them permeated by terror. And what this young man had to say when I asked him about what happened during those years is this story, which could be seen as incongruent, absurd, even comical, were it not the product of fear and silences, of half-told stories about horrible events, where many details remain hidden.

Fear is a feeling of anxiety and agitation caused by the presence or nearness of danger, evil, and pain; terror is an intense fear.[2] The dictatorship resorted to terror for silencing and paralyzing Argentine society. Studies on the psychological and social effects of political repression help us understand the mechanisms for imposing a culture of fear, which affected the whole society and left no social group or individual untouched.[3] The threat of physical pain, even the mere knowledge of the existence of torture, terrified the population. Garretón has described these societal fears in the context of infantile experiences with the metaphor of the fear of the unknown in the "dark room" and the fear of the already known pain of the "dog that bites."[4] Although publicly denying any wrongdoings, the dictatorship made sure that people had some clues of what was going on inside its torture chambers. The reason why it freed some prisoners was precisely that they would tell about their ordeals and this information would circulate.[5] Thus, survivors' stories and the rumors that circulated throughout society about counterinsurgency procedures, unexplained disappearances, and the existence of concentration camps where terrible tortures were applied fueled the fear of this "dark room."

Interviewees were aware of the mechanisms for spreading panic within the population: "People didn't think, people were afraid, because whoever dared to think was killed" (Patricia). "They imposed fear so people would behave properly" (Ariel). Moreover, comments such as "Fear is there, you can feel it in the air" (Carmen) or "They hold the fear of those days inside their heads" (Víctor) attest to the persistence of memories of terror and shed light on how young people today experience a legacy of fear. Many of us who lived under the dictatorship can still feel, breathe, and smell the fear; it is a strong and indelible memory. The events we witnessed have forever "marked" us. And the consequences of this traumatic experience seem palpable for the younger generation, which looks at us and sees the horror imprinted on our faces.

These conversations about fear are a first step in understanding what was known about the dictatorship and what young people's representations of it are. The emphasis in this chapter is on memories that convey feelings and sensations, on the emotional over the rational. It is about "what it was like to live under a regime of terror," how people felt, how people acted in response to their fears, which "survival" mechanisms they developed to cope with terror. Thus, the focus is on how the experience of living under terror had been transmitted to the younger generation, the remains of fear, and its current and future implications for Argentina's post-dictatorship generation.

The Witness Generation's Experiences under Terror

Conversations generally started by asking participants what they had heard about those years. Gloria provided a typical answer:

> I was told that anybody could be taken away. [The military] didn't look at who you were, killed you, had no mercy. [My parents] were unable to leave the house, afraid of what might happen to them. They went out but they didn't know if they'd be back. I heard that people were taken away and executed, because [the military] thought they had information they needed. And if they knew nothing [the military] also killed them. Disappeared, they never came back. It's unknown where they are. They're looking for them and they cannot find them.

(As in many other conversations, this talk about disappearances is framed in the present, as an ongoing condition without closure.)

When Beatriz, a fifteen-year-old high school student, was a small girl, she saw a television program about the dictatorship. This prompted the first conversation with her family about those years. What her parents had to say is a good example of the kind of endless lists of atrocities to which many young people had been exposed:

> It was very dangerous to be in the streets at certain hours. For instance, it wasn't well regarded if someone had a beard; or if someone had long hair he was taken to jail, tortured, and could disappear. Helicopters would constantly leave from one of the Navy's headquarters, carrying people who were thrown inside bags into the Rio de la Plata. [People] were thrown alive and drowned. [The military] would raid homes and wouldn't leave anybody alive, not even a two month old baby. And if the baby was kept alive the military would steal her. There wasn't any kind of safety. If you were talking over the phone you couldn't say anything against the government or that could upset authorities because they'd shoot to kill you. You had to be careful all the time. [The military] would kill you if you had a political idea different from theirs. It didn't matter who you were, nothing mattered to them. When they went into a house to kill a person, if they found an address book, they also killed all those who were in the address book, just for being friends or acquaintances. That is, if I saw a person once and that person gave me her telephone number, even if I only saw her once, she'd also be killed. There's no good way of killing but [the military] would kill them by torturing them, like throwing into the river a defenseless person,

inside a bag and still alive. Because it's another thing if they shoot you, you die instantly. It's wrong they're killing you, but I think it's even worse that you get tortured too. This is all I know.

The many references to address books suggest that this fear was quite widespread:

Most talk is about the disappearances of people. [The military] would go to their homes, take them away and no one would see them again, which is what happened with the majority of the people. [The military] always wore masks to hide their faces, in case that someone they couldn't catch saw their faces and could denounce them. They'd enter into the homes very violently, grab people, beat them, and do whatever they wanted. They'd look into address books and go after these people for not thinking like them, for having different opinions. (Teresa)

Many high school students talked about terror by highlighting the repression of students, the group of victims with whom they could easily identify:

[The military] persecuted the kids who were at the student centers. They kidnapped them. They kidnapped politicians who were against the regime. I think [they] also kidnapped people from different religions, all those who were against the military government, and everyone who [the military] believed was against them. There were people who didn't do anything, but were kidnapped for being members of the student center. And although they wouldn't talk [about politics] they were taken away for being suspected of having information about plots against the military, even when that was not the case. I got the impression that this is how it was. (Héctor)

Another recurrent pattern in stories pointed to the fear of being associated with people who could be targeted as "subversives." Ricardo recalled what his mother, who had been active in the Communist Party, told him:

[The military] would go to the university and search everything. My mother was at that time at the university. Thousands of her friends would tell her, "Erase my name from your address book," "Don't come back to my house to study," "Don't look at me or sit next to me." Because [the military] would go to the university and take you away from the classroom. That's the way it was. They would interrupt a class saying, "Let's see," and proceed to search everything and everyone, including the professors.

The precautions that people took to behave according to what they perceived military authorities expected from them reveal the fear of what could happen:

[My parents] always comment that [the dictatorship] wasn't a bad period for them. My father says that he was attending high school at night and [the military] took away his friends. Yes, he knew [about the repression], because he remembers having seen this. He remembers how people were taken away. He knew that he shouldn't talk more than what was necessary. He was careful in cutting his hair, in avoiding large gatherings of people, in doing everything well. (Nora)

The impunity with which military and police personnel operated added to the climate of fear:

My aunt and my uncle were engaged. [They] had a car accident, a crash against two guys and my aunt badly damaged her eye. The other driver was to blame. My uncle insulted him, "Look what you did to her." And the guy told him, "Look, I'm a cop, do you want to disappear? If you don't want to disappear don't open your mouth." My aunt and uncle couldn't do anything. (Andrés)

It seems that stories of terror also circulate within families whose members are in the armed forces. This was true in the case of Alicia, whose parents and some uncles were police officers:

I don't know why my mother is a cop. She's now retired. She's the "anti-cop," the "opposite prototype." The police do this and she does the contrary. For her, the whole dictatorship was wrong. My mother always says that she doesn't want for her children what she lived through. Even if she didn't experience it as a student, it wasn't very nice to see that they took pregnant women to the police station and nobody would ever know what happened to them. Moreover, during those times she asked for a leave of absence. In 1978 she was pregnant with me and asked for a leave because the atmosphere in the police station was chaotic. [My mother] told me this when I was in 7th grade and had seen a film at school. I asked her what had happened because I was given a survey as homework. I remember that I was told in school to ask the people around me, "How did you live the years of the dictatorship?"

Alicia had also conducted this survey among her family's friends:

I asked a person who worked at the police headquarters and who did experience that period. But he told me "I'm not going to answer this, you're too young, ask me when you're older." My curiosity didn't go away and I later asked the question again. He was one of the persons who "loaded" and "unloaded" prisoners from the trucks. It's really horrible when he talks about this. And I thought, "I'm glad that he didn't tell me this when I was thirteen because I'd have killed him." He saw people blindfolded for so long that they had worms in their eyes. And the metal wire with which they tied their hands would get into their skin. Many times [the police] had to remove the wires and took off pieces of skin. [The police officer] couldn't complain because [his superior] would [At this point, Alicia made a noise indicating he might kill him]. I asked him, "How did you manage to go through all that?" And he told me, "Tasks of my job." Many times he had to clean the blood from the police cars. Really, those who were at police stations had a very bad time because it was tragic. Police officers might not have had so much contact with, let's say, the kidnappings but yes at the police headquarters.

There were also stories of the fear under which entire communities lived, like the experiences of Irma, whose family has lived in a *villa* (shantytown) for three generations. The dictatorship embarked on a cosmetic, and brutal, "cleanup" of cities by destroying *villas* but without providing new housing to their inhabitants, thereby forcing people to relocate in shantytowns more removed from downtown or residential areas. Irma had heard many stories about it:

> During the military [dictatorship] the only thing [authorities] did was to eradicate the *villas*; they wanted to do this at any price. And the military and the police would come in their military trucks, surround the neighborhood, take everybody away, without caring if they had children, and destroy their homes. [The military] wanted to throw out my family but the neighbors organized and stayed. On any given day you'd go to work and come back to find out that they'd demolished your home, all your possessions had been taken away, and you had to go to a warehouse to look for them. I don't think this is good, to be tossed out like that during the military dictatorship, for being poor, for living in a *villa*.

Widespread repression, the inhumane treatment of those seen as enemies of the regime, and the feelings of vulnerability and impotence, thus, were strong components of the memories young people inherited about the terror.

Although it is very unpopular to publicly praise the dictatorship, I always encouraged participants to share any comments they had heard pointing to "positive" aspects of those years. The restoration of order was a most praised benefit, often compared with the chaos before the coup or current high rates of crime. During times of terror ordinary crime usually diminishes. So there were references to the criminal-free streets, with no burglaries, no rapes, and no murders—crimes monopolized by the dictatorship.

Juan's parents worked at the state-owned savings institution, where many employees disappeared.[6] They exemplify the position of those not directly affected by the repression who continue to affirm that life was not bad:

> I think [my parents] condone or condoned [the dictatorship]. The idea of the military was not right for them, but they worked night shifts, never had a problem, no one ever bothered them. They say that they were aware that [the military] took away people who weren't involved in anything. But [my parents] had no involvement [with politics], none in my family had; there are no disappeared in my family. They

lived a peaceful life. For them, it wasn't as bad as it's said because they were never stopped and no one ever came to search their house. They were never fearful and they felt safe. [My parents] are people who mind their own business and don't get involved in anything. They accept what's imposed on them. They don't question.

Mario had a comparable version of the events:

My uncle told me that he'd go to the university and, sometimes, the military would stop him; that's all. [The military] were very authoritarian. [They] would inspect things but that was all. For instance, my friend's mother told me that she'd always walk in the streets without being fearful, nothing ever happened to her, she never had a problem.

Many comments attested to the firmly grounded perception that "no involvement" (in political activities) meant "nothing to fear": "My mother didn't get involved in anything so she told me that she felt safer when she went out, there were less robberies, less rapes" (Mabel).

Similarly, when I asked who knew somebody, particularly a young person, who defended the military regime, Nora answered:

My mother is the person I know best who defends that epoch. She doesn't say, "How nice the way [the military] tortured." But she says that she was more protected. That now she's praying every time [me and my brothers] go out. That she'd feel much safer living in those times because she knows us well and is aware that we're not involved in anything strange. Maybe [authorities] would stop and check us but would realize that we've nothing [compromising]. So she'd be tranquil because no one would rob us, nothing bad would happen to us. She's the person I know who supports [that epoch]. She doesn't belong to any [political] party. She sees [the dictatorship] as a period where nothing bad happened to her; she worked, got married, and had a daughter.

However, some interviewees were aware of how relative the issue of safety was. Graciela, a fifteen-year-old high school student, described some inconsistencies:

Who told me good things about those times? To be honest, everybody, almost everybody told me the same thing: that it had its bad parts but it also had its good aspects; let's say "good" in quotes. The bad part was that [the military] would come in and kill anybody. But the good part was that you could walk safely in the streets, assuming that you were not into something that [authorities] could come after you and kill you. You could walk in the streets knowing that no one would mug or rape you, because [criminals] knew that they and their families would be killed. We could say that this was what was good. But good quote, unquote. Let's say that there was security, but security for whom? There was security for some but not for all.

Another praised aspect of the dictatorship was the economy. During the repression, the middle class enjoyed quite an economic bonanza, which may explain the longing for those times, popularly known as the "sweet money," when thousands of Argentineans were able to travel and shop around the world while other thousands were tortured and disappeared. As Patricia, a fifteen-year-old high school student, said:

> I was told that the economy was in good shape. The first time that I heard about the military was when my uncle said: "Why don't we go back to the times of the military? The economy was better." That stayed with me forever. I don't' know if this is true or not because I never asked him about the economy. But this is what my uncle, who has kind of liberal ideas, always says. He also said that the country grew more, that there was a better exploitation of resources. He doesn't defend the military but says that, in that sense, they were better organized.

Alicia shed light on other dimensions of society perceived to be working better during that period. She remembered being a child and witnessing many discussions at family gatherings:

> For instance, my cousin has been always a "subversive," that's what we call him. His father is a police officer and my cousin is the total opposite. The kid is one thing, his father another. [My cousin's] position was, "The military are sons of bitches, they killed tons of people and we're in this situation because of them." And the father maintained that during the military government things were better; for example it had been easier to pay bills. And this is something that I always remember because I couldn't believe that they'd put so much emphasis on paying the phone bill faster and without waiting in line. I was a child who listened to that and said, "Why is it such a mess to pay a bill?"

Not waiting in line cannot be taken for granted in a country where most errands have to be done in person and take hours. But it is notable that someone could point to not waiting in line to counter his son's accusations of torture and crime. In this surrealistic dialogue, inconsistencies were visible even to a child.

I was also told of a poll exploring voting trends in future elections conducted by high school students for a history class. The project was carried out in a neighborhood where many military families live. The students who conducted the survey lived in that neighborhood and were critical of the dictatorship. As Hugo, a fifteen-year-old student, explained:

> It was a school assignment. They told us to conduct a survey, go around the neighborhood and ask people in the streets whom they liked and whom they'd vote for. Many told us, "The military." And when we asked, "Why?" many would say: "Because it's

better to go back to those times, the military is much better than what we have now, at least there's discipline, there's order." That's what they said.

Since there is no "military" political party, many of those surveyed were suggesting that civilian rule is not something they hold in high regard. Students interpreted their comments as praise for a "golden past" worth returning to. And we should not overlook this longing for order. Feeling "safe" might have, for some, minimized the brutality of the regime.

However, representations of this past were more complex than a clear-cut "bad" or "good" period or fear/safety dichotomy. The post-dictatorship generation has been exposed to different, often conflicting, explanations about the events. Carmen's case illustrates how family members and peers provide multiple versions of the past:

According to what my mother tells me, life in rural areas was much better during that period. The military always brought food or medical assistance. My grand-parents were poor, had seven children and no access to health care and all that. [My mother] remembers that period and says that it was more peaceful than now. For example, there were no burglaries. But my uncle says that he'd go out at night without being sure if he'd come back. He was once with a bunch of people at a bus stop and was taken to the police station where they shaved his long hair. He says, "I hadn't done anything and was on my way to work. That's all." My classmate at the university told me that she saw her father burning books about Perón and Evita so [the military] wouldn't find anything in case they searched her home. The military came, anyway, and took away her brother but he was later released. They've told me many things.

Nora also discussed the conflicting stories she had been told:

I heard many people saying that [the dictatorship] was good because, for example, you'd go out knowing that no one would rob you and that nothing would happen to you if you hadn't done anything. And I heard from people who told me that it was terrible, that you couldn't even leave your house because it was so scary. You couldn't study because depending on what you were studying or on any document or flyer you may have, you risked being taken away and never coming back.

This multiplicity of stories is not always easy to digest. During a heated debate with his classmates, all of them extremely critical of the dictatorship, Jorge expressed his confusion:

My dad tells me, "I used to walk in the middle of the street and no one would do anything to me." My mother's friends tell me, "We walked in the middle of the street and nothing happened to us." My boss tells me, "During the military period if I was walking in the street and a patrol passed by they'd say 'hi' to me, they wouldn't do anything to me." How was it? Whom shall I believe?

Jorge was not the only participant concerned by the contradictions he had encountered. It is still too soon to assess which will be the most accepted account of how it felt to live under terror. It appears that, even among people who claim that they did not support the dictatorship, memories of order, economic growth, and stability neutralize the terror and the human rights abuses perpetrated during it. Moreover, transmitted feelings of "fear" and "safety" seem to be linked to people's involvement or noninvolvement in political activities.

Horror as Filter

We now know about the level of atrocities committed. Survivors' accounts and the discovery of corpses tell us of countless horror stories that provide a detailed picture of what repression meant. Anything was possible and we cannot classify any account as "unthinkable." However, there are stories that we might never be able to corroborate but that have become part of the collective memories of terror and are good examples of the rumors circulating, of the horror that was or might have been.

Fabiana, a fifteen-year-old high school student, shared memories of her father's pals being taken away:

> My father was young, seventeen years old, and was playing soccer with some friends. It was during the repression and [the soldiers] came onto the soccer field and took all of them. They let go my father and three other friends who had IDs. All the rest disappeared. It's not known where they went.

It is uncertain where these young men ended up. Maybe they were killed, but it is also possible that they were released and were so terrified by the experience that they decided to stay away from any public gathering. But what her father remembers is the experience of being with a group of friends who literally vanished.

The sadism of the harassment to which people were subjected is present in the story that Mónica heard from her friend's father:

> He was walking around the port with two friends when the cops arrived. There's a little balcony facing the river. They were forced to walk blindfolded on the balcony's edge while [the cops] shot at them. The shots weren't intended to hit but the blindfolded guys were walking on that edge with the river underneath and feeling shots around them. [He] says, "The feeling of impotence, because I was doing nothing, just walking. Without asking for my ID, without any warning, they blindfolded me and started shooting at me."

But not all were mock executions, and thousands of people were killed. The bodies of 30,000 *desaparecidos* are not easy to hide. Many prisoners were thrown into the ocean (the "death flights"), buried in mass graves, or burned—the *asados* (barbecue) in the jargon of the concentration camps. I also heard of bodies used in landfills, buried in construction sites, or stuffing soccer fields. Several macabre findings confirm the possibility of all these atrocities, but many of the stories I heard reveal a perception that there are bodies all over the city, all over the country. For instance, a young woman commented on her finding at the beach: "Sometimes, human bones are found in the river; the sea also brings them. Once, during my vacations, I found a femur at the seaside. And there are not that many people who drown there" (Beatriz). Rather than assuming that it was from someone who drowned—a logical hypothesis at the seashore—she took it for granted that it belonged to a disappeared person.

Certain accounts, thus, indicate that terror had altered how ordinary events and things were perceived, as if some people were looking at life through what we may call a "horror lens." A friend of Laura, who worked on the extension of the subway system, had told her of discoveries during the construction:

In the new subway, which was built at that time, there are tons of corpses in the tunnels' walls. There are tons of people buried in the cement, tons of human remains. It's assumed that they belong to the disappeared. There's coincidence with the dates [of their death and the repression]. But no one ever said anything, no one investigated. [My friend] told me that they found remains and the rumor was that they belonged to disappeared people.

Analía told me of the day when she and a friend were sitting at a public square and were approached by an older man:

There are many denunciations that nothing is being done to uncover the many corpses buried in military garrisons. I once met a guy. He started a conversation with [me and my friend]. It was very weird. He sat next to us and started talking about the times of the military dictatorship. He told us that he'd been in the military and had friends among them. And that there were tons of bodies buried in what used to be Platense's soccer field. The guy condoned what had happened during the dictatorship. And I remember being stunned because he told us about all the people taken in the death flights and that, at any moment [the military] would take power again. Something weird . . . we tried to ask him, "What's your name?" and the guy would ignore it. But I remember that after talking to the guy [my friend] told me, "There was a moment that I tried signaling at you but he was checking what I was doing and I got scared." And we both were left with a feeling of fear.

Although only full investigations and disclosure could confirm these macabre episodes, those who told me these stories seemed convinced of their veracity and had incorporated them into their representations of the past.

Childhood Memories of Terror

Horror stories are not limited to what participants were told. A few of them had amazingly vivid memories of events witnessed and experienced when they were very young. Their accounts had the photographic precision of what are called "flashbulb memories" to define memories that are a blend of personal circumstances and historical events, which are of high importance to an individual, and whose details are remembered with extraordinary accuracy.[7] These firsthand accounts of experiences under terror offer different insights than the secondhand accounts, the bulk of the stories that I heard, which were reconstructions of the past transmitted by participants' elders.

Roberto, a twenty-six-year-old student studying for teacher's certification, was from Famaillá, a small town in the province of Tucumán famous for the brutal repression that took place there. But his first memory of fear is of an event that took place when his family moved to Buenos Aires. He described his encounter with terror through one of the frequent episodes of the military stopping people for whatever reason they wanted:

> I can't forget something that happened when I was six. We were leaving the subway station. I was with my father. A guy walked next to us. The military were at the exit and made us stop. The fear we felt! I saw fear in my father's face when he stopped, paralyzed. It was because the guy next to us was wearing a long green jacket like those the military wear. So the military officer said he couldn't wear that jacket and ordered him to take it off. What I remember is what [my father], maybe joking, said, "[The military officer] liked the jacket." This is what I remember my father saying. They put the guy against the wall and stripped off the green jacket he was wearing. The feeling, I remember the face of my father because I first looked at him when [the military] shouted at us. Everybody froze. We then continued walking and my father made that comment, in a very soft voice, of course, "He liked the jacket." I felt the fear, too. Fear gets transmitted, for sure.

We speculated why his father had said that the military had probably taken the man's jacket because they liked it. Maybe he wanted to protect his son, resorting to humor to suggest that nothing really happened. But it is also possible that his father had tried to explain that the military was omnipotent and could do anything. Probably not even his father would know why he said what he did. What we know is the terror that Roberto felt and so vividly remembered twenty years later.

Diego, whose family was active in the Peronist party, remembered when he was only four years old and learned about unidentified graves (NN) where corpses of political prisoners were dumped:

> When I was a kid, I often went to the cemetery to visit our family's graves. I remember that I used to go with an uncle, who's my godfather. While we were there, my

aunt and uncle would visit the NN graves. On the way back, they used to talk about the NN. I didn't understand much what it was about. Then, as time went by, I understood.

Eugenia's memories of terror go back to when she was very young, when paramilitary gangs in their cars stormed throughout the streets of her neighborhood:

I was a kid but I remember that period. I was only three or four years old but I remember very vividly being in the street with my mother and seeing those cars with long weapons coming out from the windows. It happened twice and I think I won't ever forget them. Obviously I didn't see the men, I think I was afraid of look-ing at them. I was on the sidewalk. It seems that everything happened suddenly. I was with my mother. We live on a street crossed by an avenue [the paramilitary cars] entered in the wrong direction. I never knew where they went because I was afraid of the weapons. I think that my mother didn't look either because that's how [the military] trained people: Don't look, don't get involved. I remember this very well. The second time I was older. I think I was coming home from the kindergarten and [the military] went to a street two blocks from my house and stopped there. We heard noise of the brakes. I didn't see it. I think my mother didn't let me look. I think that during those times, beyond the walls of our house, my mother had the attitude of the whole country, which was, essentially, an attitude of fear.

Even though Eugenia is not a political activist, she told me how her own memories and the stories she had been told affected her:

Today, after so many years of democratic government, I feel safe and free to come to talk with you about this topic. At the beginning of the democratic period, and for a long time, my mother used to tell me that many people disappeared for being involved in "that whole subject" and for being an acquaintance or being in the address book of a person who was involved. Many people disappeared due to these reasons. And those things stayed with me. They stayed with me up to the point that, when I grew up and had my own address book, I even wondered if it was necessary. I reasoned, "They change the government at any time and what do I do with all these people [in my address book]; do I know them or not?" What my mother told me really got to me. I got scared.

The Legacy of Fear

In spite of the different postmemories of life under terror, fear has persisted over the years. Even though they might not have acknowledged it, the older generation showed their fears by warning their children against involvement in any kind of political activity. What had been told to young people often reveals hard-to-understand contradictions: parents who insisted on how safe it was to live under terror had, unconsciously or not, transmitted fear to their children.

Participants were very conscious of their elders' fears and there was a widespread perception that these fears were a legacy of the terror: "I think that this attitude of 'don't look, don't get close' was born during the military coup, each one minding her own business. These fears of everything that people have today started there" (Silvia). As a young woman explained while mimicking her father's voice and gestures: "My dad puts me in a state of paranoia. The other day we were walking by a police station and he said, 'Let's cross the street.' He always does that" (Claudia). By witnessing the enactment of her father's old fears, she nonetheless could only understand second-hand how terror was embodied in police stations. Laura told me about her father hiding compromising books:

> Books like [Marx's] *Capital* . . . my father has all the books by Marx and Lenin. But they're all hidden, even now. They were always hidden. We have a large bookshelf that [my father] built during the dictatorship. The shelves have room for one book in the back and one book in the front hiding the back row. Those books were always hidden. There are several revolutionary, "evil," books.

Moreover, in discussing the intergenerational transmission of fears, Laura noted how the particular experiences and attitudes of parents were crucial in influencing young people's fears:

> [Some kids] were breast fed with fear. If a kid lives in a home where her parents are terrified and don't go out at night, she feels those things. There were parents who were always afraid during the military regime. They couldn't live a quiet life, scared that "[the military] would come and take us away." When you live in fear, you transmit this to your children.

However, the continuing presence of fear among young people could be explained by either paranoia or well-founded concerns depending on the perceived dangers of the political activities in which young people may get involved. It is known that a whole generation was paralyzed by fear of physical pain. Twenty years after the coup, some participants were afraid of being tortured. And although most interviewees did not think that conditions comparable to the dictatorship could happen again, they did not discard the possibility. Since the perpetrators of brutal crimes were benefiting from amnesties, it stands to reason that "if they did it once they could do it again."

Young people's fears combined inherited and current fears. The stories they had been told were the background, the knowledge that contextualized their contemporary fears. Current fears were usually linked to concerns about ongoing surveillance by the authorities and to cases of police brutality against young people, including the crushing of demonstrations. As Analía explained:

> I think that it's fear that was somehow transmitted and has turned into a lack of participation. If you're going to a demonstration, someone always tells you, "Be careful." And all that's happening with the police helps a lot [in increasing the fear]. The last demonstration organized by a leftist political party, I think it was Quebracho, which was to repudiate the arrival of [president] Clinton, ended up with riots, people taken to jail, all the "trimmings."

Thus, old fears strengthened current fears of political participation. According to Mercedes, who at twenty-four was studying to be a professor of English:

> What happened during that period generated skepticism and despair, "What can we do?" "Look what happened to those who tried to do something." It seems that we're overcoming this now but it first generated an attitude of "It's better not to get involved, it's better to stay away. What's the point? Look at the way [those who got involved] ended." Ordinary people say this. And they're right; it's true. "They got involved and look how they ended up. I better not get involved; I better stay away." It's a matter of survival instinct.

Most participants were politically quiescent. But I share here a great percentage of the comments that I heard about the fear of political participation from those few interviewees who had some experience as activists and made references to past and present fears. Their activism included marches, demonstrations, and participating in students' centers (*Centro de Estudiantes*). These are student-run organizations that all high schools have. They offer a space for social and cultural activities, ranging from exhibits to film screenings, and including the planning of and participation in political events, either inside or outside the school. These centers were a space for activism in the early 1970s and became a target of the dictatorship.

Flor, a sixteen-year-old student, had a story about a high school sit-in illustrating how parents' fear for their children's activism is one of the predominant forms that the legacy of terror takes:

> We told everybody, "We're organizing a sit-in for this reason, these are our demands, join us if you want." And there were guys who told us, "We agree with you but we're afraid that [school authorities] would do something to us; my father doesn't want me to do this." And that day, that Saturday, all the mothers came [to the school] because we were going to have the sit-in outside the building, in the street. They told us, "Don't do that because there might be another 'night of the long sticks'[8] and the police can take you in." I went to a friend's house and her mother warned me, "Watch out, maybe the school identifies you and the police will come for you.

Be aware that if you get involved in this [school authorities] will register it." There are guys whose parents don't let them participate in the Student Center and things like that, and who supported the sit-in but didn't take part because, "Maybe my father will find out, or the school will identify me."

Although in most societies parents are, in general, concerned about their children's safety, these worries were particularly focused on the potential consequences of public activities that involved taking a political stand. Flor argued that there was no reason to be afraid and pointedly blamed those parents for inculcating fear:

[These] parents are the kind of people who say, "Don't get involved in anything." It seems to me that these are people to whom nothing happened [during the dictatorship] and don't want anything to happen. So they prefer to avoid any [political] commitment.

To be on a black list, in the wrong address book, or associated with someone considered "subversive" were real dangers during the dictatorship. Rumor was one of the means by which terror was spread. Most participants talked about current fears and some mentioned "rumors" about the existence of "lists"—using the same terminology as in the 1970s. While in high school, Marcelo was a member of the student center. His story illustrates well how rumors continue to generate fear:

I remember something very precise. I was a member of the student center. It was more of a social activity for me than an involvement for change. Our center was apolitical, without any political orientation. We did things for the school and the students. We didn't criticize important people; we could say that we didn't make much noise. We heard the rumor that they'd requested the list of those students in the center. Moreover, I think it was even published in the newspaper that the police had requested the lists of those high school student centers. And I went to talk to the Principal and he told me that nothing had happened, that no one had ever requested a list. But I felt fear then. Obviously, we knew what had happened [during the dictatorship] but we wouldn't discuss these issues openly. It's for that reason that we became fearful. I was afraid, I asked, "Why?" Many of us considered leaving the center until we spoke with the Principal who told us, "Don't worry; it's only a rumor."

Alberto, a twenty-one-year-old future teacher, explained that his Church decided to build links with certain groups in the community, in this particular case with the police. He remembered how his father and his peers' parents reacted:

We had only one talk with police officers. We approached them with the idea of what we could do for them, what they thought the church could do for them and they were very defensive. When I told my father what we did, his answer scared me. I don't remember exactly what he said but he warned me about approaching people who could add me to a list. I was a bit scared then, but not when I talked to the cops. I think that something similar happened in the other homes. We didn't discuss it as a group, yet we didn't go back.

This reaction should not surprise us, considering the fate suffered by many nuns, priests, and lay people who disappeared under the eyes of a silent Church hierarchy. It was not the first time that Alberto had been warned about the dangers of being on a "black list." He remembered another occasion:

I didn't believe it until a friend made me think that [lists] do exist. He told me that, for him, lists continue to exist. Moreover, I'd never known about the existence of lists, I'd no idea of what lists were. But the subject came up while talking to him about the gathering of signatures [for a petition at school]. According to what he told me, he believes that we still have lists today.

Hence, warnings of the dangers of participation do not come exclusively from parents. Friends or classmates also are afraid for their peers and try to protect them using the same arguments and words of their elders. Laura explained that:

My friend was afraid for me because I was in the student center and there was a period, when I was in my 3rd year that there was a lot of talk about a coup d'état, at least within my [social] circles. That there was going to be a coup, that Menem would be forced to step down, that the military were in turmoil. And my friend was afraid. He'd tell me, "What are you doing? Leave the center now. You're already on the black list. Don't play with this. Stop it. We'll have a coup and the same things will happen again."

Sometimes, fear of activism was rooted in memories of persecutions or exile that a family had experienced during the dictatorship. At fifteen, Patricia had to withdraw from her position of student representative (to the school authorities) of her high school class:

The majority [of the disappeared Argentineans] were studying at universities. This is what I was told because, at that time, my aunt studied history and was on a black list. She left the country so they wouldn't take her away and came back in 1986. Last year I was the student representative and I wanted to continue during this year. And my father told me, "Look, this is what happened to your aunt." So, I say, "Nothing happens now—supposedly there's a certain political stability, but if one day something happens and I'm in a list it could be a bit dangerous." That's why I'm no longer a student representative. Although there might be fewer risks because it's a high school, it's better to prevent them.

Nora was a member of the student center at her high school and remembers that:

> When I said that I'd been at a meeting at the student center, my mother said, "Where? Are you crazy? Look in what you get involved in. I don't want you in any mess." Sometimes she says, "Watch out what you say." And I say, "But we're living in different times." [My mother has] fear that something might happen, that the military will be back in power or something like that, and that someone will have my phone number, just because I was friendly and gave it out. And there's nothing friendly in being taken away. At first, I didn't understand why she was telling me that but as I grow up I understand better why she says this.

Interestingly, Nora's mother still maintains that those times were safer than current ones but she has no control over her fear emerging at any moment. There is an incongruence between the denial of fear during the terror and an assimilation of this fear that had survived two decades.

The pervasive memory of the dangers of being in the wrong address book translates into another concrete, and inherited, fear: the potential risks of being associated with someone who might be considered an "agitator" and could become a target of repression. Carmen explained how her mother encouraged her to be suspicious of her classmates:

> The first thing my mother told me was, "Watch out to whom you give your phone number; you don't know what might happen." She didn't say much but I think it was because of the military. If someone whom she doesn't know calls me she asks, "How do you know this person? Why does she know your phone number? Who gave it to her, you or another person?" It's constantly like this. I perceive that she's afraid that I'd get lumped with someone [involved in something risky] and that they'd come for me even if I've nothing to do with it.

Marches and demonstrations assert a political position in a visible, and therefore vulnerable, way. Taking to the streets to protest for a variety of issues, ranging from demands for higher education budgets to calls for the de-penalization of prostitution, is intrinsic to Argentina's political culture. The police often repress these public events and the possibility of beatings and being taken to jail is latent in most public gatherings with large crowds of young people.[9] And there have been some cases of young people who died in police custody during civilian rule. Alicia, who comes from a family of police officers, explained why most parents did not want their children, especially the younger ones, to go to those events:

> The past comes back. You see the current repression and you remember the repression you suffered in the seventies. You see similar things happening although not at the same level. [They] are afraid that we'll go through the same they endured, that

we'll go out one day and never come back, and [they] will wonder, "What happened? She went to a march; where is she? Who knows?" It's as if fear, the old fear resurfaces. And there are many cases of kids who died, who were killed by the police.

This allegation of police brutality by a daughter of police officers exemplifies young people's generalized opinions of the institution. Few participants had taken part in marches or been at a violent demonstration, but most of them mentioned how the police disrupted them. This is due, in part, to media coverage, which projects images of beatings and people fleeing the scene. As Mercedes explained:

[They] are always ready, even if there's no repression. It doesn't matter if it's a peaceful march; you see them wearing their helmets, riding tall horses, always ready and willing to crush you. This is what generates fear and anger. [They] are always ready to beat you.

This description of most demonstrations is quite accurate. Security forces in uniform or civilian clothes are always there, displaying their power and scaring people, "reminding" one of what can happen if things get out of control, often taking photos of demonstrators, which is another form of intimidation. This scene, threatening for those of us who remember the past repression, is also threatening for young people. Thus, young people's fear of police repression of marches is based both on present dangers and on the stories they had been told. Moreover, current repression was a reenactment of the past, a catalyst by which old fears resurfaced.

Conclusions

Different ways of experiencing and remembering terror have resulted in narratives of widespread repression interwoven with those of order. Although most stories of life under terror convey feelings of fear, at times, while listening to participants' stories, it seemed that their elders had lived in two different worlds: one where terror was a constant presence permeating all environments, illustrated by macabre and terrifying chronicles; another characterized by order, security, and economic stability. These differences illustrate the diversity and plurality of memories, the two sides of the same coin.

Many accounts transmit the panic felt by people who every day faced the possibility of never returning to their homes, often resorting to the metaphorical expression "people were unable to go outdoors." These fears also resulted in behaviors such as avoiding activists, hiding compromising books, and acting so as not to attract any suspicion. Yet, even those with "positive" memories of the dictatorship had been unable to hide their awareness of a surrounding horror, for there were no major disagreements about the brutality of the repression, only on its magnitude or on who was affected and how. The notion that the whole community was in danger, thus, is contrasted by the belief that repression only targeted enemies of the regime and that those who were not involved in political activities had nothing to fear. Hence, the various levels of perceived risk, or how close or distant the threat was felt, have originated different discourses on the transmission of fear.

If order and safety neutralized fear, we need to rethink the fear/order equation and assess the social cost that people may be willing to pay to feel safe. Recognition of the benefits of terror can be interpreted as an approval of means justifying ends or may indicate that people focused on positive angles as a shield from the fear. We may need to dig deeper into people's assertions that they were never afraid in order to understand how denial is a form of protection. Furthermore, continuing to minimize the magnitude of terror and fear may be a step in the process of self-deception by which some Argentineans develop mechanisms to defend a positive self-image and cope with a difficult past.

Studies on the culture of fear in the southern cone of Latin America indicate that, in societies that suffered generalized or centralized violence, "fear is a paramount feature of social action."[10] The voices of the post-dictatorship generation contribute to our understanding of the political, cultural, and social legacies of fear. Fear had persisted through the years. It was palpable in what the witness generation had transmitted and in what some participants experienced when they were small children. However, postmemories of terror are relevant to the extent that they shape attitudes and actions in the present and, consequently, influence the future. We need to ask what power memories of fear have in today's Argentina and in which realms this legacy affects the present.

As these conversations show, memories of terror were influencing the post-dictatorship generation's ways of thinking and acting. Specific outcomes of the remains of fear mirror quite closely how the witness generation experienced terror and the mechanisms people developed to avoid becoming a victim. Explicitly or implicitly, most parents had told their children to stay away from activities that were repressed in the past. Young people's stories also tell of the fear of repression in the present and the perception that "big brother" was observing each move. This translated into a tendency to be apolitical and to avoid public and political participation. Most interviewees were afraid to participate in student and community organizations, political parties, or street demonstrations that involve students or young people.

Many participants had been effectively deterred by warnings to "stay away," which seemed to be grounded on the memories of the 1970s—unmistakable signs that many young people had assimilated old fears. Twenty-two years after the coup, "no involvement" continued to convey feelings of safety from current or future repression. Parents also transmitted the fear of being associated with political activists as they encouraged their children to distrust potentially compromising people.

The direct as well as the "collateral" effects of terror necessarily tint processes by which communities must address the aftermath of mass violence. What these conversations tell us is that when terror is over its effects remain for years to come and, like radiation, take forms that are not always predictable. Besides, we need yet to assess the cumulative effect of being exposed to stories of horror—often fragmented and decontextualized like the one that opened this chapter—on people's perceptions of the kind of suffering they can expect—if they were capable of putting live rats in women's vaginas, what's next?[11] The fears discussed here, thus, are well grounded. Countless accounts document the atrocities committed by the dictatorship.[12] These are not fears about what "might happen," which can be found in all types of societies, but fears about what "might happen again."

It is in the context of powerful and influential memories of fear, and mindful that the post-dictatorship generation is deeply constrained from becoming politically active, that I now move from conversations about fear to conversations about societal silences, another element in the cycle of fear, silence, and knowledge.

THREE

Conversations about Silences

Introduction

El silencio es Salud (Silence is Health) read the inscription on the gigantic sign that was posted at the time of the military coup around the obelisk, a landmark monument in Avenida 9 de Julio, the widest avenue at the center of downtown Buenos Aires. Although it was part of a campaign to reduce traffic noise, it is hard not to ascribe to this slogan—especially when looking at it more than two decades later—another obvious meaning, an advisory on the benefits of silence: "Don't ask, don't listen, don't accuse."

The imposed social silence was one of the mechanisms to strengthen terror. As Taussig notes, "cultures of terror are based on and nourished by silence."[1] Silence intensified feelings of panic and was adopted by people as a condition for survival—their own or that of the missing persons (in the case of relatives of the disappeared). The feeling that something terrible was happening made people afraid of asking or learning more. People lived under a permanent double reality, witnessing the disparity between printed news and events they heard of or read between lines. The potential collaboration of doormen or the tapping of telephones made any place unsafe and made people suspicious of their neighbors or coworkers. Information was shared in private or clandestine spheres within the limited circle that people could trust.[2] As Eugenia said: "Based on terror, misinformation, who would dare to speak out at that time? Nobody." To understand the impact of the "silencing" of Argentina we must bear in mind that it is a country with a long history of vigorous public political debate. In any city or town, each café is a meeting place where all problems—of the neighborhood, the country, or the world—are loudly and openly discussed—and "solved."

In fact, silence itself was terror. This relationship between silence and terror was well understood by Rodolfo Walsh, a prestigious writer, journalist, and political activist assassinated by the dictatorship in 1977. Under the premise that terror was based in atomization and to challenge the imposed silence, he created Agencia de Noticias Clandestina (ANCLA), a clandestine news agency, and Cadena Informativa (Information Network). Each communiqué ended with these words by Walsh:

> Cadena Informativa is one of the instruments that the Argentine people are creating to break the blockade of information. Cadena Informativa can be yourself, an instrument, by which you may free yourself and others from terror. Reproduce this information through any means that you have access to: handwritten, typewriter, mimeo. Send copies to your friends: nine out of ten will be waiting for them. Millions want to be informed. *Terror is based on the lack of communication.* Break the isolation. Feel again the moral satisfaction of an act of freedom. Defeat terror. Circulate this information.[3] (My emphasis)

We know that collective remembering is a communication process that involves the social activity of people actively thinking and talking about events.[4] Since the dictatorship was an extremely traumatic and "silent" period, silences have a role in the ongoing memory construction process. One of my concerns was to assess the palpable effects of a legacy of silences, and the effect of sharing thoughts with a few people at the time of the terror might be shaping the scope of the memories circulating in its aftermath. For silence is never absolute. Rial notes that, during the Uruguayan dictatorship, people were able to create "pockets of resistance," and circles of family and friends became "barriers against terror."[5] Similarly, Passerini explains how, in spite of the apparent amnesia in the public sphere, there were "kitchen memories" preserved in Stalin's Russia.[6]

I was also exploring how silence is in itself a component and a language of the memories of this past. What is silenced is as important as what is said; what is not spoken about an event is telling something about it. While researching memories of fascism in Turin's working class, Passerini encountered the fact that interviewees refused to answer certain questions, joked, or gave irrelevant and inconsistent answers that did not mention fascism at all.[7] She argues that we cannot study memory without studying silence, for silence has a role to play in the structure of memory.[8] In his study of memories of the Cultural Revolution in China, Jing noted that memories of persecution present silences, fragmented narratives, and evasions.[9] Along the same lines, Leydesdorff uses the expression "shattered silence" to point to the silences in the narratives of survivors of the Holocaust; silences that are often a "painful noise," where certain issues that were not discussed resulted in a silence that was "deafening."[10] As we see, these are recognizable patterns in participants' postmemories.

This chapter seeks answers to the question "With whom, where, when, and how did you talk about the dictatorship?" It focuses on what was silenced or said within two main spheres, the family—including the extended one—and the school, a realm that should not be seen in isolation but as a reflection of social silences or debates in the public sphere. It explores the process by which the transmission of bits and pieces of this past challenges the pervasiveness of silences and produces knowledge of particular characteristics. It identifies young people's perceptions of the reasons behind those silences and what they made of such a lack of talk about this past.

The Remains of Silence

We know something about how the remains of fear were affecting society. But what about the legacy of the social silence imposed by the dictatorship? Are there any long-term effects?

There were many conversations about silences, themselves acts of breaking silences. The question "With whom have you talked about the dictatorship?" was often answered with expressions defining lack of talk such as "We don't talk about that," "[They] never told me," or "We don't talk much." And, in answering the question "Why people don't talk about the dictatorship?" participants described the weight and persistence of the silences by linking present silences to the past terror: "Terror and fear were very powerful and massive because, even today, there are many people who don't dare or don't want to talk" (Irma). "I think that, in many senses, the majority of people who lived that period held on to their fear of talking" (Nora). Other participants made specific connections between silences and memory: "There's not much talk about that topic because people want to forget" (Nelson).

These comments reflect a society that suffered terror and now, still afraid and incapable of dealing with it, wants to put this past behind it. Some participants expressed the belief held by some people that not talking about this past can erase it—I do not name it therefore it does not exist. Silences are thus seen as mechanisms to cope with this traumatic period. However, this was not considered an effective strategy. As Susana, a sixteen-year-old high school student, noted:

> It seems that people want to forget but they can't. They can't forget no matter how much they want to. That period and what they lost during it are engraved in them. This loss hurts. Moreover, I don't think you can ever erase memories.

Silences at Home

A pattern of systematic silences about the dictatorship was evident in all types of families—families where nothing in particular had happened, families with a disappeared relative or close friend, families with activist parents, and families that included members of the military or the police.

In homes where nothing particular happened and families were not directly touched by the repression, talk about it had been minimal. Typical comments included:

> We don't talk that much at home about military dictatorships; it's not at all a regular conversation topic, not at all. Yes, we don't talk because the topic hasn't been brought up very often. Now, or in recent years, we have started to talk more about it. (Analía)
>
> I was able to ask my grandmother [about the dictatorship]. The only thing she said is that it was horrible. But she doesn't like to talk about that. (Ester)
>
> We never talked at home. The only time I heard something was when my grandmother told me that there had been a neighbor who disappeared and was never seen again. (Luciana)

Some participants seem to have accepted silences without any questioning. But others were truly amazed at how they had been denied information about this past. As Alberto said: "I'm surprised that something that's so serious is not discussed either at home, in primary school, or in high school when you're a bit older and able to understand certain things."

In some instances, participants specifically linked the lack of talk to the persistence of fear within their family. Noemí, a fifteen-year-old high school student, talked about the first time she learned about the dictatorship:

> [I learned about it] here in school, because my mother doesn't like [to talk]. She's very afraid and doesn't like to talk. So I asked my friends to tell me about it. My family doesn't discuss those issues much. I kept on asking and what they told me was terrible. I get my information from my classmates or through news recently published in newspapers. I read that. But, otherwise, my family doesn't talk much. And I think that they don't talk at home due to fear.

Another direct link between the past and the present was manifest in comments that attribute current silences to the pain that remembering those times provokes. During a conversation at their high school, five fifteen-year-old girls (Andrea, Teresa, Ester, Noemí, and Luciana) discussed what they perceived were the reasons for the silences of their parents' generation:

> They don't like to start a conversation about that. If you ask them about it they say, "No, let's not talk about that now" and look for a pretext to change the topic. They don't like to go back to the past because they suffered a lot. Maybe they don't want to remember. Some people don't want to stir up the wounds. [They think] "it's enough, why keep on talking about the same things."

As an indication of how conflictive the topic is, there were homes where families talk about most issues but avoid the dictatorship. This was true in the case of Mónica:

> To tell you the truth, there are some friends' homes where I've heard their parents talk. They remember a lot and talk a lot about this topic. Maybe they were themselves targeted. In my family, my parents never talked to me about it. Yes, maybe they discussed all the economic problems during those times. And yes, there are documentaries you see on TV of all that process of repression. I didn't have much information [as a kid]. We didn't talk at home; even when there's much dialogue about everything, it's not about this topic.

In homes with disappeared relatives, the particular circumstances that the family endured, and how they coped with them, seem to generate silences. Marcelo talked about silences in the family of his girlfriend, whose uncle disappeared:

> [The dictatorship] didn't directly affect [my family] and, in general, we didn't talk about this topic. My grandfather, who's in favor of the military and has a pretty fascist ideology, was the only one who talked about it. He supported [the dictatorship]. I began to learn more about, let's say, the reality, through my girlfriend's family. The case of [her mother's] brother resulted in a fear of talking to people outside the family. They don't tell much about it to my girlfriend, about the search, about how much they suffered. Interestingly, my girlfriend's grandfather worked in the army as a mechanic. He was warned, "Watch out with your son; take care of him." It was a way of telling him, as a consideration for being in the same institution, "Watch out, at any moment your son will be caught." And you realize that [the father] did nothing. The son was already targeted and, in some way, [they] warned him. The relationship with my girlfriend's family changed my way of thinking, contributed to my formation. But they don't talk to my girlfriend. At no point did they tell her, "Let's sit down and have a talk; ask me." Generally, she's also afraid of asking because her mother gets very upset. When she hears about it it's only a brief comment or something that she overhears. Let's say that there's not a sincere relationship. It's as if they want to avoid the topic because it's painful to remember, because there's fear of saying, "I don't want you to know about it just in case tomorrow. . . ." I believe that the family thinks that they don't want to compromise anybody because history may repeat itself. My girlfriend feels the pain because she notices her mother's pain so she doesn't ask questions. There's no sincere talk at any point.

Thus Marcelo talked of fear and pain influencing those silences. He also implied that there was the feeling of guilt for what his girlfriend's grandfather (the father of the disappeared man) could have done to protect his son, although we now know that going into hiding or exile were the only options to protect people marked as targets.

Quite the opposite, and one of the few instances of families that talk a lot about this past, was the case of Andrea, who had an aunt who had disappeared. In her family, this devastating experience has generated talk rather than silences. Moreover, she had been encouraged to speak out and challenge those who condone state terrorism, a rare attitude among those with whom I had conversations:

Although there was always talk in my house, I started asking more things when I was about eight years old: "What happened, where are [the disappeared]?" I think that it was at that point when they started telling me what had happened. We always talk about this topic, ever since I was a little girl. We don't only talk about it but also try to discuss it with outsiders. That's what my mother taught me. Because there might be people who think that it was OK and we must explain to them why it was wrong. My idea is not to explain why it was wrong to those who think that it was wrong, rather to explain why it was wrong to people who think that it was OK.

The Malvinas/Falkland War against England in 1982, the last insane venture of the dictatorship, although not linked to fear, is another experience generating silences. Carmen's uncle fought in that war and she explained how this affected her family:

I remember that [in school] when they said "Las Malvinas" I used to say, "My uncle was there." But the teacher wouldn't say, "Let's talk," or "Why," or anything. That was the end of the discussion. For Malvinas' Day [there was] a speech, you had to buy a map and color the islands. But you wouldn't know why, what happened, what was done, why we fought, why we were celebrating that day. This adds to the situation experienced at home. My uncle went to Malvinas but we never talk about that; it's a forgotten topic, nobody talks, not even my grandparents. The only thing we always remember is when I talk with my mother and she says, "I used to cry for your uncle Jorge."

Malvinas may be a difficult issue for the soldiers who took part in it and for their families. And, as the silences at Carmen's school imply, it is another angle of the terror that society was not yet ready to discuss.

We could assume that in families with a tradition of activism there is more talk, that people with strong political beliefs who were involved in a variety of struggles would want to share these experiences with their children. But I also found silences and evasions here. Laura's parents had been political activists. This was her answer when asked about the first time that she heard about the dictatorship:

I don't know the exact moment or an approximate year. But I'd say that, at home, [there was talk] all my life. But it's not a candid talk like ours now. For example, an older friend, a friend of my mother's and mine came last night for dinner. I don't know how the topic came out while we were eating pizza. The theme was that, in

1976, my mom and dad disappeared by their own decision. They changed jobs, moved, and started again from scratch. My brother was born in December 1976. And my mother talked about when they began finding out that people were disappearing. Around 1978, a friend of my father, whose house was a hideout for ERP militants, disappeared. My little brother was named after him. I just learned yesterday exactly when and why. But I knew that my brother had that name for my father's friend who had disappeared during the dictatorship. My father doesn't want to discuss what he did during the *proceso* or what [my parents] were doing at the university. My mother and my father were leftist activists. I know for sure that my mother was active in the Communist Party but my father never wanted to talk about that. He discusses the issues in general but never his personal life. If my father had been home yesterday we wouldn't have found out [details about his friend]. He doesn't want to talk about that.

Laura could be considered an Argentinean "red diaper baby."[11] However, it took twenty years for her to learn details about her father's friend. Her father, the one who continued to hide his Marx and Lenin books, had not yet discussed his political activism with his children. We can only speculate on the reasons for those silences, which might be related to pain, anger, or frustration.

There were also silences in families that included military and police personnel. Alicia, who had been assigned in school to find out how people around her had experienced the dictatorship, commented on the silences of her father, a high-ranking police officer:

What happens is that [my father] avoided the topic, at least with his children, because he didn't like it. I should ask him now why he didn't talk to me about it at that time. He doesn't agree with everything that happened. Because of his position in the police, I know that, at some point, he must have participated in something. I'm not talking of killing someone or . . . but something must have affected him a lot because . . . maybe knowing about something, so it's very . . . you see . . . we don't talk.

So Alicia believed that her father's awareness of, even involvement in, the atrocities was the reason why he did not like to discuss this period with his children. This was obviously difficult for her, and there were silences, pauses, even omitted words, in the way she made these comments, a marked contrast with the vivaciousness with which she discussed all other issues.

Silences at the home of Mariana have a similar cause. Her maternal grandfather had been in the military. She talked about the process by which she learned about the dictatorship:

I guess that [it was] when I started high school. Maybe that wasn't the first time I heard about it but I hadn't paid attention before My personal experience is that my grandfather was in the military and, at that moment [during the dictatorship], [someone] planted a bomb in his house. In order to protect [his family] he was forced to live in a place that was not even known to my mother. He retired in 1978. This is the personal story. I learned about it recently. I was talking with [a friend], the thought stayed with me, and I asked my mother what had happened, where had my grandfather been, if he had participated in the group of the "bad ones" [adds emphasis]. So [she] told me that [story]. That was it. I didn't want to ask more because I didn't want to know, and I think that my mother didn't know much, just the basics. I don't know if I didn't continue because of what [my mother] must have felt at that moment or because I realized that I wouldn't learn much so to ask her would be a waste of time. I don't know [if I'd like to know more about my grandfather]. It would be good to learn about what happened but I don't know, honestly. My grandfather was in the military and was the kindest person in the world.

Mariana, whether out of concern for her mother's feelings or reluctance to learn more about her grandfather, had chosen to perpetuate the silences about the dictatorship and avoid any painful information that may harm the memory of her grandfather. Hers and Alicia's stories tell of the burden of descendants of military personnel who find themselves in an environment highly critical of the dictatorship and are afraid or ashamed to learn more about the activities of their elders during the repression.

A family's relationship to the dictatorship does not necessarily imply that this past is discussed and, if so, how this discussion takes place. Talks at home have often been triggered by a television program or by questions from young people after the issues were discussed at school, not at the parents' initiative. A variety of experiences and stories seem to provoke similar outcomes: powerful silences, fragmented stories, and bits and pieces of decontextualized information. These pervasive silences speak loudly of the persistence of fear, feelings of guilt, grief, despair for broken dreams, frustration, feelings of defeat, shame, uneasiness about coming to terms with this past, and the witness generation's still ongoing elaboration of the events.

We Don't Talk about That in School

The family, including the extended family, is the primary group where the post-dictatorship generation first encountered this past, even if this has frequently meant evasions or silences. But what happens in the school? How is this past silenced or fragmentarily talked about? What are the interactions between official curricula, textbooks, professors' lectures and unofficial study plans, and the often conflicting family stories that students bring to school?

What happens in the classroom is an indication of society's positions for approaching this historical period. In this more public environment, study plans or the interaction with peers could either fortify or challenge what is not talked about at home. Schools are thus laboratories to explore the dynamics of how this issue is publicly addressed and discussed. Not surprisingly, participants had much to say about the lack of talk at school, the perceived reasons for those silences, the main challenges for including the dictatorship in educational curricula, and educators' strategies for addressing or ignoring this past.

Nora's story summarizes well what seems to be a prevalent pattern in many schools. She discussed her concerns about the failure to study the dictatorship in her history class:

> Don't cut something so important as the military [dictatorship]; don't cut something like Perón. How could it be that we weren't taught that history? [I used to say that] "The country was like a person, if she didn't have memory she would commit the same mistakes." And I talked to the professors and asked them why. I was worried. I wondered, "How could it be that we are not taught this? This [history] professor was very close-minded. She always said, "Kids, I went to a nuns' school and there are things that you cannot talk about in school. You know that, in my times, if you had things that you were not supposed to have . . . well we cannot talk about that either." She used to say: "If the book stops here there must be a reason." She taught history and civic education. We were learning about constitutional rights, freedom of expression, democracy, that we're free to give our opinion. And I'd say, "How come we cannot talk?" She'd say, "Look for clippings that talk about rights, we have freedom of the press." She'd say it but without actions. We didn't talk about anything with her. All the history I studied with her was memorized.

Nora also explained differences between what is in the textbooks and what is actually taught:

> I went to a school where they use a history book that has four volumes covering the history studied in secondary school. We used three in that school. The last volume is precisely the one that talks about Perón up to the present. And this last volume is the one we don't use because, according to professors, we have no time to complete the program.

Analía talked of differences between her private high school and the public university:

> At the university, I met many people who really know what happened and who are more [politically] involved. I came from [a religious] school. We didn't talk about this topic at the nuns' school. On fifth year, the program [included] Argentine history and we didn't study the military [period] at all. It ended much earlier. I think I saw the Conservative Party governments and that was the end. We didn't even cover Perón.

It is hard to believe that the teaching of Argentine history can stop "before Peronism." But Nora and Analía were not the only ones saying that they never studied this period, even though the movement and party funded by Perón shaped the political environment of the country in the second half of the twentieth century and the first part of the twenty-first.[12] Argentine contemporary history is the last topic in high school programs. If there is too much to include in a very limited time, it should not surprise us that key events are left out and the last dictatorship becomes one more item in an appendix listing several military coups during the last five decades. Although a lack of time to cover all the topics included in study plans is a common problem, this certainly tells us something about the priorities that educators assign to certain issues. As we see, some teachers and professors make it a point to discuss the dictatorship.

Antonio, a twenty-year-old law school student, was born in the midst of the terror and finished his primary school six years after the beginning of civilian rule. This was his story of silences throughout his education:

> No, we didn't talk about that in school. I believe that in primary school we didn't talk at all about the military, absolutely nothing. I suppose that in high school we talked [about it]. But we didn't talk about the history. We never covered political history, and not at all [that period].

So I asked him whether human rights was a topic in law school and how it was covered at the private university he attended:

> Yes, Human Rights [is a topic] [and laughingly added] but not human rights violations. We talk about the different treaties and all that; we study them. But no, we never cover . . . we knew that the military had violated human rights, all types of rights but no [mention of this], no. Moreover, those professors that allowed you to bring a tape recorder asked you to turn it off when they were giving names [of those involved in the repression]. I don't think [professors] stand by what they say. If they're going to say something they should say it and then face the consequences. It's terrible.

These accounts illustrate how educators often add to the chain of silences by arguing that certain topics are not to be discussed in the classroom, planning history lessons that omit connections with the recent past, and teaching human rights theory but avoiding any examples of violations that are too close to home.

Why Silences at School?

Young people also provided some insights into what they perceived as causes for silences at school. Marcelo suggested that children were not ready for it:

> I've told you that there was no talk in primary school. It was a religious [school]. In high school I went to a public school, a school without any ideology, neither religious nor political. I don't remember talk about [the dictatorship], neither that a professor talked [about it]. We didn't discuss it, but I don't think that it was the place

to talk about it, nor were we mature enough to discuss those issues. I think that all of us had our own story and teachers perceived that [the topic] would go in one ear and out the other.

However, a generalized lack of talk does not mean absolute silence. The past had made it into the classroom, either through teachers or students, prompting situations that illustrate why it is a difficult topic to address.

Participants indicated that discussion of the dictatorship could be very painful for children with *desaparecidos* or military personnel in their families—or for the descendants of victims and victimizers. Gloria remembered how these children reacted when the dictatorship was discussed at her primary school:

> I've been hearing [about this past] since primary school because in my school some-times teachers would talk a bit about it. There are many people who endured that moment and it's hard for them to talk about this topic. [Families] that, out of fear, didn't tell their children what had happened. I suppose that there are parents who're fearful of their kids thinking about things that could hurt them, that if they tell them about a disappeared member of the family they'd do things that they shouldn't be doing, or something like that. Even today there are many kids who don't want to talk about it. I knew classmates who didn't want to talk about it, because they'd relatives or friends there, in those times, in that moment, relatives who disappeared during that period and never came back. So when there was talk about this topic it hurt them.

Gloria believed that silences within families are brought into the classroom. She also pointed to the silences of classmates with parents in the armed forces:

> I had a classmate whose father was in the military and each time that there was talk about this topic he had to leave the room or something like that because he couldn't listen. We observed, in astonishment, because when the moment arrived to discuss this issue, he left, or felt sick, or something else happened to him, always.

Apparently, the discomfort felt by children with parents in the military produces several reactions. Juan had a story from his high school about children becoming upset because the institution was questioned:

> There were a couple of discussions in high school. [The teacher] said what's gener-ally said, that people who had nothing to do with it disappeared or that it hadn't been a just punishment. OK, if they planted bombs, arrest them, prosecute them and give them prison terms. And if you've to execute them, do it and say, "We killed so and so because he planted a bomb in such and such place," rather than disap-pearing them, saying nothing, [hiding] corpses. Two or three children of military

personnel jumped in saying that no, that wasn't the case, that many military personnel were killed, that the father of one of the kids went to fight, that there had been a combat against the guerrilla forces. As if [the military] were martyrs who did a favor to society by trying to eliminate [guerrillas]. Other kids argued that there were *desaparecidos*, that the military hadn't done any favor to society by killing or disappearing people because they wanted to impose an idea. At some point, the teacher tried to stop it. And one of the kids cried, "My father isn't an assassin, he never killed anybody, all the contrary." [It was] like that for one or two classes. Then we moved on to another topic.

Furthermore, interviewees argued that there is a generalized condemnation of the dictatorship and that animosity against the military is so strong that few dare to publicly defend them, therefore contributing to the isolation of "military children." As one young woman said of her school: "If there are supporters [of the dictatorship] they must shut up because the next day they'll turn up dead at the school door" (Lucía).

A less extreme situation was discussed in my conversation with five fifteen-year-old girls. When it was proposed that plaques honoring three disappeared teachers be mounted at the school:[13]

[the children of military personnel] didn't voice their opinions because they felt in the minority, as there were more children who didn't have parents in the military. So they shut up and gave no opinion. Maybe they felt an obligation thinking that, "Because my dad's in the military I've to be against [the plaques]." I felt that the parents imposed those opinions on their children. I had a classmate who didn't agree with the coup d'état but, because her father was in the military, she kept silent to avoid disagreeing with him. Others felt that being against the coup was an insult to their parents so they defended the coup to defend their parents.

In addition, some parents complain when professors condemn the dictatorship. Not wanting to expose their children to historical explanations that differ from theirs, these parents try to influence what is taught in schools. Verónica told me about her history professor, who is a target of parental criticism:

There are problems, even with Ester. She's our history professor, who, as far as we're concerned, supports the guerrilla forces. And there are fathers who are in the military and were involved in the coup. So Ester says something, and it's very difficult to say something, to explain, without conveying a point of view. Because no matter how objective you want to be, there's always something, like the tone of your voice, which will give away your side. It depends on the events that you discuss and all that. So Ester says something and then we discuss it with our families. And parents get mad and say that other things must be taught, other points of view of course.

Verónica commented about problems another professor faced:

The geography professor was absolutely against the military. And there was one girl whose father is in the military. When [the professor] started, I don't know if to criticize but to give her opinion about the military the girl spoke about [the version] she knew, the one she had always heard at home. Then, at home, she related what this professor had said and her mother complained to the school authorities.

Some participants commented on the need for objectivity. Fernando, a twenty-year-old musician working at a computer firm who insisted he was apolitical and neutral, explained his disagreement with professors who discuss the past:

Every once in a while there's a professor who tries to test what's inside everybody's head. In my very personal opinion these are people who've kept something inside, need to talk about it, and the classroom is their forum. And what I can't stand is how these people want to influence fourteen-year old kids who are easily manipulated. Maybe the guy has no intention of influencing but he's biased. I remember a professor who gave a bad overview of the military [institution]. But I believe that there are good and bad folks and I don't like to lump all [military personnel] together.

Such comments reveal a conviction that history can and must be impartial, and a belief that teaching about the dictatorship is the result of the personal political agendas of professors who want to influence students. Moreover, Fernando suggested the difficulties in talking about this recent past:

It can be very biased if you're talking about 20 years ago, we're all alive, we're the children, and the guy who's teaching the class was there [when it happened]. It all depends on the experience [the teacher] had. I don't think it's appropriate. I think there's still hate. All our parents carry a terrible resentment.

Ignorance among students and professors about the dictatorship, and the avoidance of forbidden topics, also emerged as reasons for silences: "Only two or three [students] talked. I think there's a belief that if you don't know you better keep quiet. So they wouldn't talk because of their lack of knowledge" (Alberto). "There are some topics that are tabú in school and are not discussed. Besides, I imagine that the teachers themselves don't know that much. 'Rather than showing ignorance I prefer to be silent.' That's the way it is" (Silvia). Knowledge, thus, is seen as playing a role in encouraging or deterring discussions about this past. And it is not easy to learn about what is not discussed, a process that could be described as "I don't talk about it because I don't know about it, and I don't learn about it because I never talk about it."

Hence, there are many reasons for the silences at school, all shedding light on the difficulties in addressing this past. These include the perception that certain opinions may hurt the sensibilities of children with disappeared relatives or fathers in the military, that the topic is divisive, conflictive, and can't be taught "objectively," and that this past was too recent to discuss. In addition, some teachers avoid the topic of the dictatorship because they lack sufficient knowledge about it, or because it raises the ire of parents. Furthermore, these conversations reveal a noticeable disparity between what is incorporated in history lessons that cuts across different types of institutions, specific programs, or levels of education. Some explanations for these disparities lie in the coexistence of official and unofficial curricula in Buenos Aires' high schools and institutions of tertiary education.

Breaking Silences

The inclusion of the dictatorship in the official curriculum or in textbooks does not guarantee its study. Many textbooks have chapters dedicated to the events of the dictatorship. But, according to professors I interviewed, what is discussed in the classroom depends mainly on teachers and professors, who have great autonomy in deciding what and how they teach and are key in determining how the past is addressed in educational programs. Hence, it is not always possible to assume what a particular school will teach based on it being private or public, religious or secular, or on the neighborhood in which it is located. Depending on the teacher, there may be differences within the same school—something that I corroborated with participants who studied in the same institution.

However, different historical moments affect silences and talk. There were marked differences in the level of silence about the dictatorship depending on the age of interviewees. Silences had been more pervasive in the experience of the older students, who attended school during years closer to the actual terror. Although silences remained a consistent pattern, those attending high school at the time of our conversations had more stories of talks at school. Most of the younger participants mentioned occasions—for example, the anniversary of the coup on March 24—when, in public schools, some kinds of commemorations were held. (Private schools have their own curriculum.)

More recently, teachers and professors from various disciplines were breaking silences with homework and activities that managed to bring the past into the classroom.[14] I heard of several assignments that incorporated issues excluded from the official curricula. These can be classified into two major groups. One includes engaging in discussions generated around specific texts, such as a book or video. Or it can be a library research project. For example, Irma, who attended a high school in a working-class neighborhood, brought to our meeting a copy of the presentation she had prepared with her classmates for a group report about the dictatorship. It contained press clips of events preceding the dictatorship, of the coup, of the years of the repression, and of the beginnings of civilian rule. The project had required that students go to libraries, search for published works, and relate what they had been told at home to other opinions and records, engaging them in a process of acquiring new information that might reinforce or modify previous assumptions.

The second group of activities is geared toward making young people ask members of their family or community about their experiences during the dictatorship or their opinions about it. Alicia described one of those assignments at the religious high school she attended and how a teacher creatively bypassed restrictions imposed by a school official whom she refers to as "the nun":

> They asked me at school to conduct a survey about how [people] had lived the period of the *proceso* and their opinions about it. [I had] to ask people around me, "How did you live the years of the *proceso*?" I was twelve or thirteen [years old]. It was the teacher who did this. The nun didn't allow discussion of this topic. But this is what the teacher told us, "We cannot have a debate because the nun won't let me, but no one is prohibiting me from conducting surveys." So she did surveys.

Participants also told me about a school project in which they had to explore censorship during the dictatorship by asking their parents which topics were not taught or discussed when they were in school. Inés, Josefina, and Verónica, the students from the upper-class private school who believed that their history professor sided with the guerrilla forces, related the following:

> I remember [my father] told me about things that history professors couldn't teach, that it was very dangerous because [authorities] might catch you, about the black list.
>
> Well, regarding what they couldn't teach . . . my father told me that he studied, finished his degree, and that no professor was ever [censored].
>
> My father tells me the same. That he completed his career and was never told anything. [Professors] taught whatever they wanted.
>
> Yes, whatever they wanted. Moreover, I don't know what career track your dad was on, but mine studied law, which has a lot to do [with talk/discussions.]
>
> My mother told me that she was in high school at that time and [there were] also no [restrictions]. Professors taught whatever they wanted. But [our history professor] told us that [as a student] she had to be careful, that the program she was taught was limited.

Memories that range from the conviction that no one dared to speak out at that time to the belief that freedom of expression was never jeopardized reflect different experiences during the terror. Indeed, free speech was a respected right for those who did not challenge the rules of the game imposed by the military juntas. Over the years, I have heard many people who insist they never had any problem in saying what they wanted, an unmistakable sign that they didn't have much to say.

The value of this type of assignment is that it promotes intergenerational dialogue and challenges silences by forcing the witness generation to speak about what happened and to define where they stand in relation to this past. Since it is discussed in class, students can share the different stories they hear, including the silences, creating a microcosm of society in the classroom.[15]

Exploring textbooks and official educational curricula, thus, gives only partial insight into how the dictatorship is being studied by the younger generations. Alternative study plans demonstrate means by which educators creatively sought to familiarize their students with the past and to challenge societal silences. Furthermore, unofficial curricula add to the unevenness in what is discussed or silenced. Whereas some interviewees never talked about the dictatorship in primary or secondary school, or even in college, others were researching the period before entering high school.

Conclusions

As with fear, the silence that paralyzed society during the terror had been transmitted to the younger generation. "We didn't talk about that then" becomes "We don't talk about that now." Participants' comments suggest that there is not much talk about the dictatorship. Silence about what happened seems to be the norm rather than the exception. At times, it seemed that Argentineans were wearing invisible or metaphorical gags. It is significant how often comments such as "We never talked" or "They don't like to talk about it" were part of our conversations. The ongoing silence reveals how traumatic the events have been, suggests that, at the time of this fieldwork, the witness generation had not yet fully digested what went on, and clearly illustrates society's difficulty in confronting this too recent past.

We know that fear produces societal silences but the long-term effects of these silences are not predictable or homogeneous. However, research on other societies that experienced political violence and terror points to a link between social silence and a positive image of the past, suggesting that a "conspiracy of silence" plays important ideological functions.[16] This would imply that not talking about the dictatorship would benefit those responsible for state terrorism. Furthermore, studies reveal that memories of traumatic pasts are often repressed or voluntarily forgotten.[17] But repression also seems to produce the opposite effect. Silent events, the shared incidents about which people avoid talking, either because they are afraid or because they perceive them as shameful, may help to strengthen memories. When people are told not to think or talk about something, the repressed event becomes more deeply ingrained in their memory. In those cases, political repression results in silence on the surface but hidden suffering and a consolidation of the memory of the repressed event.[18] Moreover, people also avoid talking about silenced events because they perceive them as shameful. This voluntary forgetfulness predominates in pacific transitions from repressive dictatorships to democracies without sharp breaks with the past, as was the case in Argentina—that is, amnesties and the same institutions and laws.[19]

So which of these patterns is more prevalent in Argentina's case? How do we learn about the things we barely speak of? Although there was a consistent lack of discussion about the dictatorship, silence was not absolute. Moreover, silence is in itself a component and a language of the memories of this past. By listening to participants discuss the silence of the past, and by experiencing their own silences in the present, I was drawn to conclude that the past was present in the silences and that those silences in actuality "spoke"—and often quite loudly—transmitting memories through them. In spite of the silences, and through the powerful language of silence, we know that the atmosphere of terror was transmitted. The question becomes which versions of the past these silences are narrating. It is now time to explore what other facts were transmitted to young people and on which grounds they were creating their own representations of the dictatorship, as conditioned and shaped by the intergenerational transmission of fears and silences. It is also time to look at how what was transmitted to participants sheds light on the witness generation's awareness and denial of what was going on during the terror.

FOUR

Conversations about Awareness and Denial

Introduction

In exploring the cycle of fear-silence-knowledge, we have seen how the fears and silences of the witness generation were transmitted to the post-dictatorship generation and how they might condition young Argentineans' knowledge about the years of terror. This chapter focuses on specific facts transmitted, beyond the omnipresence of terror, and which kind of information seemed to have been assimilated better by the younger generation. It is about the magnitude and pervasiveness of the repression as reflected in stories of threats, exiles, killings, or disappearances known to interviewees' families and acquaintances. It discusses censorship and misinformation—including certain smoke screens manipulated by the dictatorship. Through the information conveyed to the participants of this study by their elders, this chapter explores society's awareness or ignorance of what was going on during the years of terror. It looks for clues to the process by which information about human rights abuses then became widely available. It explores guilt and shame. It seeks to assess how the witness generation was positioning itself in the eyes of its descendants and, consequently, identifies mechanisms of denial and self-deception.

Telling young people what happened during the dictatorship implies sharing memories and articulating historical accounts that make sense in present times. In considering how the witnesses are shaping their accounts we should be aware that reconstruction of the past to fit the present is not the monopoly of dominant sectors.[1] It takes place at various levels because it is easier to remember flattering versions of the past. In order to defend a positive self-image, individuals and social groups (including nations) develop mechanisms to cope with an unpleasant past, often revising the meaning of events and distorting their memories in systematic ways. Processes of self-deception resort to several mechanisms such as editing the causes of an event through omissions and fabrications, telling the side of the story that better fits certain interests, blowing up a historical truth into a major myth, or blaming the victim.

What elders had told participants underwent transformations. Over the years, people tend to change their way of thinking.[2] Witnesses to historical events may later question what they once asserted and, faced with the judgment of their children, tell another side of the story. Those who feel guilty for their behavior may be remaking the past to suit their current image of themselves. Likewise, there are generational patterns of self-deception because each new generation develops its opinions and holds certain values. In analyzing their elders' actions, young people may also selectively distort memory to fit their beliefs.[3] When I had these conversations, the generalized public condemnation of the dictatorship suggested that this process was going on within families where participants perceived that their elders had condoned or tolerated the repression. As time passes, young people might inquire into and question their elders' attitudes during the terror. We have already heard of the daughter of a police officer feeling uncomfortable talking about her father during the terror, or participants pointing to either a Nazi grandfather or a mother praising the dictatorship. Hence, we must look at what is known about this past with an awareness of the variety and complexity of forces and processes determining this content.

What Happened?

One of the typical initial questions I asked participants was "According to what you have been told, how would you describe to a foreigner, who knows very little about this country, what happened here at the political and social level in the second half of the 1970s?" In this way, I avoided labeling the period and allowed for any definition they wanted to give—that is, "dictatorship," "military coup," "dirty war," *proceso*. Their responses to the imaginary foreigner revealed what they had concluded were the most important facts about that period.

Participants' knowledge about the dictatorship was related to the different stories that had been transmitted to them over the years. Consequently, this knowledge was uneven and varied significantly depending on participants' families, friends, teachers, and professors or the different media to which they had been exposed. As we have seen, there were wide gaps regarding what was discussed or passed over in silence at home and in the classroom. There were children who spoke about the dictatorship at home but never discussed the subject in school, and others who discussed the subject in school but never at home.

Diego was one of the few well-informed participants. His explanation placed the dictatorship within a larger historical context, arguing that it could not be disconnected from previous events:

I don't know if I'd start with 1975. I think that it's part of a process that started before. I'd frame it within a people's struggle to be free and sovereign, and those foreign agents, at the service of a foreign power, that tried to dominate the people. So what starts in 1976 is a particular period of that struggle, which maybe was better organized with regard to tactics of repression. But it's something that started a long time ago.

Pablo was a sixteen-year-old student at a technical school. In his account, which is comparable to many others, the emphasis is on the terror, the impossibility of dissent with authorities, and the risk of disappearing:

The repression, everybody had to think the same way. If you had different ideas you were considered crazy; I don't know. It was a big big mess. You couldn't even be in the street because they'd take you away. And then you didn't' know what they'd do to you. There are people who didn't come back.

However, the focus on the indiscriminate terror can generate incredulity. Andrea, whose aunt disappeared, told me how she often thinks about this period:

Sometimes, at night, I ponder about what happened with the coup, about how tough it was. I said to myself, "They're lying to me." I need to think that they're lying to me, that it's not true, that nothing happened; but I then realize [that it happened]. I have this experience almost every week. Or sometimes I see something related to this topic and say, "No, this couldn't' have happened, no one could have that much evil inside to do what was done."

Antonio, the law school student, expressed a comparable disbelief:

When I was reading [*Nunca Más*] you think that you're nothing, that you don't exist, that they do whatever they want with you. It's terrible. It's something extremely difficult to understand. People who lived through that period, like you, maybe feel it very closely. It's something very remote for me. I cannot conceive that that happened. Do you understand? You cannot treat people like that. It's inconceivable for me. It's as if we're living in another world where that never happened.

There is no doubt that the post-dictatorship generation will have different perceptions of the dictatorship than those who witnessed it. But those differences should not be based on what they cannot comprehend because they were not there, as Antonio implies. Not having been there should not be an impediment to learning about this past. We see here that, for those who lack the necessary information, the past can turn from incomprehensible into unthinkable, almost like a chain where ignorance leads to incredulity—it never happened; put it behind you.

Participants' comments illustrate disparity and limitations in the information that had been transmitted to them. Having trouble in understanding that so many atrocities were committed may be a direct result of memories that emphasize terror without explaining its causes. Placing horrendous acts within a historical and political context does not minimize their inhuman nature but helps us to better understand why they are committed and by whom. It contributes to making the unthinkable more real, although not less abominable.

Nobody Knew (Then) but Everybody Knows (Now)

Every single one of the young people with whom I talked was aware of atrocities committed during the dictatorship and of what had happened. Without exception, they knew about persecutions, tortures, disappearances, and the kidnapping of babies. The differences were the context, the details, and the reasons given for these crimes. As Mónica, another future teacher, summarized:

> Everybody knows, everybody. It's inevitable, because either at home, on TV, or in a book, you find out about it, you constantly hear about it, information reaches you, it's inevitable. The issue will always emerge; there will always be one who lived through it, one who heard about it, always.

Knowledge about the extent of the repression was often linked to the commencement of civilian rule in 1983, the moment of official investigations and public disclosure of the dictatorship's crimes. During the repression, many people adopted ignorance, believing that the less a person knew the safer she was. According to Laura, the daughter of activists, society was divided into three groups: "Those who knew, those who didn't know, and those who didn't want to know." The category of those who did not want to know is the most interesting for me because it is an effect of terror. It defines those who were permanently living in a dual reality of knowing but denying.

Some participants had received versions indicating that society was aware of the repression at the time it was happening. In those cases, I heard different explanations about people's apparent ignorance in which fear is invariably detectable. Eugenia shared what her parents had told her:

> People knew and kept silent; they only talked inside their homes. We talked at home; everything was OK. But even so, you always had the doubt that someone

might be spying on you, that someone had managed to plant a microphone while you were not at home, that type of thing. My mother didn't go through that but those things could happen.

Some participants talked of self-denial as a protective shield. There were comments referring to the risks of knowing more than the official information admitted that illustrate the dynamics of the cycle of fear-silence-knowledge. Flor described how fearful people avoided sharing knowledge:

I think that people knew but denied it, self-denial. They didn't want to think about it. They'd tell you something and you could not tell it because you'd compromise the other person. At the same time, friends would talk about everything but not about this. And it was as if nothing was happening but each one knew what was happening.

This confusing paradox of not knowing but knowing was present in other accounts of what interviewees' parents knew. Silvia's family is a good example. While she was a child, she never learned anything about the dictatorship. By the time I interviewed her, she had had several talks with her mother:

I remember that [my mother] always told me that nobody knew at that time. She herself used to say, "It must be for something." She always tells me how engraved was the idea that people were kidnapped for "something." Although at the beginning it was not known that people were kidnapped. But I think that later people knew. She told me that they once found a girl in the neighborhood where she lived. She'd been killed in a very bad way. And [my mother] said, "It must have been for something; in which kind of mess was she involved?" Nobody knew at that time. [My mother] told me that when [the first civilian government] took power she learned about those issues and changed her way of thinking.

What Silvia's mother told her shows contradictions in how people remember: that no one knew, but she herself was aware of kidnappings and at least one killing. It also illustrates different phases in learning about the repression.

People's limited access to information was also cited as a cause of ignorance. Censorship, therefore, is the justification that people could only know bits and pieces. But we need to remember that tight censorship coexisted with rumors of terrible things that circulated quite widely. This contradictory information added to people's confusion and increased their fears. Mercedes reasoned that, probably, a significant portion of society barely intuited what was going on:

Based on my parents' experiences, I'd say that most people lived like in a cloud. Maybe they were aware that something was happening but they hadn't a clear idea of what it was or its magnitude. In 1984, with the return to democracy, they really realized what it was. I think that it might have been like when we say now, "A person was detained and died at the police station." Maybe that was the idea they had. [My parents] told me that they had no idea of what was going on. My parents, and the majority of the people, were not economists, political scientists, or something like that to analyze the policies that were being implemented. They had a superficial knowledge. In general, [people] didn't know; newspapers or the television didn't inform.

Participants also talked about what the international community knew at that time as opposed to what Argentineans ignored. While human rights groups developed strong international networks of solidarity, thousands of Argentineans were traveling—and shopping—around the world and had access to this information. So what was known overseas is important in evaluating people's actual level of ignorance. Either they never looked for this information or else they dismissed these reports as the "anti-Argentine" campaigns that the military junta denounced.[4]

Laura commented on a recent conversation during which a friend of her mother remembered the letters she received from an exiled friend:

They were talking that they only learned that people were disappearing in 1978. Her friend sent her letters from France saying, "People are disappearing, there's torture." And she'd read those letters and think, "This gal is exaggerating." Because [my friend's mother] was a political activist her friend would urge her, "Leave immediately; come here." So people in other countries knew much more than we did about what was going on.

In families where some members went into exile, young people had been exposed to firsthand accounts showing differences between what was known in other countries and in Argentina. This was the case of Sandra, a seventeen-year-old high school student:

My uncle now lives in Israel. He said that when he settled there, there was information about everything that was happening here. And there was no information about this in Argentina. Nobody knew what was going on. But they say that all over the world it was known what was happening and the extent of the repression. My mother says that she didn't know anything until it was over.

Moreover, because the dictatorship did not close the doors of the country, visitors were another source of information. This is what Analía's parents told her:

There were tons of people being tortured and dying, and many people who really didn't know anything. [Analía stresses "really"] My parents told me that they really knew nothing about what was going on. That it's surprising that during the [Soccer] World Cup in 1978 foreigners came to the country and said that there was state terrorism here, concentration camps, and people disappearing. [My parents] really had no idea of what was going on. Now, everything is coming out.

The Soccer World Cup of 1978, hosted and won by Argentina, deserves special attention. The dictatorship manipulated the national passion for the sport and used the event as a public relations campaign in which images of the population's euphoria celebrating the triumph sharply contrasted with the reality of what was going on and the atrocities being committed. The 1998 World Cup took place in France at the time of this fieldwork and, inevitably, it triggered talk about the past. Soccer, thus, became a means of breaking silences and a source of knowledge about the dictatorship.

For some, the World Cup of 1978 was a magnificent event: "My mother always says that the World Cup of '78 was the most beautiful thing that happened here" (Nora). But other comments pointed to the dictatorship's use of the championship: "It was said that we won the '78 World Cup because the military threatened all the teams" (Pedro). "I heard that the military did something, that they paid. I don't know the exact story" (Alicia). "They say that the military put pressure on the teams and all that" (Nelson). Or, as I heard during a conversation between high school students (Leo, Hugo, Omar, Ariel, Miguel): "They organized the World Cup as a smoke screen to cover up. While people were excited about the championship they didn't see what was going on." The repetition of stories that the military paid, bribed, or threatened to host and win the cup seems to be a widespread belief, which certainly attests to the perception of a dictatorship of unlimited powers.

Nelson, a fifteen-year-old high school student, commented on the use of the World Cup to defy the monitoring of human rights abuses by international organizations:[5]

> Human rights organizations came to check what was going on here. They say that the military brought the kids from the schools to participate in celebrations when Argentina won. And the kids were very happy and it gave the image that nothing was going on and that [accusations of human rights abuses] were the wild imaginings of a few.

Eugenia had heard similar stories at home and at the import/export firm where she worked:

> [My mother] considers that everything was arranged. I don't know if we can say that [the military] paid, who knows how things are dealt with at those levels, but that everything was arranged so the World Cup would take place here, as a cover up. The same applies to the euphoria of winning the Cup. My coworkers and I were talking about this year's World Cup and saying, "Argentina is playing, let's watch it." Because we don't have a TV set, we asked our boss to give us access to one so we could watch it. Automatically, one coworker jumped in and said, "I don't want to

watch the games." With our eyes opened wide, we asked, "But why?" And he said, "Since 1978 people have been captivated by the World Cup; no one was aware of all the deaths." I didn't answer him. Honestly, I was surprised that he was still hooked on that story. Watching the World Cup today isn't a cover up; it's not about forgetting. He said, "Since those times, World Cups are used to cover up other things."

Moreover, during the 1998 World Cup, the Menem administration gave students permission to skip classes when the Argentine team played so they could watch the game. This controversial measure contributed to the comparison of both championships, specifically their use to distract attention from more important issues—that is, "It brings back the memory of the one that was organized as a cover up" (Irma). Or, as Mariana, whose grandfather had been in the military, said:

> There was talk that this is the same as what the military was doing in the past; they'd say, "Today is a holiday" and cover all the problems. While people celebrated Argentina's triumph, someone in a jail somewhere was being killed. So this World Cup has brought back those issues.

Even television programs were making links between both World Cups. Mónica talked about *Zoo*, a highly popular program among the young crowd:

> For example, [*Zoo*] had a program the other day with this theme of the World Cup. About how the World Cup of '78, being the circus that the Cup is, concealed the other face of the country, what was going on. I saw only a bit of it, but they showed how a World Cup that resembles a circus blinds this country.

Other accounts linked the World Cup to the Malvinas/Falklands War as the dictatorship's key campaigns of distraction. As Luciana, a fifteen-year-old high school student, said:

> According to what I heard, many people, the majority, were obsessed by the World Cup [and] "The Malvinas belong to Argentina;" "Let's hold on to the Malvinas." They didn't realize the political manipulation that was taking place behind that. Later, after many years, they finally began to realize and said, "Wait a minute. What's going on?"

Thus, people's memories suggest that they did not know many details of what was going on, that there were events that succeeded in distracting attention from the repression, and that it took years for large sectors of society to become aware of its magnitude. Their accounts also provide clues to the process of discovering what really happened, of how they came to know and how they chose to explain this transformation to their children. However, these memories may reflect contradictions as well as matters of responsibility and guilt. "We didn't know" is the message that many parents had transmitted to their children. But, in general, their accounts reflect the confusing paradox of not knowing but knowing. Claims of ignorance, thus, seem clearly to be signs of denial rather than of actual lack of knowledge, albeit limited. We may be facing here a process in which the witness generation is distorting memory to keep a good image and fit the values and beliefs of the post-dictatorship generation. What is most disturbing in this study is that the vague explanations of the witness generation had been accepted without much questioning by young people.

As we have seen, in many ways life went on as if nothing was happening. This duality—terror/normal life—was particularly terrifying for those suffering, or aware of, the repression. However, the extent of the campaign of terror was such that few social groups were left totally untouched. Through an inquiry into people's knowledge of an actual disappeared person, it is possible to get a good idea of how many people knew of the repression as it was occurring, regardless of how many might admit such knowledge.

Knowledge of a *Desaparecido*

We may never know exactly how many people disappeared or their names, ages, occupations, education levels, social classes, or political affiliations.[6] Disappearances happened all over the country and within a wide spectrum of social groups, suggesting that knowing of a disappeared person should be the norm rather than the exception. The only official estimate, which puts the total number of *desaparecidos* at 8,961, shows that one consistent pattern was the generational nature of the activists eliminated: 80.31 percent of them were between sixteen and thirty-five years old when they were taken away. With regard to occupation, the largest single percentage corresponds to blue-collar workers (30.2 percent), followed by students (21 percent). But the category "workers" is relative, considering those students and professionals who often worked at factories to do political work. There were disappeared activists from the country's elite—in fact, many revolutionary leaders have traditionally emerged from this group, Che Guevara being a good example.

In addition to the absence of corpses, one of the difficulties of determining the exact number is that these figures are based on public denunciations but exclude those who did not have anybody to denounce them or whose relatives were terrified to do so. Three people whom I knew well remain disappeared but are not included in the CONADEP's list. The missing names in the official list of *desaparecidos* are evident. For me, it seems logical to multiply the official figure by three.[7]

Víctor explained the problems in determining the number of the *desaparecidos*:

> That was one of the goals, to create terror but that it not be discussed, so that people
> would never be able to say that something happened for sure. How do you say that

they killed 30,000 if there are no corpses? It's impossible. They had found a lot [of corpses]. Some say that [the dead] are 10,000. I don't know. According to people who have researched this, the Mothers of the Plaza de Mayo and all those organizations, there are 30,000. What happens is that estimates are based on denunciations. What about those who had no family? What if a whole family disappeared and they had no relatives because they were from another country or had their family in Bolivia? Who's going to look for them? Nobody.

Several years ago, Eduardo L. Duhalde analyzed the extent of the repression using the metaphor of a bomb explosion, arguing that the whole society was within the circle of the expansive effect of the terrorist state policies; that there was no Argentine citizen of the middle class or working sectors who did not know, directly or indirectly, of at least one case of disappearance.[8] Talking to young people fifteen years later provided the opportunity to test this statement's accuracy.

When I asked participants whether they or their families knew of anybody who had disappeared or had a *desaparecido* in the family, stories flowed about uncles, friends, coworkers, or the woman next door, stories such as "My mother was friends with a family where the children disappeared because they were studying at the university. And one night [the army] went to their home, the parents were beaten and the children taken away" (Patricia). "The daughter of one of my mother's coworkers was taken away and was never seen again. It's not known if she died or is alive, nothing" (Graciela).

Talk about disappeared people was often in the present tense, or else past and present tenses mixed and overlapped in the accounts, as if describing ongoing situations that had not yet been resolved. Irma talked of her friend's disappeared brother as if he were still the same age as when he was taken away:

I have a friend who has a disappeared brother who's seventeen. He was at home; he had nothing, wasn't involved in anything. And four or five people came into the house, took him away with a black scarf covering his eyes, and the family never again heard about him. They searched all over for him. He was only seventeen and was at his home. They don't know why he was taken away.

Several young people had known stories of disappearances since they were children. Killings, threats, or exiles within their extended families or friends had usually triggered the talk and helped to give a face and a name to the terror. A good example is what I heard during a conversation with three seventeen-year-old women (Cristina, Clara, Elsa). We were at an empty classroom in their high school on the outskirts of Buenos Aires and I had asked the question about *desaparecidos* known to them:

My aunt suffered a lot because many of her friends disappeared. That was the main reason why my uncle [her brother] left the country. They always told me all that.

In my mother's family, in particular, they were very affected by it. My uncle and my aunt, one left the country and my aunt told me that, practically overnight, she lost all her friends and didn't hear of them ever again. My aunt cannot believe that she's alive now, she cannot believe it.

My grandmother's nephew [disappeared]. He had a wife and a baby. And, it seems that the wife wasn't home and he was taken away. They went to his house one night and took him away.

My mother's cousin disappeared and his corpse was later found inside his burned car. He's the only relative, but there are many friends of my mother and of my aunts and uncles.

Tons of my mom's friends also [disappeared]. But, well, my mom shut her mouth and, rather than lose her life, she chose to remain silent.

What these participants had been told illustrates how repression affected larger sectors of society and suggests that there is more talk within families than the pervasiveness of generalized silences indicates. Young people may say "we don't talk about the dictatorship," but when they are asked about a particular issue, disappearances in this case, their answers indicate that there has been talk about it.

Lucía was a fifteen-year-old high school student and hers was another case where disappearances hit her extended family, her mother's friends, and her friends' homes:

My grandmother has two disappeared sons. The case is that I have a grandmother who isn't really the mother of my mother. But, since I was born, I consider her my grandmother. Supposedly, I have two disappeared uncles. And my friends' parents have acquaintances that disappeared. My mother knows people who disappeared.

There were accounts of entire families being persecuted and eliminated, such as the one told by Teresa, a fifteen-year-old high school student. Although it is not clear how some details of this version were known, considering that everyone wound up dead, this was the story circulating in her family:

I have a relative who's *desaparecida*. I was told about some distant cousins who used to go out every night and paint political graffiti in schools, and they were persecuted. Their mother disappeared; she was raped in the presence of the children. The children were very traumatized by this. Later on, the children were killed.

The responses of Josefina, Inés, and Verónica, upper-class young women studying at a very exclusive private high school, are examples of how repression crossed socioeconomic levels. All three had a story of killings and disappearances. Verónica's was a confusing episode going back to the Cuban Revolution:

I have a distant cousin whose parents were killed in relation to Che [Guevara]. The father was a guerrilla. Both his parents were killed and he went to live with his grandparents. He was two years old. Then the grandfather died and now he lives with this grandmother. But he lives a lot with us because the grandmother's economic situation is very bad. [His parents] were killed, I don't know why. His father was a guerrilla. [My cousin's] name is Ernesto, like Che. He's angry about what happened but has learned to cope with it. His father was killed in Cuba. I'm positive that he wasn't a member of the guerrilla forces during the military coup.

Owing to the ages of the protagonists—the cousin was in his twenties and the Cuban Revolution was in 1959—the events may actually be related to the Argentine dictatorship but assigned to another, more remote, and maybe more celebrated, historical moment. Whatever the story, the family had not discussed it in detail, creating this confusion of dates, guerrillas, countries, and social struggles. This mix-up shows the unreliability of memories, how events get unintentionally confused and accepted as truth. This can happen within small groups—that is, the family—and larger communities, as in Portelli's analysis of Italian workers' memories confusing the date and circumstances of the killing of an activist and illustrating how events are reorganized and distorted.[9]

Josefina talked about one of her mother's classmates:

My mother told me that she had a friend who went to school with her, a classmate who also was a guerrilla. She then had a baby girl, because she married another guerrilla. And both of them were killed. And before the military caught them they gave the baby to their parents. I don't know if hers or his. Well, [the mother and father] disappeared and I've no idea what happened later with the baby.

Inés had this story of a murdered guerrilla in her family:

I have a cousin, from my mother's side, who lives in Brazil. My mom had no involvement with anything but her cousin wanted to contradict her parents and became a guerrilla. She and her husband were both killed in their house and the baby survived because [the military] didn't see her. That baby is my second cousin who now lives in Brazil with her aunt and uncle. They told me the story of this cousin who was coming to visit. I was a small child, maybe six years old. She was seven. They tried to explain to me that [she and the other children in the family] were not siblings but cousins. And I didn't understand why they were cousins if they lived in the same house. When they came to visit, [my parents] explained to me that her parents had died because there were problems in this country and they'd been killed.

The explanation of why Inés's aunt became involved in armed struggle had been stripped of any political resonance and turned into a daughter/parent's conflict. We will never know what the real motivations were. But it is interesting that the family denies the possibility that the young woman was involved in a cause for which she was ready to give her life.

This was not the only account in which small children's confusion with any alteration of traditional family structures triggered talk about disappearances. This was Andrea's puzzle in relation to her disappeared aunt:

> I have a disappeared aunt, my cousin's mother. So my cousin lived with my grand-mother and I wondered, "How come my grandmother, who's my dad's mother, is my cousin's mother?" I thought that my grandmother was my cousin's mother. I was very confused. When I was about eight I began to ask, "What happened? Where are [the parents]?" I think it was then that they started telling me what had happened. I'm constantly surprised because they always tell me new details. I think I know everything and they always tell me more. I have a box where I keep all the things that I find, such as newspaper clippings and other stuff. A few days ago, my father was looking for the exact date on which my aunt disappeared. And when I see my father open two huge boxes and start pulling out writs of habeas corpus, I realized that there are many things I didn't know.

Losing someone important was not limited to a relative or a friend. There were also accounts of professors and mentors. Fernando, who refused to criticize the dictatorship, knew many details about the repression and had this story to tell:

> My mother suffered [the repression] like everybody. People running away, she lost friends. My aunts and uncles told me about people in the neighborhood who disappeared. "Do you remember XX? He's gone." A classic story of my mother is about a nun who was her religion teacher and disappeared. [My mother] tells me about this because it was an important case. She adored the nun because [my mother] was about my age, in her twenties, very religious, and the nun was her mentor, the kind of relationship that you have with priests. And [the nun] disappeared and my mother wanted to kill herself.

Some participants knew about disappearances through their classmates. Marta went to one of the top high schools in the city (Nacional Buenos Aires), where many students disappeared. This seems to have shaped the weight of the past on the new generations of students. This was her story:

> In high school, I met many friends with exiled parents who lived overseas for ten years, and also with parents who were in jail. That's why I say that [school] is where information started circulating for me. A friend of mine introduced me to an acquaintance of hers whose parents, his mother, father, and some aunts and uncles disappeared. It was a big family. His grandmother left and now lives in France. And this guy is living here and had a very tragic history. He was born in captivity and was given away to a prostitute.[10] And he grew up with the prostitute without knowing

that she wasn't his mother, a pretty awful story. Then [his biological family] found him. But even now he's not doing very well. He had a bad time.

Juan had first heard about disappearances through his parents' landlord, when the family lived in the coastal city of Mar del Plata:

My parents rented a store whose owners had moved to Mar del Plata because their sister had disappeared. These two guys, who at that time were around twenty-three or twenty-four-years old, had moved with their parents to get away from all the harm there was here, to forget a bit about all that. And they told me what they'd gone through with their sister. I was around eleven, ten years old. [They'd tell me] that they still didn't know why it happened, that the sister wasn't involved in anything strange. But I think that she studied at the university, philosophy or something similar. And that maybe she had the kind of ideas that could've been the reason why she disappeared.

Eugenia shared a story from her neighbors:

Our neighbor has a daughter. The military took away the daughter's husband. He was taken away at dawn. First was his sister, who was a medical doctor. She disappeared because she made a mistake. We know for sure that she had no subversive ideas or anything like that. But she knew people who were subversives and had planted a bomb. And the one who planted it was badly hurt. They were neighbors and knew each other so they went to her looking for her services. And she cured him, as a professional, fulfilling her obligations as a medical doctor. From that moment on, she realized that she was being followed. We know this because she talked to her brother the day before disappearing. She went to work and never came back. And they searched and searched for her but she never appeared. She knew that she'd cured a subversive. The family and those who knew about it assumed that this was the reason. A few days later they came for her brother. He wasn't yet married [to the neighbor's daughter]. They stormed in like in the film *La Noche de los Lápices*, that while you were sleeping they knock down the door and take you away. It was like that. To be honest, I don't know if he had a problem like torture and those things. He was taken away and was kept a couple of days blindfolded, being interrogated and that kind of thing. Then they realized that he had nothing to do with it and he reappeared alive. But I can assure you that he's not the kind of person that you say, "Oh, good, what a normal guy he is."

This account of repression targeting relatives of the suspected "subversives" incorporates the issue of those who survived torture. There are no official records of these cases, and oral history projects offer one possible way to learn about them. The high number of *desaparecidos* suggests that not many were tortured and released.[11]

And, unless the former prisoner speaks out or initiates a legal action, there is no way to know how many cases might exist. At no point during our conversations did I ask participants whether they knew of someone who had been tortured.

I heard of people who honor their relatives and friends who disappeared by naming their children after them. In those cases, the story of the disappeared person in particular and of the repression in general is transmitted to the children from the time they are very young. Sara, a fifteen-year-old high school student shared this story about her mother, who had seen many classmates disappear while she was studying architecture:

> My mother told me many times that she had a friend—that's the reason why my brother's name is Pedro. [Her friend] was nineteen, twenty years old, and he was one of her few friends who wasn't an activist. But he was one of the first to be taken away and they never saw him again. She loved him very much and my brother is named Pedro for that reason.

The presence of the absent people was indeed widespread during our conversations. It was a relentless, never-ending series of stories, even if they were just a fragment of the estimated 30,000 *desaparecidos*. The majority of participants had heard of at least one concrete case of disappearance. This suggests that their elders knew of these disappearances at the time they were happening. The expansive effects of the terrorist state policies that Duhalde analyzed had been intergenerationally transmitted and prompt us to question the assertion that society did not know what was going on.

Conclusions

We have identified some of the main facts transmitted about what went on during the dictatorship. Our previous discussion highlighted the interconnections between fears and silences in shaping knowledge of the repression. Exploring young people's reconstruction of this past, their postmemories, allows us to assess what the witness generation knew during the terror and the process by which it was conveying its experiences. If the witnesses still carry fears and silences we have to evaluate how this affects the generational history they are writing and society's memory construction process.

There was an evident unevenness in knowledge among participants. Some of them could give only brief summaries of the terror highlighting the brutality of the repression and its apparent arbitrariness; others gave accounts that revealed a deeper knowledge about the period; yet others told stories illustrating a confusing absence of contextual information resulting in major distortions, even incredulity. These differences were usually related to what had been discussed or silenced within the family or at school. This pattern seemed to cut across socioeconomic or educational levels.

Even if there was no talk at home, young people had access to information through friends, professors, classmates, or coworkers—the other memory communities. The main differences in levels of knowledge of the terror were between those participants with political activists in their family and those without. There had also been more talk in families where relatives or acquaintances disappeared or had been persecuted and escaped into exile. Being savvy about Argentina's politics and direct knowledge of victims of the terror seem to define the content of the memories transmitted.

Because interviewees were "gray zoners," their stories tell us what the average family or person knew during the terror. Many parents had told their children that they did not know what was happening at that time. Censorship, misinformation, or the distracting role of such events as the soccer World Cup and the Malvinas/Falkland War explain this ignorance. But I cannot avoid being extremely skeptical when people insist that they did not know. Some levels of ignorance qualify for the category of "innocence as sin," to borrow words from filmmaker John Sayles, who has argued that people have the obligation to know what their government is doing.[12] Interestingly, Argentina's *The Official Story*, winner of the Oscar for best foreign film in 1986, two years into civilian rule, was an endorsement of generalized ignorance. Set in the last months of the dictatorship, it is precisely about a history professor who has no idea of what has been going on around her.

By looking at society's awareness of what was going on during the terror we can evaluate how the witness generation was positioning itself within the historical events of the dictatorship and in the eyes of its descendants. We find hints in the process of learning about human rights violations, the switch from "nobody knew" (during the dictatorship) to "everybody knows" (based on the information that circulated in the aftermath).

Young people are telling us about their elders' memories, necessarily shaped by contradictions and feelings of guilt, responsibility, and complicity. Claiming ignorance at the time of the dictatorship might honestly be due to a lack of knowledge but it may also be self-denial. People do not want to feel guilty for what they knew if they did nothing to stop it. And shame is another important element contributing to denial. There are also the sequels of processing the intense fear they felt. Fear of acting at that time may translate into attitudes of victimization years later and also into denial of having known, if the fears have not yet been recognized and processed.[13] Therefore, we need to pay attention to how the experience of witnessing and simultaneously denying the horror is affecting people today. Feelings of guilt and complicity have an effect on the memories of both the witness and the post-dictatorship generations.

There are indications that young people had accepted the justification of ignorance during the terror. I was often surprised by participants' insistence on justifying what their elders told them. For instance, by accentuating certain words and clearing their parents from any responsibility, such as "[my mother] was a police officer and she *never* participated in anything," or "[my parents] *really* didn't know anything" (my emphasis). But participants often perceived that people knew and that self-denial was a protective shield, which would explain the confusing paradox of not knowing but knowing that is detectable in many of the accounts that they had received. The large selection of stories about *desaparecidos*, persecutions, exiles, or killings known to participants' families or friends allows us to evaluate the extent to which the repression affected the whole society and how close the bullets were felt to be by the average family. Almost everybody had an anecdote about a distant relative, a neighbor's niece, or a parent's classmate. The manifest pervasiveness of the repression contradicts the claim that people did not know and favors the assumption that ignorance was adopted as a survival tool.

In spite of fears and silences, the past has made it into the present. Judging from the stories that have been transmitted, stories of surprise break-ins, detainment, disappearances, torture, and death at the hands of government agents, there is no doubt that participants were aware of what life under terror was like and of the human rights violations that took place. Knowledge of the dictatorship was uneven and, as we have seen, the witness generation was still processing these events and facing the problem of justifying itself for what it did or did not do and of being confronted by its descendants' questions. Terror emerged as one of the most vivid memories, but the consumption of the details of the atrocities had not been matched by an analysis of its causes. As we move into a discussion of impunity, and society's outrage or apathy toward it, we explore more deeply how fragmented and decontextualized knowledge about this past determines people's attitudes and actions.

FIVE

Conversations about Impunity

Introduction

We have discussed the fragmented knowledge that young people have of the past and have linked this to the legacy of fear and silences. This chapter is about impunity. It explores the cultural scenario of the lack of accountability in a society where hundreds of *represores* were benefiting from impunity laws.[1] It discusses young people's feelings of impotence and anger at the absence of justice. It examines patterns revealing a major and lasting distortion of ethical and public values, what I describe as the "normalization" or "naturalization" of living with major human rights abusers, who circulate in public places, appear on television talk shows, become politicians who run for and hold office, or are licensed to parent the children they seized after torturing and disappearing their biological parents. In parallel to participants' comments on the legal aspects of impunity, I look at how they experience living in a society where these killers and torturers live normal lives, and at how they react to their presence.

Impunity is not only a legal matter. In the late 1990s, Argentina seemed to be in transition between a culture of fear and what might be called a culture of impunity. Impunity pervaded all layers of society and it was a component of the still contested "consolidation" of democracy. The examples were countless: hundreds of torturers and assassins were free, corrupt politicians and corporations did not suffer major consequences for their "white collar" crimes, and there were unsolved mysteries of politically motivated crimes. The latter included the murder of teenager Maria Soledad Morales in dubious circumstances, incriminating relatives of prominent politicians; the execution-style murder of photojournalist José Luis Cabezas; the bombings of the Embassy of Israel and the AMIA (association of Jewish organizations)—crimes of which young people had direct knowledge.

The pervasiveness of impunity undoubtedly influenced people's attitudes toward it, which were manifested in indifference and an amazing degree of tolerance. I do not mean that people did not care. Public demonstrations or polls showed that large sectors of society condemned the crimes and demanded concrete responses from the authorities.[2] But one of the characteristics of living within a culture of impunity is that people are so overwhelmed by the everyday character of abuse that they seem apathetic to current forms of violence and repression. At the time I had these conversations, the capacity for indignation or outrage seemed to have been drastically minimized.

Let us take as an example the police's violent crushing of demonstrations at the time of this fieldwork. I participated in a human rights demonstration against torturer Peyón that was brutally repressed. Some Mothers of the Plaza de Mayo were beaten and a couple of young activists were taken to the hospital. Although the media reported those incidents, apathy seemed to be widespread, even among those who were highly critical of police brutality. While it was surprising to see how a society that had experienced such a brutal dictatorship could be so indifferent to the present violence, I perceived that an excess of abuse could lead people to detach themselves from it as a survival strategy.

Impunidad: *The Cultural Scenario*

The cultural scenario of impunity has its complexities, as apathy and tolerance may indicate an effort to go on with everyday life in the best possible way. Despite the apparent apathy, young people were conscious of the absence of accountability for the dictatorship's crimes. Furthermore, the opening of new trials for the kidnapping of babies and the international campaigns to bring the criminals to face trials in other countries were contributing to making impunity even more visible and difficult to hide.

Analía elaborated on the political context and pressures that characterized the process of legalization of impunity, first under the Alfonsín administration with the impunity laws, then under the Menem administration with presidential pardons to the *represores:*

> A trial for the military juntas was too much to handle for the first democratic government. Pressure must have been very strong for "the Turk" (nickname given to president Menem) to let them out, no? And, after that, now there's a big push for justice. But many interests must be at stake, many political pressures because it's not that everybody is washing their hands. The Mothers of the Plaza de Mayo are pressuring at the international level so the *represores* go to jail. [Judge] Baltasar Garzón is pressuring in Spain to put them in jail. And the government doesn't respond. Do you understand? I think that the government is an accomplice of what's going on,

but you've to consider that Alfonsín was the first democratic government, not to justify [the impunity laws]. But now, time went by. You cannot keep on covering what has been publicly denounced. There are international demands for justice. Society already knows what happened. There are no longer ways of covering it up, except as it's being done, which is with absolute impunity.

There was a perception of anger in society and of the need for justice to calm this anger. But there seemed to be a generalized feeling of impotence manifest in the recurring comments I heard: "It's over," "It's too late," "What can you do now?" Juan expressed these beliefs:

I don't see any benefit in pursing investigations. Many years have passed. Now, I'd concentrate efforts on more urgent issues. If there were no investigations at that time, I don't think we can find out that much twenty years later.

In addition to the many years that have passed and the perception that there is not much to be gained by pursuing investigations, the quality of punishment already given to *represores* was widely cited as a factor that strengthened disbelief in any possibility of justice. The reasoning was often based on the fact that those who spent some time in prison in the first years of civilian rule were kept in luxury "country club"-style facilities. Moreover, those prosecuted at the time of these conversations were given house arrest on account of their age (more than seventy years old). This benefit, which is not usually granted to ordinary criminals, is a 1997 decree issued by President Menem—a sign of the continuity of impunity promoted by civilian governments. But these arguments overlook the hundreds of *represores* in their fifties who, if tried and found guilty, still could spend a couple of decades in jail. It is not that young people ignored this fact, but there was a focused iconization of evil and discussions usually referred to the few well-known faces and names, such as Videla, Massera, and Galtieri, members of the military juntas, or individuals with a particularly atrocious record, as in the case of naval officer Astiz.

As Víctor reasoned:

Unfortunately, there's nothing you can do now. I don't know if I'd put them in jail after 20 years. How long can Videla remain in jail? Five at most and in a VIP prison. Then he'd die. They should've been tried at that time.

For Jorge, the futility of current prosecutions was also due to age:

What do you want? To put them in jail after twenty years? What for? It's over. I don't get it. The guys are seventy years old. Put them in jail and that's it or let them live their last years in their homes. They have forever the burden of their consciences.

At a very lively discussion, one talking londer than an other, four fifteen-year-old high school students, Patricia, Beatriz, Graciela, and Fabiana, described a powerful apparatus of impunity and reasoned that pressing for accountability is a dangerous and hard-to-win battle:

> The fact that they pardoned the military is like saying, "That's it; it's over." I think that if the government had any intention of doing something, Videla and all the rest would be in jail where they belong, not under house arrest, even if this is according to the law. I'm not interested in the law in this case. They should be in jail.
>
> Before, you lived watching out for what was going to happen to you, and today you live watching out that it doesn't happen again but also that there's justice.
>
> I don't think that there will ever be justice. Honestly, I don't believe in justice. They always say that there's justice and there isn't.
>
> The Cabezas case.
>
> For me, justice doesn't exist, at least in Argentina.
>
> The Maria Soledad case.
>
> There are tons of cases, and because there's no justice we have to make there be justice. I don't believe, nor think that I can say, "Good, OK, there's no justice, OK."
>
> There's nothing to be done.
>
> Don't say that.
>
> For me, justice doesn't exist. Because justice is always a cover-up, the most powerful and the judges solve everything with money. For me, the word "justice" doesn't exist. It's something I've never seen so far. According to what I've been told and what I've seen, justice doesn't exist.

As some of these comments suggest, the omnipresence of impunity for past and current crimes and the lack of political will to allow prosecutions might have convinced many young people that justice does not exist and that it may not be worth struggling for. This can be described as a process in which anger easily dissipates into fatalism.

The Torturer Next Door—Living with *Represores*

One symptom of the normalization or naturalization of living with *represores* is the development of an unhealthy acceptance of the social spaces they have been granted. The participants and I discussed at length the ambivalence between public outrage and tolerance, as well as the effects and reactions that the *represores* provoke.

The coexistence with these major human rights abusers has resulted in situations where former victims have met their torturers face to face. As Miriam Lewin, who met her torturer, "Tigre" Acosta three times, has said: "I always fantasize about making a scandal. But I never do it because I feel that no one around me will react; they'll look at me as if I'm crazy."[3] One of these episodes took place during the fieldwork. Silvia had heard about a woman who met her former torturer, "el Turco Julián" (his real name is Julio Simón) at a bar in downtown Buenos Aires. She expressed her indignation about this incident:

> I was shocked by that woman, I don't know if you heard about that woman who, in a bar, met the guy who'd tortured her. I heard this on the radio. [The torturer] left because the bar's owner asked him to leave. [The torturer] even told her, "Be grateful that you're alive," and I don't know what else. I'd break his face, grab him against. . . . On top of that the guy said, "To be honest, I don't remember you." And then he says, "Be grateful that you're alive."

However, most *represores'* faces were not well known, and it was difficult to evaluate public reactions to their presence in the urban landscape. So far, those who were recognized were increasingly facing harassment, insults, and physical assaults, mostly by young people. We need to remember that the CONADEP avoided printing in its report the names of the *represores*, a quite significant omission. In quite the opposite way, the South African TRC identified and made public the faces of the perpetrators. One of its goals was precisely that those who had committed human rights violations should come forward to expose their crimes.

Publicized encounters with the well-known *represores* prompt us to ask how many of them do people meet everyday without being aware of it. Three participants had met dictator Videla in a public place. Lucía remembered an episode from her childhood by which Videla's face was engraved in her memory:

> For example, I don't recognize Galtieri. I wouldn't recognize him if I saw him on a bus and sat next to him; [although] his name may sound familiar. I'd recognize the faces of Videla or Massera but no one else. Videla because I saw him once at the bank, my mother looked at me and said, "See that man Lucía, that man's a son of a bitch." I was around five and said, "Ah, ok." My mother told me that it was a kind of "*milico*" [derogatory term for military] bank and [Videla] was surrounded by a bunch of women gazing at him. There are tons of people who admire them. When I saw Videla he was with a bunch of old ladies. You know those situations where it's evident that he's the only man and a group of women are saying, "Ahhh?" That's how they were. I didn't understand anything. I remember my mother telling me, "See that man Lucía, that man's a son of a bitch." I remember his face, everything about him, the image. But I don't remember what happened afterwards.

Eugenia described her encounter with Videla, the anger that she felt, and her perception that people hate these criminals.

> [It was] one of those buildings that are old and very beautiful, where elevators have iron gates. The elevator comes down; the people inside leave. I was going to take the

elevator and saw someone coming in. I looked and it was Videla with another guy. It was seven years ago. I recognized him because I believe that he generates hate in me. He doesn't generate anger but hate. I looked at him and he made a gesture for me to go first. And I said, "No thank you." I didn't put on any special face. Besides, the guy doesn't know me to recognize whether or not my expression was one of hate or something like that. But my "No thank you" was my polite way of saying. . . . Wait, I'm lying. I told him, "No, I'll go later." Afterwards I thought, "I didn't thank him as I normally would with any person to whom I say yes or no when they offer something. I thought it over, "I couldn't thank a person whom I consider an assassin. I don't have to thank him. Thanks for what?" So you project it to the fact that, regrettably, they're free. So it's the social condemnation of scorn. Do you understand? Maybe they don't experience it that way. Maybe they're happier than me, I don't know, and maybe tomorrow that hate will turn against me. But I think they must feel it. Yes, I think they must feel that people hate them and keep their distance. I sense that.

Another encounter with Videla was brought up during a discussion on what to do if one meets the *represores*. Relating his experience with Videla, the neighbor of one of his friends, Jorge illustrated his argument that people shy away from defying them:

Maybe you're next to [the torturer] and it doesn't affect you at all. At most, you'll insult him and that's it. You won't have the guts to confront him. No one [dares]. I experienced this. I went in the same elevator with Videla and this guy who's a [political] fanatic but he didn't even say hello. The first time that I went to my friend's house I had no idea that he lived there. [My friend] told me, "Do you know who lives in the 6th floor? Videla." I didn't know why I had to show my ID and sign a log when I entered the building.

These "meeting Videla" episodes illustrate different reactions that the *represores'* presence in public places provokes in people: some honor them; others remain indifferent, feel anger, or are intimidated.

We discussed whether people were aware of and bothered by the hundreds of torturers and assassins who may be the nextdoor neighbor, the family doctor, or the person at the next table in a restaurant. Laura, who was very upset about this, argued that:

People aren't conscious of this. They don't stop to think about it. Because if you think of the number of torturers and assassins that are free and walking around the streets, you want to kill yourself, you want to kill everybody. All those who were part of the *proceso* are free.

So Laura perceived that, faced with impunity, people choose to ignore some of its effects. This attitude may be a legacy of the "ignorance-as-survival-tool" that many adopted during terror. Furthermore, she speculated on what she would do if meeting *represores*:

If I see him on the street, I wouldn't walk by him as if nothing happened but rather shout at him, "Assassin, son of a bitch." Neither would I beat him because I don't think I have to hit him. I'd put myself at his same level. But [I wouldn't] let it go by. As when Massera went to a military officers' club and some left the room. But, before [leaving], I'd walk by his table and tell him, "You're a big son of a bitch, etc., etc."

Imagining reactions to these encounters is a way of reflecting on the various instances in which people can meet face to face with a torturer. I wanted to know how participants felt about torturers and their willingness to accept, challenge, or isolate them. So I asked them to figure out how they would respond if they found out that their neighbor was a torturer and whether they would prefer to know or ignore this fact. Laura had this to say:

There's a guy who owns a maxi kiosk [like 7/11 stores] and was a torturer during the military period, another jerk. I don't know him or where the kiosk is located. But my horrified friend told me that the other day. She said, "I won't go again to that kiosk." I don't think I'd move [if I had a torturer in my building] but [I'd slip] a note under his door everyday, or ring his bell at two or three in the morning, whenever I want. If I'd live in the same place I don't know what I'd do, honestly, I don't know.

When I talked to a group of four high school classmates, their opinions were split between wanting to know and not wanting to know that their neighbor was someone who had tortured and killed. Liliana candidly stated: "No, I wouldn't like to know because I'd have to move." And Héctor believed in the power of words to isolate *represores*: "Every day, I'd slip a note under his door reading, 'Assassin, mother fucker.' So he'd feel really bad and be forced to move out, to leave the neighborhood."

Although several participants said that they would prefer to be aware of the presence of torturers in their neighborhood, they were not clear on how they should proceed. There were comments revealing how transmitted fears could be a deterrent for actions to denounce them or limit their social spaces. Teresa was one of those opting for ignoring their presence:

I'd be scared. I'd be very scared if they tell me [he's my neighbor]. Maybe [the torturer] realizes that I know [about him] and I risk my life. What if something like the military coup comes back and, because I know [this], "pa pum" they kill me?

While her fear was based on the possibility of a new wave of repression, she was reproducing the belief that the less you knew the safer you were (during the terror).

We can see a latent feeling that any public action against the *represores* was being registered in a data bank, ready to be used if the occasion demands. Fears were also grounded on what could happen at the time we had these conversations, which reveals a perception that criminals still held power. As Josefina said: "I'd be afraid; I think I'd prefer to move immediately. I know that nobody would buy the house. But I'd be afraid that he might come after me and torture me." Although the reasons for those fears varied, there was a recurrent similar solution: it is better to ignore the fact that torturers are among us. The limited knowledge about the past was reinforced in the present by attitudes promoting the concealment rather than the disclosure of the truth.

There was also mention of fear as something that torturers might feel. This was Marcelo's reasoning:

> They're the ones who should be afraid now, the ones who should be careful. Because, after ten years in which we made many mistakes, we're living now a more consolidated democratic period. They were prosecuted; they were pardoned. It's like now they're free but up to a certain point. Any wrong move and the topic comes out. Whoever says, "I'm pleased that I killed so many people" is criticized by public opinion. I guess that they must be walking around afraid because anything out of the ordinary that they do triggers the reaction of the media against them, adverse public opinion, the mothers [of the Plaza de Mayo] are always there.

This was one of the few comments I heard about the *represores* being afraid. I see this as a perception that *represores* might not be comfortable with the rejection they feel and the signs of growing social condemnation for their crimes. But the proposed harassment of the torturers was, in general, subtle when compared to the nature of their crimes.

Represores had gained another social space by securing a presence in the communication media, be it on television screens, on radio programs, or in press articles. Some journalists' distorted concept to objectivity, based on their concern to present "all sides" or, more despicable still, in the search for higher ratings, may explain the presence of former victims and their torturers on the same television programs.[4] However, I heard comments advocating the *represores'* right to free speech. One of these heated defenses took place during a discussion about the presence on a television program of the particularly infamous torturer Turco Julián (the same one who met a former victim at a bar). On one occasion, this torturer had used a television talk show to claim that, during the repression, the norm was to kill, that he had tortured with a *picana* (an electric prod), and that he would do it again.[5] According to Jorge:

> It's OK [that he's on TV]. It's not bad, because we all have the right to give our opinion. Free speech is for everybody. Whatever the guy was in the past is his problem. Regrettably, you have to let him voice his opinion, because you cannot refuse this right to anybody. Wasn't Astiz a *represor*? And the press talked to him and the guy

spoke. Journalism has nothing to do with this. You've to interview both the good and the bad guys. He was a *represor* and you can interview him. Why wouldn't you? Why not? You're a bad journalist if you don't write the article. If you've to write the article you do it, period. Whatever you know, after the interview, you can tell him, "You're a disgusting mother fucker." But first you must do it.

It is interesting that in discussing journalistic integrity, Julio mentions the Astiz case, which had taken place earlier that same year. Astiz went on record with a journalist saying that he was the best-trained person to kill politicians and journalists.[6] Astiz's outrageous declarations, unlike Turco Julian's, resulted in legal proceedings against him for the apology of crime. However, there is a difference between objective reporting and giving assassins a forum for justifying and advocating their crimes. The issue is not that the *represores* receive media coverage but within what context this coverage takes place. By aiming to present different "opinions," certain media coverage has resulted in giving acknowledged bestial criminals an equivalent moral stature to other participants, which gives them the power to influence the public. This potential to influence may be momentary but immensely disturbing. *Represores* should be allowed to speak as torturers and assassins but not as upgraded voices to celebrate diversity.

The Torturer Is a Kind Parent

In most societies, only those considered to be potentially fit and loving parents are granted the privilege of taking care of its most vulnerable members. Children are taken away from unfit parents. Allowing *represores* custody of the estimated five hundred babies they seized as part of their "spoils of war" is another major sign of their acceptance as respectable individuals. The issue of the torturer as a kind parent deserves special attention. It symbolizes, probably better than anything, an acceptance that criminals have the right to a social space that is not behind bars. Unquestioned acceptance of the quality of parenthood that torturers can provide seemed quite widespread—a paradoxical contradiction considering the generalized indignation concerning the brutality of their crimes.

Some of the arguments for appropriating these children are, at best, sickening, such as naval officers explaining that they did not kill pregnant women because they were against abortion.[7] That did not stop these Christian men from torturing pregnant women and killing them after they gave birth. They even developed specific torments to torture the fetus such as inserting a metallic spoon in the vagina until it touched the fetus and then applying a *picana* to it.[8] Some supporters of the dictatorship continued to reason that they "saved" these children from death, gave them a good education, and prevented them from becoming guerrillas as their mothers wanted them to be.[9]

Stolen babies—most of them in their twenties at the time of our conversations—can be identified and returned to their biological families, the goal of the unyielding struggle of the Grandmothers of the Plaza de Mayo.[10] What should be done with these children was an extremely controversial issue that stirred up fierce debates, even when the adoptive parents were the selfsame individuals who tortured and disappeared the biological parents. These debates centered on what was best for the children and revealed a quite generalized acceptance that torturers can have a second life as kind parents. The media were influential actors because their coverage, which provided a basis for society to discuss the issue, usually emphasized the plight and love of the adoptive parents, but totally and inexplicably excluded from these accounts the political dimension of the crimes against these children. During this fieldwork, Videla was placed under house arrest for his role in these crimes, and this was a recurrent topic in our conversations.

Alicia provided many details about the complexity of the issue:

It's a very difficult topic. Because what's at stake here are the kids, although now grown-up. For me, what Videla did isn't right, because he stole them and that's wrong. I agree that it was better to give [the babies] to other persons rather than kill them, but these kids had other family. Beyond the fact that the parents were kept in captivity, these children had a grandmother, an uncle. And the rationale that if they brought up a subversive child, they'd bring up a subversive grandchild, isn't a valid justification. Really, rather than killing them I think it's perfect that they were given away to others. They saved their lives, quote, unquote, but they deprived [the children] from their past; they live in a lie because they don't know who they are.

In spite of her clear analysis of the problems caused to these children, Alicia thought that they should stay with their adoptive families, an opinion shared by many participants:

We need to assess how beneficial it's for the now grown-up child to learn that he's really the son of a disappeared or to continue believing that he's the son of the [adoptive] father. It's very tough. We know of people who find out that they're adopted when they're older and that their [real] parent wasn't an assassin or anything, and they get very upset, angry, and hate everybody. To find out that you're the child of a *desaparecido*, that your father probably killed your mother or father, that you've lived twenty, twenty-two years with lies. You ask yourself up to what point is it good to give back the children their primeval identity. You put yourself in the place of the kid. I think that it would be horrible for me to find out now, at nineteen, that my parents are not my parents, that my father probably killed my father. I'd die. I'd hate my own parents, even when they raised me, I'd hate them. And I'd also hate those who told me that the guy who raised me killed my dad.

Several cases prove that returned children do not hate the relatives who found them. But Alicia brought up a recurrent pattern among participants: the personalization of the experience. They put themselves in the situation of the stolen children and analyze the cases with an extreme emphasis on the individual psychological factors. The personal and the emotional take priority over the crimes committed. This is reflected in opinions that it is preferable to leave the stolen children with torturers rather than causing them the trauma of discovering the truth, even when this truth concerns the role the adoptive parents had in the disappearance of the biological ones.

The concept of obedience to authority was also mentioned in evaluating the torturers' moral standards. Juan illustrated the belief that someone can obey orders to torture people to death but be a loving parent of the illegally appropriated children of his victims. Moreover, his views on torturers' transformations and human rights campaigns as personal vendettas support the benefits of continuing with the spiral of silence and denying these children the truth about their story:

> I'd forget about that topic. Or I'd investigate where [the children] are and if they're OK, without telling anything to the kids. If you see that they're doing well that's all. [The grandmothers] want to take the kid away and hurt the torturer but they hurt the child. What they want is to win by taking [the kid] away from the torturer, "We won, we have the kid now." If the person changed, after many years, finally they treated the kid very well. Maybe [the torturer] was under pressure to torture. He either tortured or was tortured himself. And if he raised, took care, and is giving the kid a good quality of life. I'd find out if [the kids] are doing okay, what happened, everything. If the kids are doing well and are happy where they are, I wouldn't tell them the truth because it would hurt them.

Lucía, who had met Videla at the bank when she was a little girl and had in her extended family a Mother of the Plaza de Mayo, also pointed to the benefits of silences and ignorance:

> Put yourself in the shoes of a child who has a very happy life and through that test [DNA] discovers that he was a baby stolen by the military. Sometimes it's better to deny reality and go on with your happy life. You're screwing up the life of a kid. Because it would destroy my life to find out that my mother is not my mother, that I was stolen by the military, that my parents don't exist, that my mother . . . it's horrible to find out that. I don't know what I'd do, won't say. I wouldn't like to be forced [to DNA testing] and I don't know if I'd like to find out. These kids, with their military parents would be able to go to the university, have a career and a life. If you take away those kids, where would they go? To an orphanage?

Lucía analyzed the issue as if it were an everyday case of adoption, seeing only the pain and ignoring its roots. Her mentioning of the better standard of living that torturers can provide illustrates how the economic dimension can override ethical concerns. References to orphanages seem to ignore the existence of biological families.

Carmen was extremely interested in this topic and had followed media coverage of prominent cases. She referred to the famous case of the Tolosa twins, seized by police officer Miara and often referred to as the Miara twins, whose mother, father, grandmother, and the midwife who assisted in their delivery remain disappeared. Carmen's remarks show well how the media play with emotions and simplify or partially hide the reasons for the suffering they expose:

> When I heard of the Miara twins, who were with a former police officer, I said, "Poor kids," I burst into tears. I identified with them. I watched every [television] program where they participated, searched for all the newspaper clippings. They'd go on a TV program. They wanted to be with their parents but their grandmother and uncle wanted them. [The twins] were living with an aunt. And I said, "Poor kids, they don't know with whom to identify." At the same time, their father, the ex-cop, would say, "You've to come back because I give you clothes, I give you all this but they don't." So the kids were very confused. I felt, "Those poor kids don't know what to do." An unknown person comes, because the grandmother is a total stranger to them, don't tell me about the blood and all that; she's a total stranger. I don't think they have to be with the grandmother. Even if they say that's the biological grand-mother. My mother always relates this to my situation and says, "What if your father comes now?" Because I haven't seen my dad in ages, it has been almost twenty years. So [my mother] says, "What if your father comes?" And I say, "He's a stranger to me, I won't go with him." It's the same with this person. You were raised by this person who gave you love. In spite of how he got you, he treated you well. You have an image of this person. It's very difficult to, overnight, move in with your grand-mother who's someone alien to you. It's going to be very difficult for me to change my position regarding this. Because if you are eighteen years old, as the twins were, how could you be told, "These are not your parents. I'm your grandmother, I'm your uncle. Your mother was killed this way or that way." You create psychological conflict for the kids.

We have here yet another instance of personalizing the issues by identifying with the stolen children of the disappeared, as if there is no difference between a father who left his family and the torturer who took his victim's child. These are not regular cases of adoption. Rather than the talk being about what was done to those chil-dren—the root of the problem—the focus is their future suffering if they are removed from the adoptive parents, even if the adoptive parents were the ones who eliminated the biological parents.

There were other opinions about the twins' situation and their refusal to undergo DNA testing: "Well, it's their decision. If they want to forget and don't want to know about their past, not because of fear but due to shame or something. It's up to them" (Pedro). "Maybe they love that guy a lot and don't want to know about his life, what he did" (Nelson).

Because of the ongoing search for these kids, new cases continued to emerge. As Marcelo noted:

> Even nowadays we keep on finding people. For example, the bass player of *Los Pericos* [musical group] had a disappeared brother whom he found, by chance, last year. He found him alive, but he'd been given away to a family and never knew that he was the son of *desaparecidos*. There must be a lot [of people] like him.

How many children of the disappeared live in ignorance of their true parents' identity is not an easy question to answer. But we talked about a related issue: the suspicion among many young people that they might have been the stolen child of disappeared parents. There were indications that these concerns were widespread among Argentineans in their twenties. Juanita Pargament, a Mother of the Plaza de Mayo, told me of young people who approach their organization seeking to clarify their doubts.[11] While collaborating with a human rights Web site, I once opened an e-mail addressed to the Mothers from an anguished young man who had agonized for years before approaching those who could help him investigate his origins.[12]

Alicia, the daughter of police officers, talked about doubts among the children of military personnel:

> Any child of military personnel of that period doubts if those are her parents. I put myself in their place. Suppose that my dad was a military officer during the *proceso*. So I'd wonder, "I'm nineteen years old and I can be the daughter of a *desaparecido*." Who dissipates this doubt? When you're a small kid you always have the idea that, "Ah, I'm adopted." You imagine that because you heard once [about] adoption. "[My sibling] looks different than me; I'm adopted."

Many people can probably remember learning about adoption and wondering whether it had happened to them. But these twisted cases of "adoption" add new dimensions to these doubts. Laura imagined the reactions of young people facing this situation:

> Sometimes I find myself thinking; it's not that I'm always delving into the same topic, but I think about these kids. The shock of finding out that the person who's raising you and always gave you the best, loves you, and takes care of you is a torturer and assassin who killed your real mother and your real father. In addition to finding out that your parents aren't your parents, you find out that the one who pretends to be your dad assassinated and tortured your mom and dad. What's to be done with these kids? Psychological treatment for life won't suffice.

Sara was one of the few participants challenging the torturers' rights to keep the children:

> [We need] investigations. The good thing is that organizations such as HIJOS and Mothers are investigating. They search for the children, try to locate them. Honestly, I think that if you find them . . . As I was talking with my brother the other day, he said that there should be mandatory DNA testing for those who refuse to do so. Because when you discover a stolen baby and the person refuses the testing, the military has already screwed up her or his life. And it's good that people know this.

Hence, although there was consensus on the traumatic aspects and the suffering involved in the process, some interviewees supported the Grandmothers' right to take back their grandchildren. They argued that torturers should not retain custody over the stolen babies and investigations must continue to verify the identity of these children and return them to their biological families. But this is an ongoing process and aberrant details keep on emerging. Time will tell whether they alter perceptions about torturers as kind parents. One year after these conversations, witnesses publicly described the "distribution" and appropriation of babies by Navy officers: "The only children that were valued were those that were recently born and white. They used to get rid of the oldest. I know that they killed some boys no more than ten or eleven years old. The babies were given as if they were just little kitties."[13]

This is not the first time that children were separated from their biological families for political reasons. The Nazis gave to German families over 200,000 Polish children.[14] Children also disappeared in El Salvador and Guatemala during the armed conflicts of the 1980s.[15] But, consistent with its strategy of "leaving no traces," Argentina's dictatorship implemented a peculiar campaign for the systematic seizing of babies: a "baby factory" where pregnant prisoners were kept alive until they gave birth.

Conclusions

In this chapter we have explored the cultural scenario of legalized impunity. Young people's stories revealed how they are experiencing the lack of accountability as an everyday occurrence. A culture of fear had been replaced by a culture of impunity.

Participants had much to say regarding any hope of altering the current environment. A generalized anger and indignation over the absence of justice coexisted with strong feelings of impotence before the futility of current prosecutions. There is no doubt that young people were horrified by the dictatorship's crimes. Both rational analyses and emotional reactions demonstrated that participants were highly critical of human rights violations. Nonetheless, their apathy, tolerance, or hopelessness toward the absence of justice and the societal spaces that had been granted to the *represores* contrasted with this and may be a good reflection of how society in general was dealing with these issues at the time of this fieldwork.

I have defined this process as the naturalization or normalization of living with major criminals and human rights abusers. Certain opinions on concrete issues show an alarming acceptance that the *represores'* place may not be behind bars. They range from calls to respect their right to free speech to the acceptance of torturers as legitimate and kind parents to the children of their victims despite how *represores* seized the children and the expense to all involved.

Many of these attitudes evince a distortion of ethical and public values that cannot be disconnected from the effects of state terrorism over the social body. How can we explain this? Did people give up any possibility of justice? Are people still afraid of the *represores*? Do people condone or justify the crimes, even when they publicly deny doing so?

Postmemories of terror were shaping the attitudes toward impunity and accountability discussed here, but the pervasiveness of impunity can generate either apathy, as reflected by hopelessness, or it might invigorate calls for justice, prompted by the feeling that "It's enough." Thus we move on to explore social indifference toward the repression and toward the issue of justice through the views of the younger generation.

SIX

Conversations about Indifference

Introduction

"If only people knew . . ." Unfortunately, the notion that public awareness of mass violence and repression could deter them remains—quite often—wishful thinking. As for the causes of indifference, a multiplicity of factors are at play, ranging from political interests to fear, and including individualism or sheer approval of the perpetrators' crimes. Furthermore, indifference is not limited to the times when the atrocities were being committed. There is another phase to it, one that relates to the aftermath of the terror, the tortures, and the killings. It is reflected in a society's stance toward impunity and accountability. But there are links between the lack of justice and indifference. As we have seen, living under a culture of impunity provokes feelings of anger, fear, and impotence, which easily turn into cynicism and apathy.

This chapter explores indifference as a human rights concern through the importance of this traumatic past in young people's lives and their attitudes toward it. It looks for answers to the questions "Why bother?" and "So what?" It focuses on the younger generation's interest—or lack of it—in learning about the dictatorship and participating in struggles for accountability. I am talking of knowledge linked to action, as a tool to understand political processes, to defend one's rights, and to exercise a responsible citizenship. These conversations also seek to assess what value young people ascribe to justice and their attitudes toward it, including active participation in related political activities. Thus, I was interested in how participants perceived society's role in this process, in how the experience of this traumatic past was shaping a new breed of citizens who would either tolerate impunity or press for accountability.

The Value of the Past

To some extent, the significance of any historical period depends on the value that it has in the present. In one way or another, the dictatorship marked the generations that lived under it. How young people relate to this past, thus, is influenced by many factors, including the relevance that it had for their elders, the information they received, and its importance in relation to the many problems affecting their lives today. We cannot explore societal indifference without acknowledging that, for young Argentineans, the future was at best problematic. It was a generation torn "between indifference and indignation."[1]

I was concerned with the meaning that this past had in their present. I looked for answers to the questions: What determines the value of this past? What influences young people's interest or apathy regarding these issues? Do they think that it is important to know about this period? What is the relationship, if any, of knowledge to political participation? I also asked participants to think about what they perceived to be the current climate of opinion in their own generation and in society in general and to consider the reasons for these attitudes.

In discussing the value of this past, there were spontaneous and recurrent references to memory. Participants brought up the risks of political amnesia and stressed the importance of remembering so "history won't repeat itself." They did not doubt that this past was important and that societies must keep alive the memory of their traumatic events. Even those who were very candid in stating their lack of interest recognized the dangers of indifference. As I was told: "I don't want to find out [what happened] but I know that this is dangerous. The future is built with the past" (Mariana).

Mercedes, who was only ten years old when she used to read the newspapers with all the details of the trial of the military juntas, elaborated on the dangers faced by amnesic societies and the arbitrariness by which societies decide what to remember:

> I think that the events of the dictatorship left a mark that will remain, in my opinion, forever. Many generations will be influenced by, will suffer from this mark. These are indelible marks left by the military government. This should suffice for us never to forget this. That's why we don't forget, beyond all the grief it left. If I forget that fire burns, I'll put my hand back in the fire and burn it again. That's precisely the objective. If I forget that when they were in power the military massacred, tortured, assassinated and did all the atrocities they could, I'll repeat the same mistake. This is the issue; we should always have in mind what happened so it won't ever happen again. Look at how North Americans won't give us a break with the Vietnam War. They made all the movies, books, and serials they wanted. It was a deep wound for them and no one dared to say, "OK, it's over, let's forget." They've been remembering and commemorating it for over twenty years. I think it's something natural

for any human being at the individual level and for societies, to remember the major tragedies, the major sufferings from the past so not to endure them again.

But the consensus on the need to remember did not necessarily translate into interest in this historical period. During our conversations, we discussed the many forms that apathy takes and the reasons for it. It is here that we can observe constant references linking interest to particular social groups and categorizing memory communities.

Some interviewees brought up the issue of societal silences about this past and linked them to the lack of interest. What is not talked about, what is not perceived as relevant by the family, the community, or what is not taught in school, appears, therefore, not worthy of being explored. Leonardo explained how personal experiences and the circle of people surrounding a person influence interest toward particular issues:

> There are two well-defined sectors. I think that the people who had time to talk and learn are interested in knowing more. But there are other people in whose homes they never talked about it and who don't care. They look ahead and that's all. They're wearing their blinders. It's not circumstantial that there are those who say: "OK, it's over." I think that having many people who are not interested was intentional. The project was to forge a mass of people who're not very interested in looking back, to whom the repression is presented as something that's finished. But it's not circumstantial that people don't want to know or think about other things. At least, this is what's said. [They] want people to believe that that won't happen again. The intention is to plant this in people's minds, "Don't worry, we are in a democracy."

Many participants pointed to other priorities created by a not very promising future, including the difficulties of making ends meet under deteriorating economic conditions as an important cause of indifference. As Analía summarized: "I have the impression that everybody is very worried about what's happening now and they're not willing to participate or make a commitment to other kinds of activities."

Antonio had no interest in the events of the dictatorship and explained the frustrations and individualistic drive that he perceived in his generation. He also linked apathy to impunity, suggesting that indifference is a consequence of impotence and disillusionment, factors that add to the uncertainties of the future:

> I don't think you can go on delving into the past. What happened is over and we need to struggle for other things. I come every morning by train [to the city]. Do you have any idea how depressing [it] is to ride this train and see the faces of the people who travel in the mornings? You've no idea of what that is. They're dead, dead, that's it. It's terrible. Waking up at 6 am, traveling packed in that train that overflows with people. You look at their faces knowing that they'll work for

$300 a month and might spend half of it on the train. I'm twenty years old; I've only been working for seven months. And to see people who are ten or fifteen years older and think that that's what is waiting for me. Is this a first world country? Is this a country that's improving? They cannot keep lying to us. I don't know what others have told you but I'll bet that 90 percent are not interested in politics. It's one of my conflicts; I'm in law school and I'm not interested in politics and these two things go together. For many people from my generation this [past] is a very distant subject. We discuss that we're twenty-years old, that we're beginning to live our lives and we don't know where we're going or what's going to happen to us. People my age are only interested in themselves; nothing else matters. I care about myself and two or three persons I love. I don't want any problem. No one cares about what happens with the rest. Because if you don't think this way you have to think like the Mothers of the Plaza de Mayo and take to the streets for twenty years without achieving anything. It's more productive to think the way people think now. I'm not telling you that it's better or worse. Twenty years in the street for nothing. This is why we now think only of ourselves. I try to do my thing in whatever way I can. I try to live my life, to look for the things I care about, to see how I can get them. Then, everything may go wrong but that's another thing [he laughs] it's Murphy's Law.

It is worth noting this reference to the Mothers of the *desaparecidos'* apparently unsuccessful quest for justice. These bits and pieces of information allow us to assess attitudes toward, and relationship between, human rights activists and society in general. For another viewpoint expressed was that indifference, specifically regarding political participation, was rooted in the belief that someone else is doing the job that needs to be done. Alicia brought up these concerns and discussed human rights activism:

I think that interest in what happened depends on the values you have, the social group to which you belong, and the people with whom you socialize. Maybe I oper-ate within a group with specific values. For example, in the scout group certain values are fundamental for us. That's why this topic is of interest. The idea is not to lose the memory of what happened, it's to know about it and remember it so there isn't another coup d'état and we endure the same that happened before. But it seems that everybody says, "Why should I go if so and so will go; the Mothers of the Plaza de Mayo, all those go. So, why should I go? Others are going." And if the 33 million [Argentineans] would think like that we'd be lost. I think that's what goes on.

I heard several references to an apolitical younger generation. Although it is normal for young people to have other priorities in their lives, there were indications that, in some circles, the dictatorship is seldom a topic of interest. One discussion between Andrea, Teresa, Ester, Noemí, and Luciana, fifteen-year-old classmates, illustrated the reasons for this perception:

> From what I've seen, I thought it was here in this school but I spoke with guys from other student centers and they told me that, always, at the meetings they organize with the Grandmothers [of the Plaza de Mayo] or to watch movies there are always the same faces, always a few. I don't think there's much interest. I always see the same faces here at the student center or wherever I go. It angers you that there are always the same faces and that there are no more. It's a minority. Those guys [from the other school] told me that you could see that only ten or eleven kids from the whole school had gone to see a beautiful [human rights] exhibit, with stunning photographs. It was an exhibit about identity. I loved it but there were either older people, or the organizers, or guys from the student center.

> I think that people our age aren't very interested in this topic. It's more what they ignore than what they care about. If I'd have to estimate a percentage, I'd say that only 30 percent are interested.

> I see that, if you introduce the topic, some may start talking and get interested. But, in general, they're concerned with the present, with discos, concerts, or music.

> I wanted to say that when I talk with my friends from the neighborhood and bring up this issue, they say, "No, no, it's over, let's not talk about it." And I say, "It's not over, it's the past but we shouldn't . . ." [and they go on] "No, no, let's make plans for Saturday, let's go out to eat pizza" and all that. They don't care that much.

The primacy of superficial topics needs to be connected with this generation's lack of utopias. There were links between indifference and helplessness through comments suggesting that apathy was a consequence of people's resignation to the current political and economic system as the only one possible. The lack of dreams or the impossibility of social change seemed to act as paralyzing devices.

Diego grew up listening to political discussions and had probably heard many stories of frustrated projects. His words were very revealing of a generation that had inherited a feeling of defeat, was not interested in knowing more about things that they could no longer change, and had nothing in which to believe:

> Most of us have given up. So there's no desire to know about something that could have been or didn't happen. This might imply the responsibility of continuing with a project. Nobody challenges globalization; the free market is a fact. So, it's over; this is the only possible country, the only possible reality. This is what's being imposed on us and we've been gradually assuming it.

Mercedes discussed indifference along similar lines, bringing in past frustrations and linking them to current apathy:

I think that there were many years of fear of [the repression]. We don't have that fear today but there's disbelief, despair. I think [they] have resorted to other means. For example, the same system that annihilated a generation has appropriated that generation's symbols: Evita [Perón], Che [Guevara]. It's like it's over now; we were left with nothing. We're left without the people who at some point fought for something and without the referents that those people had. Through the school and all the rest, we're only left with a profound ignorance and social apathy.

Some participants related interest in the past to social class, revealing assumptions that upper classes are more apathetic because they suffered less during the repression. For Mónica, class was a main factor influencing divisions among young people:

Our generation is split. There are two sectors. It's divided among people who are probably better off and live in a bubble, a capsule. I don't know for sure but I think that there are main differences based on economic factors. There are other people whose parents were more touched by what happened, and might look for more information. But those who always lived well, never had problems, or weren't affected stay away from these issues, aren't interested. There are many people who refuse to listen because they say, "It didn't happen to me."

Another argument advanced was the generational basis of indifference. A recurrent comment was the perception that the events of the dictatorship were very distant and not an issue for those who did not live under it. This is how some fifteen-year-old classmates, Leo, Hugo, Omar, Ariel, and Miguel, explained young people's disconnection with this past:

I think that [young people] are interested in other stuff. They don't give much relevance to issues related to this past. They think that the past is over and they must live the present.

They take it as another experience.

I think that, among young people, [we think] "It's OK, it's over, and we must try to avoid its repetition." It's a period that we didn't live through so it didn't affect us. At least, myself, I don't think I have a relative who was kidnapped.

The generational component of attitudes of indifference was also expressed in relation to those who lived under terror. Víctor, who was twenty-one years old and one of the coproducers of a community radio program, was keenly interested in the dictatorship. He pointed to the lack of interest among different age groups:

> I think that those in their twenties are very interested. Maybe they didn't live much of this period and were a couple of years old when this happened. But I think they're interested. I don't know if the younger ones are. I don't think so. I think they're not interested because it happened long ago. I hope that young people will become interested because they're the ones who could do something. Older people lived through it. It's like they can't or don't want to do anything.

Thus, either because people were not born then or because they had too much of it, Victor worried for a generalized apathy with its consequent lack of political participation.

There were also links between indifference, the excess of abuse, and widespread mistreatment as an everyday occurrence. Feelings of impotence and doubts about what difference individual actions can make were a recurrent observation. According to Silvia:

> We're used to doing nothing. I see an announcement of something and [I think], "No, I'll stay home, what's the point of going?" We're really used to that, to doing nothing. We're so used to being mistreated and [saying], "Well, it's OK." Even in a bus, people push you, they step on you. And if you complain the same passengers turn against you. So I don't complain and keep on going like that, each one minding her own business; that's the way it is.

Thus, pervasiveness of impunity, excess of abuse, lack of utopias, or the demands of everyday problems that do not leave time and energy to worry about this past are all reasons that young people perceived as explaining indifference. Participants further argued that people's attitudes seemed to be conditioned by the memory communities to which they belong, be it related to generation, families' experiences during the terror, or social class. Let us now move into the other main concern in exploring indifference: the value that justice had for the post-dictatorship generation.

The Value of Justice

What about indifference in relation to struggles for accountability? Practically all the young people with whom I talked were critical of impunity laws and pardons and thought that those responsible must be punished. This is consistent with what the national polls had documented regarding public attitudes throughout the process of legalization of impunity.[2] But the issue is how opinions that justice is necessary translate into actions to bring it forth and what people are willing to do to press for it.

We have seen how the pervasiveness of impunity had convinced many young people about the impossibility of justice. But in spite of the generalized skepticism, most participants were aware of how beneficial justice could be for society. Their arguments often claimed that amnesties and pardons were strategies for forgetting. However, there were different opinions on how to keep memory alive and deal with the wounds inflicted on the social body, with references to the benefits of either keeping the wounds open or closing them. The metaphor of opening or closing wounds compares to, and links to, the idea of an open memory, an activist memory at the service of justice. This is in the mission statement of an Argentine organization created in 2000, precisely called Memoria Abierta (Open Memory), integrated by the country's main human rights groups.

The benefits of open wounds and the link with memory were articulated during a conversation with fifteen-year-old high school students Andrea, Teresa, Ester, Noemí, and Luciana:

> To forget would be the worst.
>
> Wounds have to remain forever open so we can remember them. We forget scars; time erases them. I don't know why Menem pardoned the military that had been punished by Alfonsín. Because, directly or indirectly, they're responsible.

Other participants talked about closing the wounds but insisted that only justice could do this. Sara speculated on possibilities for healing and also noted differences between the attitudes of those directly affected by the terror and other sectors of society:

> For me, the ideal is memory, but in order to move forward not backwards. The idea is to have justice, to send the military to jail with life terms, and that the past remain present in people's memories. Because this is the first thing you learn. Why do we study history? To avoid repeating the same mistakes! Supposedly, studying history we don't repeat the same mistakes that we committed during the last two thousand years. A nation cannot advance if it's constantly reopening wounds. The idea is to close that wound. And, yes, the anger against the military is going to remain in our elders' generation, in my generation. But it's going to soften in the next generation. You cannot change the feelings of people who lost their children, friends, husbands, uncles, nephews, whoever. These people have the right to feel rage toward the military.

Many participants stressed that justice was a condition for advancing toward the future. Their position challenged discourses of reconciliation based on closing the book on the past. This opinion was present even among interviewees who believed that it made no sense to continually talk about what happened. For them, the official condemnation of the crimes was essential to strengthen society's moral values:

> The priority is to capture the guilty. We'll know who the guilty are. Then we should discover where the corpses are so they can rest in peace and their relatives can also

have peace. And then go on with life, rather than continue like this, knowing nothing, because we know nothing. (Silvia)

[Those responsible] have to be in jail. Whoever steals a piece of bread to eat goes to jail. Doesn't he? If you steal bread you go to prison, if you steal a million it's a bribe. In order to placate people, everybody must know that these people are in jail paying for what they did; that if you do the right thing you'll be fine but if you do the wrong thing, as they did, you go to jail. It's necessary to shake up things so they fall where they belong. (Antonio)

There were, however, comments suggesting that justice was an obstacle to avoid. Fernando defended his attitude of indifference and compared his vision of life with that of activists whose parents disappeared:

I see that the guys are obsessed and might waste their youth for that reason rather than living an innocent adolescence. Maybe it depends on the possibilities. I lived it that way but maybe they didn't have the opportunity. I feel pity in seeing twenty-year-old kids who are blinded by hate. They cannot have a good life; they don't live in peace. And I feel sad about that. Take a guy from HIJOS He has a terrible need for justice. He wants to capture the guilty. Someone like me wants to live in peace, as detached as possible from any confrontation or argument. My philosophy is to live and let live; let's not bother each other. How can we both fit? There's no room. Time is the solution. That's why I insist that my children will be the generation that will calm down, because I won't inculcate anything to them. Others may inculcate but in a lesser proportion of what was done to them. The problem is the pain, the suffering of the people. Pain will gradually disperse.

We do not know how many Argentineans are this passionate in their conviction that the best response to the disappearance of 30,000 people is indifference, impunity, forgetting, and the passage of time. But it was the best-articulated defense of the benefits of political amnesia that I heard. Furthermore, by pointing differences between the HIJOS' "terrible need for justice" and himself, Fernando's comments touched on key issues regarding society's role in struggles against impunity.

Who Is Responsible for Seeking Truth and Justice?

Indifference was also an issue with regard to the question of who has the right and the responsibility to demand truth and justice. Participants' opinions on the roles that they saw for themselves and for society were revealing of the position that the younger generation was adopting, either as actor or spectator. These tasks seemed to be reserved for the "direct victims"—survivors or the relatives of the disappeared. It is "their problem"; if it did not touch you, if you were not there, you keep a distance.

We discussed the struggles of the Mothers and the Grandmothers of the Plaza de Mayo, and of HIJOS, the organizations of mothers, grandmothers, and children of *desaparecidos*. I heard many opinions highlighting the relevance of these groups for the collective memory of society and to challenging political amnesia. The Mothers, in particular, emerged as indefatigable memory-keepers and the embodiment of the struggle for accountability. Most participants considered that the relatives of the *desaparecidos* should continue to demand accountability. Nevertheless, they often put a wall between society and human rights groups. Comments such as "It's their own history" or "It's logical that they demand justice," illustrate that, although they may agree with the struggle, participants often disregarded any role they, or society, could or should have in it.

Héctor, a sixteen-year-old high school student, noted that people tend to detach themselves from problems that they do not perceive are affecting them and pointed to the distinctions between direct victims and society at large:

> Many people who didn't lose a child say, "It only happened to them [victims/relatives]; I look into another direction. It happened to them and not to me." But it might happen to us as it happened to the Mothers.

Not all participants individualized the problem as being exclusively of the victims' relatives. Some evinced awareness of the broad effects that the dictatorship had on the social body. They believed that the issue should concern everybody and that it was society's duty to demand accountability. As Pablo argued: "This is society's problem. It's the environment that surrounds us. I live in a society and whatever happens there also affects me."

Flor insisted that society's participation in the struggle for accountability was crucial to achieve its goals:

> It has to be a social and collective effort, not exclusively of the Mothers. Otherwise, nobody will pay attention. Everybody says, "OK, I agree, if they want to do that, let them." But it should be "We do" rather than "They do."

However, the belief that society should participate actively in the search for truth and justice brought an important issue into our discussions: who in society has credentials to pursue these tasks? There emerged a pattern of firsthand experience, either of having suffered it more directly or of having witnessed the terror, which seemed to mark divisions and determine the role that different sectors could and should play. (An extreme position on society's lack of credentials was revealed by the comment, "Who I am to judge [the torturer]? There's God for that" (Nora).)

The different attitudes among the witness and the post-dictatorship generations were illustrated by Analía:

> I've the impression that, excluding the people who lived through it, there are only a few who'd commit themselves and participate in a struggle that doesn't touch them

closely and personally. I think that the ones who're most involved with that are the people who really lived through it. The rest of the people don't care that much. But, watch out, I don't think the country would put up with another dictatorship.

Jorge suggested that only those who experienced the repression could judge:

Let the people who lived through that judge [*represores*], not just anybody. Because I cannot judge them. On the other hand, one who lived it, "OK, you did this to me, pay for doing this." But it would be because I know what [they] did and not because I'm playing by ear.

Sara had comparable comments and, when asked about the victim's relatives' struggle, candidly argued that she had no voice:

I don't think I can speak out about it because I didn't go through the same and I don't have a kidnapped child. So, if they feel that this is the way to show their pain and their protest, let them do it. From my point of view I think it's exaggerated but I know that I don't have a say because I wasn't there during the *proceso*, my child wasn't kidnapped, and I didn't loose a close relative.

The lack of credentials was not limited to participants' perceptions of their limitations owing to "secondhand" knowledge or "playing by ear." Some of them mentioned how their elders often ignored their opinions. Eugenia told me about people who disqualified her opinions because she was a little girl during the dictatorship:

It bothers me when I speak and say things, and I'm aware that I have a big mouth, but what I have to say is based on facts. If it's about a documentary I didn't invent it. So it bothers me that I'm told, "You didn't live through it so you cannot speak about it." Like I'm not granted the right only because I wasn't a direct participant.

The question of credentials, thus, is a complex issue that might shape attitudes of indifference. If only those who were there can demand accountability, the younger generations or the future ones are excluded from pursuing justice. It also suggests that those who are neither direct victims nor witnesses are disqualified from talking or writing about the dictatorship, from transmitting knowledge about it, or from judging the events that took place.

Conclusions

These conversations shed light on young people's levels of interest and apathy toward human rights concerns, as well as on the many shapes and roots of indifference.

We heard of the priority of other urgent issues, an apolitical and apathetic youth, the belief that someone else is doing the job, resignation to constant abuse, a lack of credentials, or the acceptance that impunity was integral to the current political and economic system. We have seen how ways of remembering shape attitudes. The different memory communities once again became visible in the discussion of social indifference, the relevance of this past, and the value of justice.

Indifference may also be explained by generational factors, revealed in the perception that young people are very distant from the events and that "having been there" is what determines people's interest. We must link this argument to the ongoing memory construction process, to how knowledge, or lack of it, determined how young people were inserting themselves into the historical process. For we should look at indifference in relation to memory, paying special attention to how the past is used in the present to link memory with action. If young people feel left out, this may be encouraging their apathy. The equation could be expressed as "If I cannot play, I will remain spectator and, eventually, lose interest."

The cultural and social effects of legalized impunity influenced indifference. Impotence often translated into apathy, as evinced by the pervasiveness of the feeling "Why bother if nothing can be done?" Belief in the need for justice but the awareness that it might not be possible were factors influencing the widespread fatalistic views that many participants expressed when discussing accountability. If young people feel that nothing can be done, we should not be surprised by comments revealing impotence, frustration, exhaustion, or a "disempowering cynicism."[3] This is not to be confused with the quite different step of condoning impunity.

The legacy of silences was contributing to minimizing the relevance of the topic. These silences, as we have been pointing out throughout these conversations, cannot be disconnected from the remains of fear. In exploring the social constructions of indifference toward mass violence and repression, Ronald Cohen categorizes the roles of silence, which include silence as endorsement, objection, ignorance, ambiguity, absence of voice, and silence in response to the dangers of expression.[4] I would argue that participants' stories reflect consequences of the transmission of silences and tell us that, in the aftermath of the terror, we can recognize some of the roles of silence in shaping young people's apathy and inaction. It suffices to mention ignorance and the perceived lack of opportunities for voice and action as main components reflected in the discussion of credentials.

Apparent or real, indifference was present in many discussions. There seemed to be a generalized perception that politics, including the dictatorship, was not an issue that interests young people. Some comments even suggested that people were being encouraged not to look back. However, this view contrasts with how most of the young people with whom I talked actually engaged in the discussions. Furthermore, interviewees made it very clear to me that young people and society in general do care about what happened and that their indifference is only apparent. Most of them agreed on the value of this past and on the need to remember it.

In spite of the disbelief in the possibility of justice, participants praised its value and pointed to the dangers of closing the book on the past. But critical positions toward impunity coexisted with an apparent indifference, pointing to a gap between opinions that the perpetrators must be punished and what people are willing to do to prosecute them. Discussions on who should struggle for justice revealed a strong perception that this task was reserved for the direct victims of the repression rather than matters of public interest that pertain to state institutions and civil society. Issues of truth and accountability were often individualized and their systemic nature ignored. Moreover, this reveals a lack of generalized awareness of the effects that the repression had on the entire society—a typical comment I have heard over the years is "The military didn't do anything to me." On the other hand, arguments favoring society's participation in this process show that the categorizing of human rights violations as private or public concerns was a key and ongoing debate.

I should conclude by pointing out that one of indifference's most troubling outcomes is the reinforcement and encouragement of a bystander role for society. Most participants praised the need to remember in order to avoid the repetition of the crimes but remained spectators in ongoing struggles for accountability. This is especially detrimental for the formation of new citizens among the post-dictatorship generation. The Mothers of the Plaza de Mayo claim that they have become the symbolic mothers of 30,000 *desaparecidos*. They refer to this as "the socialization of maternity," meaning by this that they demand justice in the name of all the disappeared and not only for their children, that their struggle has a collective rather than an individual basis.[5] Maybe what is needed to reverse society's bystander position is to follow the Mothers' example: collectivize accountability and claim that we are all mothers, fathers, sisters, brothers, daughters, and sons of *desaparecidos*.

We are aware of how participants experienced the lack of justice and we know how this affected sentiments of indifference. It is time to discuss prospects for justice. Attitudes toward the human rights violations committed and the perpetrators of those crimes would be key in either reinforcing a culture of impunity or developing a culture of accountability.

SEVEN

Conversations about Justice

Introduction

In the cultural scenario of Argentina in the late 1990s, "accountability" seemed to be an alien word. But impunity wasn't taken that lightly. As we have seen, young people's feelings of frustration and manifestations of indifference contrasted with the strong conviction that justice matters. In spite of the generalized skepticism about the possibility of justice, there was an awareness of its importance to society. Moreover, in 1998, debates over accountability were reinvigorated because some *represores* were being sent to jail for the kidnapping of children, a crime not covered by the impunity laws, and legal proceedings were initiated in foreign countries.

Comments made by high school students Leo, Hugo, Omar, Ariel, and Miguel attest to resentment in society and awareness of the urgent need for justice:

> I think that sentencing the military to many years in jail would calm much, much anger [in society]. Many people would feel relieved. Because, how can you tell the people whose son was killed, "This guy? No, we don't have any charges against him?" How can you tell them that? Yes, [there's anger]. It's also impotence, more impotence than anger.

Coming to terms with the aftermath of a violent past often entails calls for reconciliation and pleas for forgiveness that translate into amnesties. This has been a prevalent pattern in Latin America's new democracies, where calls for justice for their dictatorships' crimes rarely match the demands for accountability for Nazism's crimes. Moreover, the praises for reconciliation, as in South Africa, often fail to acknowledge that it is a hard-to-define concept whose benefits are not always very clear. But impunity may be a risky choice, the long-term effects of which we still know very little about. As Mahmood Mamdani warned, with regard to Rwanda, "The alternative to justice is not reconciliation—it is revenge."[1] In Argentina, there have not been cases of revenge or of people taking justice into their own hands. However, the prospects of ending legalized impunity were not so promising at the time of these interviews. It was easy to conclude that not much could be done that would successfully secure a culture of respect for human rights.

So I asked participants what actions they would recommend in pursuit of justice more than two decades after the coup. I encouraged them to consider the relevance of investigating the past and sentencing the culprits, considering what they believed was best for the country. This chapter reveals participants' answers to the question "What would you do if you were minister of justice?" It is about assigning guilt and responsibility for the crimes of the dictatorship and determining a just punishment for those crimes.

What these "legal advisers" had to say sheds light on how the post-dictatorship generation was conceptualizing justice. Their opinions help us to better understand how processes of collective memory construction work in the aftermath of violence, the links between memory and action, and the implications that particular ways of remembering have in the pursuit of truth and justice.

Whom to Punish for Past Human Rights Violations

Defining whom to punish starts by assessing the crimes committed and identifying who should be held accountable for them. The opinions of a group of fifteen-year-old girls, Patricia, Beatriz, Graciela, and Fabiana, were representative of generalized beliefs:

> [There's need for] a serious investigation . . . because there're some people whose names are known. It's another thing that [authorities] don't divulge [these names] or cover them up. But those known to be guilty, those who were really involved in that, let justice be done and put them in jail.

> The issue is that we still don't know. Also, it was such an ugly, harsh, and hostile period for the whole country. We know the main facts but we ignore many details. We only know about three leaders well, but those weren't the only ones. Certainly, there were many more.

Calls for further investigations reflect an awareness of insufficient information to determine who should be punished—a consequence of the partial official truth about this past. Interviewees had very clear opinions, as was evinced by additional comments by Leo, Hugo, Omar, Ariel, and Miguel during a passionate discussion that was hard to follow:

> First [the accused] have to testify.

> A trial first and, afterwards, we'll probably have more people because [other] names will be revealed.

Take Astiz, for example. I don't think [the accused] will say, "I'm the only one, nobody else [participated.]" I think that when people testify under pressure they give away information in order to alleviate their guilt: "I'm not the only one to blame, so and so was also involved."

We need to find out who all [the guilty] are. I cannot say, "You look like a bad guy; come here." The first thing is a full investigation.

Without full disclosure, those to blame are mostly leaders and scapegoats. However, much could be achieved with the investigative information gathered by human rights organizations and governments' political will for official prosecutions, the latter still lacking at the time of this fieldwork. As these students suggested, once you open the box, the accused themselves would cooperate.

According to Alicia:

I wouldn't last more than two days in that position [minister of justice]. I'd move mountains without worrying about the consequences to find the guilty and make them pay for what they did. To keep going in circles after twenty years, twenty-two now, over a matter, which we all know well who the brains were behind all this. In one way or another we know that Videla was involved, we know who they're. But everybody's covering them. The army's also covering them.

The lack of sufficient information did not stop participants from assigning responsibilities for the crimes. In fact, the greater the knowledge of the different actors involved in the dictatorship—as was the case with a few more informed interviewees—the broader was the list of those who should be punished for actively supporting the repression. According to Ricardo:

Half the population of the country should go to jail. For the *proceso* and also for the "special benefits." There are many who made big business during the *proceso* and now they're no longer military, they're businessmen. During the Malvinas War people donated jewels, gold chains. Where's that money?

The recycling of assassins and torturers into business executives is another chapter of the aftermath of terror. It suffices to mention torturer Cavallo, who in 2000 was captured in Mexico, where he was the director of the National Registry of Vehicles. The episode certainly raises many questions regarding the "laundering" of assassins and the international angle to this process.

But identification of the guilty was not usually that broad. Marta's comments illustrate well a more generalized position when talking about "all" those guilty:

It's like [authorities] close the doors. It's very difficult because you've two laws, "Due Obedience" and "Full Stop," a bunch of closed cases that you cannot reopen; it's closed, pardoned. I ask for trial and punishment to all those involved. I'd forget about the Due Obedience, absolutely all those military, the Montoneros, everybody, all the torturers and assassins.

Andrea presented a similar rationale:

That Due Obedience law! I'd have liked that all the military would've been brought to trial, from the one who tore down the door to enter into a house and took the person away, even if he didn't torture. I think that all military personnel, from the one giving the orders to the one at the very bottom, should have been tried. And, if they hadn't disappeared, those who were killed also should've been brought to trial. I'm not saying that they were saints. I believe that someone who kills must be prosecuted.

These comments illustrate two main referents mentioned during our conversations about guilt and punishment. There is the "Two Devils" theory, whereby the "bad guys" are basically the military personnel or the guerrilla forces, and which assumes that all the victims of the repression were armed combatants involved in violent acts. There is also mention of the impunity law obstructing prospects for justice popularly known as "Due Obedience," whose acceptance or defiance deserves closer examination.

On the Acceptance of "Due Obedience"

Although obeying orders to commit crimes against humanity is in violation of international law, this did not stop the first civilian government from excusing torturers and assassins under the premise of "Due Obedience." Beyond legal concerns, what matters is how this rationale had been accepted or rejected by society. To my surprise, "Due Obedience" was a recurrent framework for ascribing levels of responsibility. Beatriz's analysis of a military officer summarizes well the opinion that many young people had about the military institution:[2]

I saw a television program where a military officer said that he'd done what he did because he'd no choice; he had to obey. Because of the mentality that the military have, the military were created to obey. It doesn't matter which orders. If you say to a soldier, "Shoot yourself in the head" he'll do it because a superior is telling him to. So if his superior tells him, "Go kill your family" he'll kill it because they're cold, because they were trained to be cold, to obey, and only to obey. They don't care how many they've to step over; they don't care at all. They care about doing a good job. And their mission is to obey and that's it.

This conceptualization of military personnel as machines trained to obey suggests that people can see them as disgusting human beings but understand, and even justify, that they were forced to commit crimes, that there was no way out. It also implies tolerance for the military's claims that they were just obeying orders, doing "their job." Beatriz's comments are also revealing of how people may interpret major human rights abusers' statements to the media. Television screens offer them the possibility to "write their memories" of the dictatorship, including vindicating their actions, showing repentance, or playing victims. Furthermore, as Portelli notes about Italians' perceptions of Nazi Germans as machines and beasts, this stereotype serves to portray their criminal acts as natural and to shift the guilt onto the victims.[3] In other words, what can you expect when you deal with obedient beasts?

So the soldier is trained to obey—"He had to obey." But was it impossible to disobey? Were there other options such as early retirement, transfer, or leave of absence? It is true that the repression was organized and implemented in a way to taint everybody's hands with blood. There is no doubt that pressure was exercised, although I had no luck finding published accounts of cases of military officers who were punished for refusing orders. The absence of these records means either that there were no such cases or that they have not been documented. The exception is Paoletti who refers to a few police officers who were tortured or who died in confusing episodes (e.g., during an alleged confrontation with "subversives" who may have been killed by the same police, a naval officer who disappeared, and some military officers forced to retire).[4] But what did participants know about these issues? What were their opinions regarding the possibility of disobeying?

There were particularly interesting discussions at a public high school attended by several children with military personnel in their families. It was the appropriate environment to explore how this particular memory community—"military families"—was transmitting details of the soldiers' duties during the terror. As I heard during a conversation with five fifteen-year-old boys, "Maybe those who beat others were ordered to do so. Maybe they didn't want to but were ordered to do so and their superiors were the main culprits."

Noemí, a fifteen-year-old student at that school, summarized well the views of several of the students I interviewed:

> I don't blame everything on the military. First, because the military were manipulated. Second, there were many soldiers who were walking with their children in the street and were killed. I'm absolutely against the coup but I don't blame everything on the military. Many [soldiers] didn't want to do what they did but they were forced. Some of them who dared to say, "I won't do that" were killed together with their families. Many say, "The military, the military," but the truth is that not all soldiers are to blame.

We should point out that the many relatives of military officers who were killed by guerrilla forces amount to five children and three wives.[5]

The discussion with other fifteen-year-old young women from the same school, Patricia, Beatriz, Graciela, and Fabiana, was particularly illuminating on the perceived dangers of disobeying, even when noting that some torturers had no problem performing their "job":

> I don't justify them at all. But we only look at the families that were completely destroyed because they killed everybody. That's terrible; it's the worst thing they could've done. But I believe that, beyond the fact that some military personnel have weird minds, because to do what they did you have to have a weird mind, the military officer, who was under the orders of his mentally twisted superior, probably must have felt very bad at the idea of killing a two-month-old baby who wasn't involved in anything. That's why they didn't kill them and why they adopted them or gave them away to avoid killing them. You cannot put everybody in the same bag. Some of them are insane but others acted under pressure, because if they didn't do what they were ordered to they themselves would be killed.
>
> But if you're a man and have what you have to have in the right place you say, "I don't care."
>
> Yes, but they kill all your family.
>
> But it isn't easy to kill a two-month-old baby.
>
> There were those who, under that heavy pressure, killed themselves afterwards. They'd kill a whole family and after realizing what they had done, in spite of the orders that they had, they then killed themselves. It's not so easy to kill so many people by orders of someone who is your superior.

These comments are indicative of a discourse that reinforces and justifies "Due Obedience" based on the ferocious retaliation toward the disobedient soldier. To my knowledge, there are no published accounts of cases of military officers who refused to follow orders and whose families were killed. As for cases of suicides, if some torturers and assassins indeed killed themselves we still have not seen their suicide notes acknowledging that their feelings of guilt were the reason.

Alberto remembered discussing the impunity laws with his classmates while at high school:

> And some said, "No, he had to obey, the one who ordered is the one who should get it." But, let's start all over, who ordered? I don't know if they defended the military but some said, "I think the one [to get it] should be the one who gave the order and not the poor guy who was ordered and could be killed for refusing."

Another relevant conversation was that between Guillermo, a twenty-year-old computer major at a private university whose father was a retired military officer, and his best friend Fernando, who constantly strove to be neutral. The tense tone of the discussion, the silences, and the doubts showed how tough the topic was for both. According to Guillermo:

> The military, those at the bottom, under the pressure of a superior did what the superior told them because they knew that refusing meant that something bad

would happen to them. At that time, [military] jobs sucked. If you didn't do it you didn't have money for your family, no food for your children. If [they tell you] at gunpoint, "Go and steal." Or imagine yourself in the future as a father, "I know who you are, that you've four kids, that you live in that place. If you don't do what I say . . ."

We do not know whether Guillermo had discussed this topic at home. But being raised within a military environment had probably shaped his opinions that orders to torture were part of a job that "sucked." Fernando accepted his friend's arguments but, like other participants, noted that some may have tortured without major pressure on them:

One thing is if they tell you, "Beat the shit out of someone." Another is if they tell you, "Pull out her nails, burn her eyes." You see? There were two kinds [of torturers]. There was the guy who was ordered, "Pull out the teeth of that guy without anesthesia," and he did it [without being pressured]. And there was the guy who [hesitated and] was told, "Listen, if you don't [do it] you won't find anybody when you return home."

And this is what Juan, a supporter of the death penalty who knew in detail the dictatorship's crimes, answered when I asked him whether he would execute the *represores*:

I wouldn't, because I'd be acting like them. I'm in favor of the death penalty. I'd apply it in some extreme cases, like rapes to minors and things without sense. I think they were forced. It's not that they did it because they liked it. They were also forced. There's a book that says that those who refused, or treated prisoners well, something like that, could also suffer punishment. I believe that they acted under pressure.

Many of these comments were made by participants who were children of military and police personnel or who had friends and classmates who were. This suggests that the sources of this information might be conversations within military families, widespread rumors, or media declarations by *represores*. Several interviewees, however, took these stories as truth. It is hard to think of more extreme human rights violations than those that occurred under the dictatorship. The idea of sparing punishment in these cases shows how well accepted the notion of obeying orders is and reinforces the notion of "Due Obedience." Moreover, I couldn't find any "book" explaining the risks of disobeying. But it is hard to assess how widespread the beliefs are that there was no way out for the torturers, that there were many casualties among military families, that those who refused to obey were killed together with their families, that they stole babies to avoid killing them, or that the belief in unbearable guilt of some *represores* caused them to commit suicide. The absence of official records suggests an evident distortion of the past within certain circles or memory communities.

Whom to punish, thus, was subject to debate and varied from a handful of leaders who gave the orders to half the country's population for condoning, tolerating, or refusing to recognize the horror. Divergences could be solved with investigations and the assignment of culpability. But once that were to be established, another crucial problem would need to be solved: how to punish the guilty.

How to Punish for Past Human Rights Violations

We know that a high percentage of young Argentineans wanted the military to be punished. For example, a poll conducted during this fieldwork (July 1998) found that 85 percent of those aged eighteen to twenty-nine thought that dictator Videla should remain in jail for his responsibility in the kidnapping of babies.[6] But participants' recommendations revealed the different meanings of punishment, which, although predominantly framed under the rule of law, included the disturbing consideration of "revenge" torture. However, two main levels emerge in analyzing approaches to punishment. One is emotional and based on feelings of anger, indignation, and impotence. It includes what participants would like to do. The other is rational and it is what they would really do. These contradictory levels coexist in statements such as "I'm against the death penalty but I'd kill them all."

Modify the laws

So how would these legal advisers deal with impunity laws? Eugenia was the medical school student who had refused to share an elevator ride with Videla. Talking about *represores* jailed for stealing babies, she was one of the participants proposing reforms to the legal system:

> Modify the laws and look for [the guilty] as they did now to [Videla], who's finally under arrest for something that wasn't covered by that [impunity] law. I'd break with the current justice system to allow legislation that can be retroactive. Do you understand? To start all over the legal process, to annul Full Stop and Due Obedience, beginning from scratch with the investigations that took place so far and the ongoing ones. At that moment, maybe a short time had passed and we didn't know as many things as we know now. I'd do something that would make it possible to say, "[Laws] are nullified; justice made a mistake with you and many others." It's not the same after all the years that have passed. There's now more precise data. And maybe we've things to say, not in my case but kids whose parents disappeared can now talk, can say, "I've informed opinions, ways of thinking." They couldn't before; they were no one but kids drifting at the mercy of whoever got them. I believe that all these people should be granted the right to talk.

The impunity granted by the laws could be solved by their annulment, an option already considered at the time of fieldwork in a bill introduced but not approved. Eugenia, like other participants, was aware of these debates. Moreover, she understood that accountability was an ongoing process where the final word had not yet been said, where new actors and information could foster significant changes, where the post-dictatorship generation should be granted the right to have a voice and be heard.

"Sliding scale" jail terms

Determining jail terms for the guilty was the punishment of choice for this group of legal advisers. In analyzing their recommendations, we should bear in mind that the few *represores* who had served time or were under arrest at the time of fieldwork had been given a very special treatment, mostly "country club" accommodations and house arrests, followed up with pardons. The following comments represent well a generalized call for prison terms:

> Never the pardons. No such thing as saying, "OK, it's over, let's start again from scratch." No, because there are people who're suffering due to those times. I'd look for every one, each person, for all who participated, find out what they did; I'd investigate carefully everybody who took part. And I'd lock them up for life, inside, locked up, well locked. And neither VIP [status], armchair, nor staying in bed. Another thing, I'm not God, because God is going to [punish them]. But here, on earth, this is our law. They've to pay with something. Much worse is what my uncle, a former cop, says, "If I know of anyone who rapes my daughter or my niece, or whoever, I'd do to him the same thing that he did." I tell him "That's resentment, you don't have to pay with the same token." [He says], "So he feels what the other person felt." I'm not for [the guilty] feeling what the victims felt, I'd rather he be locked up thinking about what he did. Kill him with his own madness. (Carmen)

> [Jail them] without the possibility that someone comes after two months and releases them, because that's what happens. (Susana).

> Life terms to the ideological perpetrators. But I'd reduce a bit the punishment to the material authors. There's now a method of house arrest. I don't think it should be this way. They [now] have a house, can watch TV. If it's jail it has to be [jail]. Neither VIP salon, nor anything like that. (Miguel)

In fact, most participants would like to see the *represores* jailed, in regular prisons, like ordinary criminals, and would like them to remain there. They were outraged by the privileges granted to human rights abusers and critical of the pardons for the leaders of the repression. In assigning jail terms, they overwhelmingly stressed the need to establish culpability accurately in order to give the deserved punishment to each person found guilty. One basis to determine sentences was the difference between being the planner or the executor of the repression, undoubtedly related to the acceptance of Due Obedience.

Death penalty

Although there is no capital punishment in Argentina, there was a generalized wish to see the *represores* dead, expressed in comments such as "I think that we should kill them all. We should cut off the hand of those who steal. That's the way it's for me. If a person killed another one, why not? Besides [he] didn't kill only one" (Carlos).

Only a few participants favored the death penalty. Diego, a Catholic activist, was one of its few proponents:

> I come from a Christian-Catholic formation. So the issue of death and judging about other people's lives is conflictive. But I think that there are cases where there's no other option. I suppose that God, in his mercy, can forgive anybody. But, as a man, I cannot forgive certain guys. I don't pardon the life of those who were in charge of the government, from Videla up to now. The thing to do is line them up before a firing squad and execute them all—the members of the military juntas, Alfonsín, and Menem (first two civilian presidents). They were the visible faces. Either you're stupid and I kill you for being stupid or you're an accomplice who also deserves to be put to death.

Diego was emphatic in his conviction that many of the guilty needed to die. And his argument for eliminating the former leadership highlighted its responsibility either for action or omission, as he had argued about the Catholic hierarchy. I should also point out that he was one of the very few participants who included the ministers of economy during the dictatorship and a civilian administration (Menem) among those to be executed. This criticism extends to the rampant corruption and the devastating effects of the neoliberal economic policies implemented by the dictatorship and the post-dictatorial civilian governments, therefore making a specific link between state terrorism and economic policies.

Torture them

Many interviewees wished physical suffering to the *represores*. Supporting torture as a fair punishment is undoubtedly a disturbing consideration. But it was a first reaction during many conversations, such as that between five high school classmates, Leo, Hugo, Omar, Ariel, and Miguel, which illustrates well the kind of arguments for and against torturing:

> Torture them as they tortured others.
>
> I'd just cut off their heads, cheaper and faster.
>
> We'll first cut out the tongue, then an ear.
>
> No, it would be foolish to lower yourself to their same level.
>
> Let's kill them little by little.

Doesn't change anything if you torture them. I don't know how to explain it to you but whatever was done is done; it's pointless.

It's not worth it to torture them so they experience what other people experienced.

Many comments advocated punishments based on "an eye for an eye." One rationale for torture, thus, was that torturers must pay with their own suffering, feel what their victims felt. As I heard during a conversation among fifteen-year-old Andrea, Teresa, Ester, Noemí, and Luciana:

I'm not in favor of violence. But I think that, to the military who did this, we should do the same that they did to all the *desaparecidos*. I don't agree but I think it was a horrible act and we should do [the same].

It was not often clear whether interviewees would actually condone torture or whether it was just a wish prompted by their indignation at the nature of the crimes. However, I would like to share opinions from two young women who strongly advocated torture.

Flor was sixteen years old, from an upper-middle-class family, living in an affluent neighborhood. I also talked to her mother, who was very worried by the intensity with which her daughter expressed her hatred against military personnel. This was Flor's recommendation:

I accept it and totally agree with people who would torture them. I wouldn't have the hate to torture them, to dig a knife through the flesh and hear it go clack clack. But it would be great if the child or the mother of a *desaparecido* were to have the opportunity to torture them. [Torturers] should be killed. I absolutely favor revenge. If I don't avenge, I owe something to the people to whom something was done. If you lock them up, they're the ones who then rape others in jail. They're the ones who rape, beat, and hold the power in jail. They put rats inside women's vaginas! It's revenge for me. I couldn't torture because I don't have enough hate. That is, I'd lack the necessary hate to dig the knife all the way in. Obviously I'm in favor or their being killed. But if it had affected me and I had sufficient hate, I'd kill them myself.

Flor was full of rage, and torture was for her a matter of hate. This explains her belief that only victims' families could take care of this task, even when there had not been a single case where victims' relatives have taken justice into their own hands. She also linked justice with revenge, something that needs to be analyzed because justice-seekers have often been accused of being revenge-seekers. Flor's use of this word may be due to a discourse she had assimilated or could mean that she was convinced that the lack of justice calls for revenge.

Elvira was a twenty-two-year old, from a working-class family, living in a working-class neighborhood. She looked straight into my eyes and calmly said:

> I'd torture Videla, in particular. I'd apply torture to him because that's the same thing he did. He tortured the people who were kidnapped, tortured them so they'd give names of other people who were their allies. They were not released until they were tortured or gave away names. With the rest, just trials and jail terms.

By targeting Videla, the ultimate symbol of the repression, Elvira's recommendation can be read as a public scolding rather than a decision to torture back. But it is precisely her decision to punish the other culprits with prison that made her call for torturing the leader so strong. Hence, two very different young women were the most serious proponents of torture. I had no doubt they really meant what they were saying.

Let others decide

Jail terms, the death penalty, and torture were not the only punishments recommended. Another pattern that emerged is the assignment of a bystander role for society. Participants urged that trials and other legal proceedings be replaced by giving the *represores* to the victims' relatives, by "throwing" them into the hands of ordinary criminals in jail, or even by some divine justice.

Many interviewees recommended that the victims' relatives should decide or carry out the punishment. Advocates for this option reflected upon parents, children, grandparents, close relatives, and the ones who they considered had suffered the most.

> Let them feel the same that the mothers who lost their children or grandchildren feel, see how they can handle that. (Nelson)
>
> With those military men who tortured I'd ask the mothers of those who were tortured what they want to do. [I'd do] whatever they think is just, whatever they want. (Héctor)
>
> I'd give those proven guilty to the child of a disappeared father and tell him, "He's yours, do what you want with him, he's the one responsible for your not having your mom and dad." (Laura)

As with the suggestion that direct victims have the necessary hate to torture, these options assign families the burden of administering justice. It may be that they are seen as worthy of a louder voice in this debate or may exemplify distrust in society's legal institutions.

Awareness of the brutality that goes on inside prisons was the basis for proposing that punishment be administered by other prisoners, evincing a generalized belief that *represores* were repudiated by society and ordinary criminals would take care of them. For example:

> I'd put them in jail with guys who steal, sell drugs. They themselves would torture [the *represores*]. (Andrés)
>
> Let them be raped by the other prisoners. (Pedro)
>
> I would've put [Videla] in the regular prison. It's a fact that in the regular prison he would've suffered the consequences. If he hadn't been in the VIP wing, he would've probably suffered a serious beating, and maybe something more. (Alicia)

Víctor rationalized throwing the *represores* to the lions:

> I'd put them together with the prison population. Let's see what they can do there, whom they torture. I'd jail everybody, any soldier who carried a gun, not only the visible faces like Massera or Videla, and not in the VIP wing. I'd put them with other inmates to see what happens to them. Let's see if they feel what torture is. I can assure you that torture in jails can be worse than what [the military] did. Put them together with the assassins, the rapists and see what happens, what they feel.

I even heard of the need for supernatural forces. Laura, although not a death penalty advocate, would like to "kill them all" and longed for a supreme power that would make the criminals suffer:

> I wouldn't shoot him one shot at the heart so he instantly dies, because the guy didn't kill the 30,000 that way. The guy tortured with electric prod, pulled out nails. It wasn't a soft method. So I want them to suffer until they die. I wouldn't torture them, I wouldn't pull their nails, neither would I send people to do that. I'd love that there would be divine justice so he'd catch one of those plagues that can last for a year, and that the guy would agonize, lying in bed, vomiting blood and things like that. Ideally, I'd send them to jail so they can rot there and catch tuberculosis.

These options evince a pattern of individualization and personalization of punishment. By this I mean that some participants considered that particular individuals, be they relatives of the *desaparecidos* or ordinary criminals, could be trusted more than the legal institutions to administer a just punishment. What these metaphorical ministers of justice clearly showed is anger and impotence for the pervasiveness of impunity, often manifest in a quasi-schizophrenic position by which they showed an absolute commitment to the rule of law and a strong wish that those guilty suffer physical pain, but avoiding the official sanctioning of torture or the death penalty.

International law

Perhaps the strongest hope for justice at the time of these conversations came from the provisions of international law and the promissory globalization of justice, in particular for Judge Baltasar Garzón's moves to extradite *represores* to Spain.

According to Marta:

> I'm surprised with Judge Garzón. How come we, the people who really suffered the *proceso*, do nothing? How come a Spanish Judge . . . ? I think it's great. Sometimes, we don't take ourselves very seriously. How little we do for ourselves. I'm even ashamed.

Analía also commented on Garzón's quest for justice and the Argentine government's responses to him:

> And now, with Baltasar Garzón and his trials for the Spanish *desaparecidos*, and due to all this when the president travels people all around the world are demanding justice for people who disappeared here, it's like all this emerges again. So, one also knows about what happened because of what's going on now. Baltasar Garzón is applying pressure from Spain so [the *represores*] go to jail and the government does nothing. Do you understand? I think that the government is very much an accomplice of what's going on.

Antonio, the law school student, reflected on the weight of international pressures for justice and how Nazi criminals who escaped to Argentina continue to be hunted:

> Because in order for someone to open his mouth we need someone from outside to say it first. If not, nothing happens. Look at that guy [Nazi criminal] who was living in Bariloche.[7] How many years before he dies? Five, ten? They caught him, took him away, and jailed him. They didn't say, "Poor guy, he's going to die." No, the guy killed. Nothing happens here. "Let's focus on other stuff." That's the way it is.

Lucía commented on military officers "wanted" in several countries:

> Besides, not everybody in the military can leave the country. Tons of them have open legal cases and as soon as they leave Interpol catches them. So they cannot escape. They can't say, "I will live in that place." They can't because they'll be caught.

Sara, her friend and classmate, also part of this conversation, further elaborated on international justice limiting the *represores'* enjoyment of their impunity:

> I read about the problem in the magazine *Tres Puntos* that my mother buys. The expression that they use in some articles is that Argentina will turn into a tremendous *aguantadero* (hide out) of people wanted by Interpol that cannot leave. It's the military officers that are wanted. There was a map of Europe and it signaled with arrows, those from here who assassinated and are wanted in France, Sweden, Finland, Norway. They showed the different European countries whose citizens were killed here and were initiating trials. There were like one hundred seventy more cases.

These were indeed the times when the possibility of international justice was a main disruptor of the *represores'* impunity. Argentine politicians' political will to enforce justice was still weak compared with the obstinate efforts of foreign prosecutors.

Conclusions

I have explored here how participants conceptualized justice and would punish those responsible for human rights violations. Throughout the discussion of these issues, I have identified some patterns that can be seen as a result of the fragmented knowledge about the dictatorship. What these "legal advisers" had to say not only demonstrated how limited the possibility of any future justice seemed but also revealed the generalized conviction that those responsible must be punished. Practically all of the young people with whom I talked were very critical about the lack of justice.

The discussion on accountability provided interesting clues on how the younger generation evaluated the need for justice and what the concept meant for them. In spite of the impunity and the corruption of the legal institutions, most participants revealed a strong respect for the rule of law. This is particularly relevant to the outrage they expressed over legalized impunity, the malfunctioning of the justice system, and the privileged treatment given to the few criminals who served time.

The debate on who should be punished revealed how opinions and attitudes were shaped by the acceptance of dominant discourses. One influential parameter was "Two Devils." For most participants, the guilty were the torturers and assassins, or the guerrilla leaders. Only a few included other supporters of the dictatorship among the guilty. In doing so, they often made links between corruption and human rights violations, pointing to those who amassed fortunes during the terror. Enlarging the list of those to be punished highlights the need to uncover those sectors that should publicly acknowledge their levels or responsibility, a process that was not taking place at the time of these conversations.

Participants' opinions also evinced a generalized belief in different layers of guilt. "Due Obedience" was a discourse that seemed to have been accepted by a surprising number of the young people with whom I talked. The belief that soldiers are obedient machines who would do whatever they are ordered to do, and that it was not possible for them to refuse orders, shaped debates over the assignment of guilt. The acceptance of this concept suggests resignation to impunity based on official discourses. For although the law and human rights activists might challenge obedience as an excuse, society may be accepting it. Obeying orders, moreover, may have been for many soldiers a matter of pride. Let us remember Eichman's insistence during his trial that obedience was a praised virtue.[8]

If torturers and killers were indeed strongly opposed to what they were doing but carried out their orders because they were terrified, we should today—more than twenty years later—be listening to hundreds of them denouncing the atrocities they were forced to commit. This is not the case.[9] Hence, it makes sense to assume that either they were not forced or that they continue to be afraid of any backlash against military personnel who dare to break a code of silence—another angle of the legacy of fear. Both explanations are extremely disturbing. Similarly, the acceptance that the stealing of babies was a way of saving them raises the issue of why these *represores* do not come forward now to explain that they seized these babies to save their lives and give them back to their biological families. Moreover, if there are indeed cases of military personnel who disobeyed and had members of their family actually tortured and killed, this is still an unexplored and secret history.

Deliberations on how to punish considered a wide range of options. The more troublesome area is undoubtedly the idea of torture as punishment, a recurring first reaction. In some cases, participants were very serious about it. This may indicate a transmission of an ideology of repression justifying the torture of the enemy. In other cases, advocating torture seemed more like a wish—an issue that also needs to be analyzed—and their peers were the ones who, during discussions, noted the irrationality of becoming a torturer to punish torturers. I can only speculate on the reasons for an apparent acceptance of torture. It can evince how repressive ideologies and sentiments are widespread within society—that many people may carry "a torturer within." As Pilar Calveiro, a survivor of the dictatorship's torture chambers, writes, torturers are ordinary persons, not a special breed of monsters; this is precisely the terrifying fact.[10]

We should highlight the fact that abiding by the rule of law and recurrent mentions of investigations and trials marked the tone of our conversations about justice. This is probably one of the most interesting outcomes of a generation so used to abuse, overwhelmed by impunity, and apparently indifferent to the events of the dictatorship and its aftermath. There were clear differences between what they would like to do and what they would actually do. Even when many respondents expressed their desire to punish the *represores* with the same token, at the time of defining what they would really do, most of them switched from "an eye for an eye" to investigations, trials, jail, and, at most, the death penalty—a punishment supported by only a few.

Accountability, however, is a long and ongoing process, and young people's opinions of and actions for this process are highly relevant. The children of yesterday are today's and tomorrow's voters, activists, or indifferent citizens. Struggles for accountability are not limited to the courtroom. Building political momentum and pushing lawmakers are also society's tasks. The voices of the post-dictatorship generation will have weight regarding matters of justice. They have a crucial role to play in intensifying demands for accountability and securing an end to impunity.

It is now time to focus on the different media that, over the years, have continued to construct, transmit, and reconstruct the memories of this past. For young people's postmemories are based on intra- and intergenerational dialogue, education, and the communication media. The issues that we have discussed so far are related to a variety of media, which were key sources and referents in the memory construction process.

EIGHT

Conversations about the Communication Media

Introduction

I have shared what participants knew about the dictatorship and how this knowledge seemed to be shaping their opinions and actions. But how did they learn what they knew? How do we identify which sources transmitted the memories that shaped their representations of this past? How do we recognize the realms of memory that codify and symbolize it? Among fears and silences, and in a fragmented and decontextualized mode, the past had made it into the present. How this happened is the question that the following pages seek to answer.

This chapter looks at the roles that a broad spectrum of the communication media was playing in transmitting and reconstructing the events of the dictatorship. It explores the different sources on which participants based their knowledge, the major historical referents, the many voices and images that, over the years, have informed their way of thinking. It discusses the various texts and cultural artifacts that constitute the dictatorship's "textbook": television programs, films, popular songs, monuments, and sites that symbolize terror such as the former centers for torture and extermination.[1] I was interested in looking at how the media were providing historical referents, setting up agendas, reinforcing or challenging societal silences, and at how participants interpreted and were affected by particular representations of the dictatorship.

We know that a society's memories are transmitted, modified, and preserved through talk, that collective remembering is a communication process. It is in this discursive construction and reconstruction of what is remembered or forgotten that the media play important roles in incorporating memory issues into the public sphere and shaping the ways that societies remember.[2] There are differences between having a "direct" and a "mediated" experience of events, the latter being the case for the post-dictatorship generation. There are connections between the offering of particular historical accounts and remembering a particular version of the past.

Halbwachs, considered the first serious explorer of the social frameworks of memories, highlighted that the media contribute to the construction and reproduction of collective memories.[3] Writing about individual remembrance as the intersection of collective influences, he noted how people often present, as deeply held convictions, thoughts borrowed from a newspaper or a book without being aware that they are but an echo. Judging from my own experience, I often find that what I remember about the dictatorship incorporates new information that I have acquired over time. This reminds me of the Vietnam War veteran who said that what he remembers of what really happened during the war is mixed with what has been said about the war.[4] We should be alert to this combination of personal experiences of the past with more contemporary knowledge in the many stories that participants heard from their elders and the media.

There are a number of pertinent analyses of the media's role in the memory construction process. They range from Anderson's study on the press and the formation of national identity to Dayan and Katz's research on communities united by media events, defined as those rituals of millions of people simultaneously doing the same thing—for example, watching the broadcast of the Gulf war.[5] Studies on how societies remember their traumatic and violent pasts illustrate how historical accounts offered by the media shape memories and reinforce beliefs, as with students who learned about the Spanish civil war through textbooks and media images.[6] There are also studies about the offering of changing historical versions of the same event—some of them analyzing French and Spanish war films and revealing how different social groups symbolically reconstruct their past. Thus, French films on the Algerian war show how, over the years, the conflict has been represented in different phases—that is, focusing on silence, amnesia, or individual memories.[7] In the United States, there are studies about the Vietnam War reconstructed as docudrama and of how these media images are sources of historical information.[8] Other studies have focused on films about the Holocaust, discussing, for example, debates between historians and media scholars on how *Schindler's List*, as a form of historical "writing," contributes to the transformation of our understanding of history, and how the film shapes memory and national identity.[9]

However, even though this chapter focuses on the media, I should point out that memories are transmitted over time through three main sources that overlap and mix: intergenerational accounts, formal education, and the media, a process well illustrated by Susana:

> I'd find out [about the dictatorship] through the television. And I'd then ask questions at home. During anniversaries, the TV tells how all of that was, what

happened. So I started to ask questions and began to find out. Moreover, at school, professors who were there at that time talk about how it was. They tell us how they lived and all that. That's how we keep learning more.

This combination of sources emerged constantly: the family discussion prompted by a television program, a newspaper article, the film watched at school, what a professor or classmate said, the street poster where someone read about a demonstration, a concert organized by a human rights group, the former torture center around the corner where an aunt lives, or the building where a neighbor was killed during a military operative. It is not possible to determine with exactitude where and when something was learned. Similarly, proposing direct links between the exposure to a particular message and the reactions provoked by it would be an inaccurate simplification of an extremely complex process.

The focus here is on participants' descriptions and interpretations of a number of texts and the reactions prompted by them. These accounts are tinted and filtered by the passage of time, so we are talking here of memories of encounters with the media. To convey the broad spectrum of media that participants mentioned, I explore several examples, each one illustrating different angles of what media messages were conveying. In analyzing each example, I emphasize particular elements, but all of them could be examined from other perspectives. What ultimately matters is identifying what information constitutes the dictatorship's "textbook." The chapter provides some background on the mainstream media coverage of the dictatorship and its aftermath. It looks at television, focusing on both news and entertainment programs. It discusses films and popular music. It analyzes the geography of terror, or how this past is topographically encoded in many places.

Mainstream Media and the Past

We could summarize mainstream media coverage of the dictatorship by a switch, over the years, from silence to a growing flood of contested commentary. During the years of terror, the media either acted as the regime's de facto propaganda agency or remained silent as to what was really going on by obediently echoing the official version of events.[10] There were indeed restrictions on the press and approximately 100 journalists remain disappeared, but the media played an important role in legitimizing the dictatorship. At the beginning of civilian rule, there was wide coverage of the dictatorship's crimes, characterized by a sensationalist approach to the issue.[11] Macabre reports provided details to shock but failed to provide the necessary information for a critical analysis of the events. Horror became a profitable business for the same media corporations that had previously praised the dictatorship and may have turned many people into consumers of human rights atrocities. Then, the issue gradually faded until a new phase commenced in 1995 when former Navy officer Scilingo confessed to his participation in aircraft flights where political prisoners were thrown into the ocean alive.

Media coverage of the dictatorship had continued to intensify. The new legal causes initiated against *represores* were one factor. But the media had also installed the past into the public sphere by turning into a political forum for human rights debates and battles. Several significant moments in the public disclosure of information about the dictatorship took place during television broadcasts, with millions of Argentineans watching and participating in these collective rituals, which were veritable "media events." In 1995, the same television program was the stage for the *mea culpas* of Army chief General Balza and Montoneros guerrilla leader Firmenich. A few torturers had confessed their crimes on television, a phenomenon that was coined as the "end-of-century confessional."[12] This resulted in the media often performing as symbolic courts of law, albeit without the necessary legal consequences.[13] Additionally, on some occasions, torturers and their victims have been invited on to the same television program.

At the time of the fieldwork, the past was definitely a manifest presence in the media. One night I was going to an *escrache* (demonstration) organized by HIJOS in one of the several Buenos Aires' buses with electronic bulletin boards that continuously give news headlines. One of the items that I read during that ride was that a midwife had been summoned to testify at one of the new trials for the kidnapping of babies. Going to a human rights demonstration and reading information so related to it gave me the feeling that I had been transported back in time to the commencement of civilian rule rather than being in 1998, twenty-two years after the coup.

In evaluating media coverage of the dictatorship, participants were, in general, very critical of the content and style of mainstream media reporting, which they categorized as fragmentary single-issue, sound-bite style, profit-driven, sensationalist, lacking in context, and aimed at reinforcing certain agendas.

As Nelson explained:

> I learned about other things the day that [the media] talked about [Videla] but, afterwards, they stopped. For one day TV and newspapers covered Videla and Massera exclusively. They talked about them in the news, in entertainment programs, in the newspaper. And then, the day after, as if it had been a dream, they stopped talking [about it] and continued with another topic.

Nelson was not alone in noting that the presence of the past in the media was conditioned by which other events were competing for front-page positions. At the time of this fieldwork, Videla was jailed and for two weeks the media talked only about Videla; the Mundial (Soccer World Cup) started and Videla completely vanished from the headlines to be replaced by intense reporting of the tournament; the Mundial was over and another single event dominated the media.

Some participants highlighted how the sound-bite style that characterizes this coverage produces scattered information that is difficult to understand. According to Mónica:

You watch TV and there's Videla and a pile of data about that period, but the information isn't connected. It may seem that way to me because I don't know that much about the topic. But if you listen [to broadcasts] the facts are disconnected and it's hard to get to the heart of the matter. This is what happens to me; I don't know with you.

The comment is very revealing of the way memories were being transmitted. We know that silences and the lack of contextual information had resulted in a fragmented knowledge of the dictatorship. This was the foundation upon which young people assimilated the new facts to which they now had access. But the media seemed to be offering data without the elements to facilitate a comprehensive analysis. For those who relied on the media as their main source of knowledge about this period, the information conveyed was practically useless.

Moreover, participants' skepticism toward the country's main institutions included a poor opinion of the media, which they saw as being composed of corporations that would do anything to increase ratings and profits. I was told that journalists who were keen to shoot disturbances or police raids that might occur covered human rights demonstrations. Ricardo shared an interesting anecdote:

Disturbances sell. I remember going to a march and, suddenly, having journalists running after us. We were at a march; I remember it was in Plaza de Mayo. I wasn't looking and, all of a sudden, the guy who was next to me said, "Run." And we started to run. And then I looked back and saw thousands of journalists running. I stopped and, of course, they were focusing their cameras on me. So I left. But those who stayed wondering what was going on got their faces on camera. It was a row of journalists with cameras and narrators. And you could see that the police was behind the fences. A total lack of control! Because one can turn, throw a stone, and that's the beginning of the mess.

Journalists looking for a riot, ready—and eager—to record disturbances? I participated in a human rights demonstration that was violently repressed and for sure the media were there. And their coverage of the repression contributed to shaping specific versions of the events. Regarding this incident, the chief of police's version, broadcast by the media, was that demonstrators were throwing stones. From what I saw, and according to other witnesses, no one threw a single stone. We do not know which images were used by TV broadcasters to support their claims—maybe it was stock footage of violent demonstrators. But Roberto repeated almost word for word the broadcast police report, which he had obviously and easily accepted as the truth:

I saw it on TV. [Demonstrators] started throwing stones at the police. The police were around the corner of that house. I don't know very well how it happened. One of the kids hit a police officer and that was the beginning. I saw how one of the kids was pulled up and dragged by his hair.

Alberto, who was also part of this conversation, pointed to the particular agenda that police repression at demonstrations might have and how crucial media coverage of it is:

> I think that's what goes on. We go and peacefully demonstrate in order to voice our opinions. Someone, who's purposely sent to do so, infiltrates us and throws a stone. So the police has to repress because we're all creating a brawl. That's what goes on. With all the good intentions there's someone who infiltrates us. Or the police themselves instigate the violence so [demonstrators] respond violently so that later what appears on TV is, "Subversive groups, whatever, did such and such." Rather than, "These people who think in such and such way, went to do this and that, but then something or other happened, and this was the outcome."

Television

I have chosen television, the most pervasive communication medium, to illustrate roles that the mainstream media play in the transmission and construction of memories.

TV: Source of Information/Conversation Trigger

Memories of participants' first encounters with this historical period reveal the recurrence of television as a primary source of knowledge. This is illustrated by statements such as "The first time that I heard about it was on television" (Ariel); "I felt curiosity after watching a film or something else on TV" (Gloria); "I know about the Mothers through seeing them on TV" (Carlos); "I learned about the trials [of the military juntas] through the media" (Marcelo).

On some occasions, participants had reacted to information in the media by wanting to learn more and asking their parents questions, often triggering conversations on a topic that their families had not previously discussed. Beatriz explained her reactions to a television program:

> The first time that I heard of the military coup was on television. It was a documentary about the coup. I was nine or ten years old. I asked my mom and dad what was this about and they explained to me a bit about it.

The importance of television in prompting curiosity was also present in comments by Pedro, an eighteen-year-old high school student:

> The topic was discussed on a program. I didn't understand a thing so I asked my mom about it. But she wasn't willing to tell me much. I think it was for an anniversary.

I'd never been interested about this issue but, at that time, I was interested in anything that was shown on television. So I'd ask about different things and my mother usually answered me. She did answer me about this, but didn't say much.

Pedro's account of his mother's limited explanations is yet one more sign of the pervasiveness of silence and the transmission of incomplete information. Several participants noted society's inability to address this past. That was Leonardo's concern:

It's up to us to investigate, to discover things. I think that it's good that this issue is being addressed again. Even to arouse a pinch of curiosity in people, a fragment of information to make them curious. I believe that, today, any kid who hears [the name] Videla on TV is going to ask his father, "Who's that guy, why is he being sent to jail?" Or maybe he doesn't ask anything but will be curious to find out about him. I believe that's good. What I don't know is if we're all prepared to answer him. That's the problem, the lack of preparation [we've] to answer this question. And more than once you don't know what to say so you just reply, "Some guy."

His observations were consistent with other opinions linking the lack of discussion to ignorance. Obviously, the problem of incomplete answers to young people's questions is not limited to the subject of the dictatorship. But the beneficial effects of the post-dictatorship media coverage of the past may not be matched by people's capacity to deal with it. An inevitable effect may be a continuation of the transmission of silences.

In spite of these problems, participants saw the media as powerful agenda-setters and as extremely helpful for familiarizing the younger generation with human rights issues. For example, while I was discussing the marches of the Mothers of the Plaza de Mayo with a group of high school students (Elena, Pedro, Héctor, Nelson), one of them noted the relevance of the television coverage they received: "Maybe a kid sees it on TV, becomes interested, and starts finding out about [this past]. So young people become more interested and we can do something [about it]."

TV: Reactions to Torturers' Presence

Television was giving the younger generations access to the mentality and ideology of torturers and assassins. The impact of the firsthand accounts was far greater than that of a secondhand story of the past. Television was showing what these men had to say about the dictatorship fifteen years after the beginning of civilian rule. In some cases, they had not only committed horrible crimes but also were proud of them and ready to strike again. Thus, their declarations were reminding society of the caliber of the criminals who benefited from amnesties.

One example that allows us to analyze torturers' presence on television is the recurrently cited program of yellow journalism icon Mauro Viale that was brought up in our discussion to illustrate the superficiality with which the dictatorship was often discussed. This leading trash talk show, as defined by participants, seemed eager to turn human rights crimes into a "hot" topic for the sake of profit. Viale had confronted young people and *represores*.

Marta shared the annoyance she felt:

A couple of times, I saw the topic being treated on television with excessive frivolity and lack of respect. I remember that I saw it once in Mauro Viale's program. This was a while ago. It was pathetic. I was angry and ashamed. How can he be so insensitive? How can they play with this? That program was like a game. There was a military officer who'd been a torturer and *represor* during the military dictatorship discussing with three kids, three teenagers. It wasn't serious. I saw it as a lack of respect, as they often do, not only with this topic but also with the majority of cases presented in this program. But I was very upset that they focused on this, because this isn't a joke.

Beatriz, a fifteen-year-old high school student, remembered the occasion when Viale invited children of *desaparecidos* with the torturers. The television set became the stage for having the victims' children facing their parents' victimizers. This time, the episode setting had provoked the popular wrestling match so common on certain talk shows:

On one side, there were the children of the disappeared, of the parents who were killed. On the other, there were the military and the people involved in [the repression]. And they ended up beating each other up in that [television] program. It was a mess.

However, even if the atmosphere created by the program host had offended the participants of this study, I did not perceive any signs of indignation over the fact that victimizers and victims had been given an equal forum to discuss the dictatorship. This might indicate that, for participants, the problem had been style rather than content and may illustrate acceptance of the belief that torturers have the right to fair treatment by an "objective" media, as previously discussed in the context of impunity.

TV: Entertainment Programs and the Past

The presence of the past in television is not limited to news programs or talk shows. Television can trigger talk about the dictatorship through a program that is not addressing this topic—and is not even being watched. Sara had an interesting story about family talks prompted by what her neighbors used to watch. The program was *Brigada Cola*, apparently a bad production but a very popular comedy with high ratings.[14] Sara said that it was intended to be a funny show about a military battalion whose soldiers carried toy guns, "struggled" against bad guys, and chased women wearing bikinis. These were Sara's memories of her first talks about the repression:

> I know that there was a *proceso* that was terrible, that thirty thousand people died, or they're disappeared but it's known they are dead. My parents have been telling me this since I was a kid. I remember that my mother would tell me those things during the time that a television serial called *Brigada Cola* was being aired. I'm ashamed of that TV serial. It was about some military. I didn't watch it; I didn't like it and watched *The Simpsons*. But we'd listen to our neighbors watching *Brigada Cola* with the theme song blasting from the TV. So my mother would tell us what the military had done. This is the first thing that I remember. We'd lie in bed in front of the TV with my mom and my brother to watch *The Simpsons*, but we listened to *Brigada Cola* during the advertising breaks. If I switched to *Brigada Cola* during the breaks, I remember that my mother would tell me, "Don't watch these things." First, because it was bad and second because she didn't want me to see a serial based on the military. She said that a military dictatorship had ended ten years ago. My mother was very hurt seeing that Argentine society could give such high ratings to such a serial, even by the idea of having the military as protagonists and main heroes.

Sara's mother worried that this packaging of the military as charming, well-intentioned soldiers was sending messages that countered negative images of the military institution.[15] But these conversations based on what other people watch on television illustrate the need to keep an open mind when trying to assess which media texts address this past or function as its conversation-triggers.

Film

As is the case with television, films play an important role as source of historical knowledge, be it the official history, the counterhistory, or the memories of certain groups.[16] Films, as representations of historical events, have certainly shaped the way we imagine the past. Filmmakers are producers of history in forms where the actual events are often modified, edited, and dramatized.

The analysis of historical films usually focuses on the decoding of the messages that the images convey (e.g., the accuracy of the historical facts portrayed) and on how audiences interpret and are affected by those images. For example, Rosenthal, discussing reality-based fictional films, argues that *Gandhi* or *Malcolm X* sold fiction as truth but are "germinal films in the formation of public opinion and attitudes toward key historical political issues," such as civil disobedience and black pride.[17] Ferro, in looking at the relevance of films in bringing issues into the public sphere, highlights how, in the year of the release of *Reds* there were a greater number of published articles about the Soviet Revolution than at any other time.[18]

But the fact that films are fictional recreations of the past does not minimize their function as history "textbooks." It is not that easy to identify the films about the dictatorship. As a few participants noted, the dictatorship is present in many, or most, contemporary Argentine films.

According to Marta:

We always discuss with my brother that, at some point, the *proceso* appears in most Argentine films. In general, it's always present in some way or other. Some are children of *desaparecidos* or are exiles. [The *proceso*] is always part of one of the film's themes.

Juan, a fan of Argentine cinema, also argued that this presence is manifest in the recurrence of certain themes, even in those films not explicitly dealing with these events:

Most Argentine movies, either casually or in-depth, touch the issue, all of them. Solanas's *Sur* is mostly about it. I love that film. *Buenos Aires Viceversa*, which is the best film, either foreign or Argentine, that I've seen so far, also deals with it. Everybody has a past that has to do with the *desaparecidos*. Almost all the movies [do]. If I think about all the movies and try to make connections, at some point they name the *desaparecidos*, or someone has a past story, a disappeared relative, was tortured, or something like that. Or they mention the epoch referring to it as awful times: "Do you remember that we couldn't do anything?" But all the Argentine films that I can remember touch the issue; and I see most of them because I love Argentine cinema.

The first national production to address the dictatorship was *The Official Story*, winner of the 1986 Oscar for the best foreign film. It is about the kidnapping of babies from prisoners who were then disappeared. The film, set up during the last months of the dictatorship, tells the story of Alicia (a history professor), her husband (a supporter of the dictatorship), and their adopted daughter. The central narrative is Alicia's awakening from total ignorance about what has been going on through the suspicion that her child might be the daughter of a *desaparecida*. This implies addressing her husband's complicity, the anguish of the families looking for missing children, and the dilemma of keeping or giving back her daughter to her biological relatives.

Not many participants had seen it. The older ones were about ten years old when it was released but some had watched it on television and video. Some of the few comments that I heard suggest that the film may have successfully promoted the concept that people did not know what was going on during the terror. Marta saw her family reflected in the film:

The protagonist, the woman, reminded me of my mother. There's a part where you can see that she was completely blind about what'd happened, completely naïve and blind. This reminded me a lot of my mom and my dad.

Thus, this film could reinforce the belief in society's ignorance and serve to calm any remorse for not having done anything, therefore discouraging the questioning of past roles. In other words, it can be a tool for a collective self-deception process, or a reconstruction of the past to defend a positive self-image of an uninformed and innocent society: we did not know, therefore we have no responsibility.

I also heard comments indicating that the film may have shaped opinions regarding kidnapped babies. Carmen, who considered that these children should remain with their "adoptive" families, remembered her feelings when she saw it:

> What touched me the most is when I saw *The Official Story*, the film that won the Oscar. When I saw that little girl, I remembered all the babies, all the pregnant women, all that they had endured. I don't get it, I can't understand how someone who wears uniform, who belongs to an institution and all that can have such a rotten mind. When I saw the little girl I said: "Poor girl, she has no family, she doesn't know who her parents are, her grandmother is struggling for her." But I also said: "These parents also love her. This kid has two histories the one before and the one after her birth. I don't want either family to suffer. I put myself in both their places." I saw it with an aunt, a friend of my mother, his mother, and my mother. When we were driving back home, they commented, "What these military did!" And I said, "The girl has to stay with the parents who have her." And my mother said, "Do you think she should stay? And the grandmother? What do you say about her?" And I said, "I want her to stay with the parents with whom she is now." That was the only thing I understood.

Carmen had seen this film ten years before our conversation. When she argued that stolen children should stay with torturers, she seemed to have had firm convictions about the issue since she was a child. Her reactions to this film suggest that it might have influenced her way of thinking.

But my question about which films about the dictatorship the participants had seen was usually answered with *The Night of the Pencils*, a major historical referent for most of the young people with whom I talked. The "Night of the Pencils" (September 16, 1976) was when ten teenage fine arts students (hence the reference to "pencils"), who were political activists, were abducted by security forces. All of them were brutally tortured; three survived and the rest remain disappeared.[19] The events have become the symbol of repression against students. The film is a very intense and dramatic production that conveys in a very graphic way state terrorism's methods to eliminate dissidents—terror, paramilitary groups storming into houses in the middle of the night, torture, rape, murder, disappearances. Practically all interviewees had seen the film and remembered a story of watching it with family or friends.

Many participants indicated that they had learned about the dictatorship through this film (as 74.7 percent of 500 college students answered to a survey poll conducted at the University of Buenos Aires).[20] For example, Carlos, a twenty-one-year-old clerical employee at an advertising agency, mentioned the film when he discussed the repression: "They came to your house, kidnapped you, took you away; I don't know, I rely a lot on *The Night of the Pencils*."

Television broadcast of the film had often prompted family talks. Mónica shared her experience:

> I remember well the day they showed it on TV. I was very young; I might have been ten years old. I told you that we didn't talk [about the dictatorship] at home. But the day *The Night of the Pencils* was shown, I remember that my mom made the three of us—I have two brothers—and my dad watch the movie. She told us, "We're going to watch this film." She knew what the film was about and wanted us to see it. "Let's see what happened." I remember that we watched it and we all cried. It was very powerful for me. I was too young and to see how they tortured, how they took people away. I didn't understand much because I was only ten years old. But it touched me a lot. And afterwards we talked. My mother told us some things. Based on the film she told us what had happened during those years. Yes, I remember now that it was very strong for me. Because watching something like that when you're a kid is too tough.

The use of the film as a handy device to educate, illustrate stories, or validate words attests to its value in filling a gap in available images documenting the repression.

However, there were comments illustrating that the older generation may be unprepared to address the issues the film portrays. Graciela described a talk with her father while watching the film. It is an example of how the transmission of the atmosphere of terror often lacks information that can help young people to grasp the "why" of what happened:

> [Prisoners] were beaten, all women were raped, some of them were pregnant and [the torturers] stole their babies. And I asked my dad and he told me that during those times you couldn't even go out of your house because the military would capture you and maybe you'd disappear and would never be seen again. Either they killed you or took you away. There were concentration camps. The movie was very good because it showed everything, with many details. I wasn't afraid because that epoch is over and now there's democracy.

Peers had also been influential in turning the film into an important source of information. Accounts of watching the film with friends and classmates reveal that it has generated strong emotional reactions and talk. Gloria remembered the anguish she and her friends had felt:

> We had a conversation once the film was over. We were hurt by the things that had happened; because we couldn't believe that so many young people had been taken

away and all that was done to them. They were imprisoned and [the military] wouldn't give any information. They were all disappeared even when they were alive.

We will return to this film. Because it is one of the most quoted "historical documents" about the dictatorship, it deserves special attention when discussing representations of horror, the theme of the next chapter.

Music

There were frequent references to music as an influential medium through which young people were learning about the dictatorship, revealing the existence of an alternative public sphere created around recordings and concerts where this past is present. Apparently, counterculture music focuses on the issues currently affecting the younger generation and also on the dictatorship and its aftermath. Police brutality, in particular against young people, continues to be a problem in post-dictatorial Argentina, where police officers are commonly referred to as those of the *gatillo fácil* ("easy trigger"). Thus, by addressing contemporary violence—a subject with which most participants were familiar—these songs help in establishing links with the past and in the understanding of the dictatorship's repression.

In Argentina, the *rock nacional* has traditionally been immersed in the social reality—"rock" is a word popularly used to include a variety of musical currents such as hip-hop, heavy metal, rap, or punk. It emerged in the 1960s and underwent different phases during the dictatorship. At the beginning, rock concerts were one of the few public gatherings in which young people could participate without risking repression. It almost vanished during the terror's worst times—absolute censorship, musicians forced into exile. It then reemerged during the Malvinas/Falkland War, when, as a "vindication" of national culture, only music with lyrics in Spanish was allowed to fill the airwaves. But, although it was promoted by the dictatorship, rock became a realm of resistance and opposition.[21] As for the role of popular music in remembering violent pasts, studies ranging from Chile to the Holocaust confirm its importance in this process.[22]

Participants highlighted the informative role that music plays in transmitting historical information and noted how receptive they were to these messages: "Sometimes you learn through musical groups that play themes about the coup d'état and tell you what went on" (Nelson). "Music gets to you; you learn through it, even if it's not obvious. It stays with you" (Pablo).

The events of the dictatorship are present in many songs. I was told that some groups that play this type of music have members who had been directly affected by the repression. One of them is *Actitud Maria Marta,* a hip-hop rap group with a duo of female vocalists, one of whom is the daughter of a *desaparecido*. Most of their songs relate to the dictatorship repression and address this subject in a very direct style.

I heard many opinions about the group, ranging from appreciation of their directness in conveying their political message to criticisms of the vulgarity of their language, including that it is too strong, even violent.

Marcelo noted how the group turns concerts into forums to discuss human rights:

> The songs are very strong. If you listen to them you'll hear anything and everything. On their album cover there's a photo of members of the military junta with a huge turd in between them. They criticize [the military]. It's not humorous, it's strong, harsh. It's kind of gross but it's true. They do good songs and good music. In their concerts, they usually speak about the issues before singing.

Analía, obviously impacted by their music, highlighted the anger the musicians transmit:

> They do protest songs against the military and talk about the disappeared and all that. I believe that one of them is the daughter of a *desaparecido*. It's very strong music, quite violent. I heard them and it caught my attention because there's hate, anger in it. You listen to them and you fill yourself with hate and rage, you want to go out and kill.

Another group recognized for denouncing the dictatorship's crimes in shocking style was *Todos tus Muertos* (All Your Dead)—a name loaded with symbolism of the massacre that took place in the country. During my conversation with Pablo and Héctor, they stressed the musicians' background, the appalling images of the group's videos, and their value as information tools:

> Their videos are very impressive. Disgusting. They show such things, like when [the military] tortured and killed people. They show people on their knees being executed by gunfire. These videos are something. But it's ok, they inform, although they don't show them very often. They show them at 3 AM on cable music channels. The musicians of *Todos tus Muertos* are from a shantytown. They began playing music there and they "crossed over" through the music. So they must know, have to know a bunch of stuff.

The credibility of the group seems to be reinforced by the fact that violence is not alien to its members, who sing about what they know well. Furthermore, these comments illustrate an appreciation of musicians as organic intellectuals, which I perceived in several of the young people with whom I talked. The authority of the message seems to be based on the credentials that their origins and experiences grant to its authors and performers—for example, being born in shantytowns or having disappeared relatives.

Nora, who even sang some of the lyrics while sitting at a coffee shop, talked of songs about the cruelty of a dictatorship that sent young soldiers to die in the Malvinas/Falklands War, the promoted euphoria around the Soccer World Cup of 1978, and the presidential pardons to the military juntas:

> Lerner has a beautiful song called "Pardon." During the Malvinas War, Andrés Calamaro came out with the song "One Thousand Hours," which says, "The other night, I waited for you for two hours under the rain." It talks about the snow; it's dedicated to the young men waiting for their dead in Malvinas. He also has another song that says, "I'm from the Mundial' 78's generation," and talks about society experiencing paranoia and suffering.

The Mothers of the Plaza de Mayo are well aware of the value of music in reaching young people. One of their communication strategies is to organize concerts with the participation of many of the musical groups mentioned by interviewees. These concerts attract large audiences, but I found different opinions on their efficacy for human rights campaigns.

Analía was skeptical:

> I don't know if everybody participates. I don't know if they all adhere to the cause. It seems that [people] go for the music rather than to support the Mothers of the Plaza de Mayo. I believe that the convocation has a relative value.

But other opinions indicated that these concerts might act as memory activators in a society where people are encouraged not to look back. According to Silvia:

> I think that the majority adheres to the concerts' goals. Besides, I believe that [concerts] are organized so people won't forget about those things, although people don't care that much. Everything in society is done so people won't think. There are the fashions, taking care of your body, clothes and all that.

Along the same lines, some comments suggested that concerts fulfill an educational role. As Alicia noted:

> People in power are not very interested in young people knowing what happened and making this past part of their own history. This is why I approve of those musical groups that speak [about what happened].

Concerts, thus, opened spaces for the reflection and discussion of human rights issues. At least, they put them on the agenda and helped to build bridges between activists and those who might have gone exclusively for the music but would listen to what artists they admire have to say. Some musicians were taking care to transmit this past through a medium and a language that the younger generations can relate to. In bringing back this past, popular music was writing memory and helping the post-dictatorship generation to rewrite its history. Although it is hard to assess the popularity of these musicians—no sales figures, music reproduced and distributed through alternative networks—there was evidence that some of them were very popular and that the music counterculture was keeping the spirit of resistance it showed during the terror. This suggests that we need to carefully scrutinize the apparent apathy of young people toward the events of the dictatorship. Young people participating in these concerts, singing and dancing to the beat of these songs, were also remembering this past.

Geography of Memory—"Landmarks" of Terror

We know that a society's memories have spatial frameworks and are encoded in topographic sites. Geography carries historical references; it is a structure for remembrance and people locate their memories within places such as a public square or a factory.[23] What went on in Argentina has left indelible marks on those sites where terror shook up the community. In the city of Buenos Aires, raids on homes, schools, and factories, shootings, and paramilitary gangs driving around town characterized the urban landscape during those years. Memories of terror are engraved in the many buildings where counterinsurgency operations took place under the terrified gaze of witnesses. To this we may add police stations, garrisons, and other now sinister buildings that housed the centers where prisoners were tortured, murdered, and disappeared. These sites symbolize terror and have become historical referents of this past. But, what role(s) do they play in society's collective memories? What reactions does their presence provoke?

I have my own memory of my building's door having been broken the night of the coup by a squad that came looking for union activists. From day one, my home and neighborhood were marked by terror. And I heard other stories about places that are symbols of horror for a particular family or neighborhood. According to the official statistics 62 percent of *desaparecidos* were taken away from their homes in the presence of witnesses, 24.6 percent from public spaces (e.g., streets, buses), 7 percent from workplaces, 6 percent from schools, 0.4 percent from military or police headquarters.[24] There were always witnesses, even when they looked in another direction or closed their doors and windows to avoid hearing the screams. How many relatives, neighbors, coworkers, classmates, people riding the same bus, passersby have witnessed kidnappings, assassinations, disappearances? How many streets, houses, apartments, offices, factories, and classrooms are imprinted with terror and evoke that past to whoever was there at that time, whenever they walk by or whenever something triggers images and sounds of that particular moment? Today, all of them have a story to tell.

Patricia's parents witnessed the storming by a death squad of their neighbors' home. She explained how that street and house became a mnemonic referent for her parents:

There was a house next to where my mother lived. My dad and mom, who were dating at that time, were one day outside her house. Suddenly, a police patrol car arrived loaded with armed policemen. They stormed into the neighbors' house and started shooting. [My parents] went inside their house. Everybody in the house died. My mother always tells that the police went in and started [shooting] without checking if there were people there. She told me this the other day, while we drove by. And I was stunned by my mother telling me "I was there, next to it; I saw this and that." She told me that because my father asked her "Do you remember what happened here?"

Listening to this story, it was obvious that the episode was very vivid in Patricia's parents' memories. As with the many stories of disappearances that I heard, the topographical marking of those stories that are waiting to be told could draw a map of the spatial frameworks of memories of the repression.

This map is already being traced and has some key points marked on it: the buildings that housed torture and extermination centers, the approximately 340 "clandestine detention centers" that functioned in the country during the terror.[25] Their relevance as historical referents was manifest in participants' mentions of them. Some were about El Olimpo, the torture center perversely nicknamed after "the home of gods," which continues to house police offices.

Nora commented that one of the first things that she heard about the repression was linked to this place. Something about that building prompted her curiosity and she remembered being a child demanding explanations from her mother:

My mother's cousin lived around the corner. Each time that we went [to her house] I asked, "What's this, what's this?" [My mother] told me, "Here's where the military tortured those they took prisoner." It stayed with me. For me, that place is sinister. Whenever I pass by I remember and I imagine [what went on]. So each time that we passed by I asked [my mother] again and again "What's this?" because when you're a kid you want them to repeat things over and over, "The place where they tortured people." I remember this now.

Silvia also mentioned the sinister specter of the site and the reactions its presence provokes. She passed it by bus every day and, remembering the suffering of those who were victimized within these walls, used to say to herself: "Mother fuckers, there were people here that. . . ." Moreover, the embellishment process to which El Olimpo has been subjected offended Silvia. The entrance now has a fountain with a little angel and some ceramic tiles with the image of the Virgin of Luján, the most venerated among Argentinean Catholics. As she said: "It's insane, super insane. They put [the little angel] at the entrance, gates, and a little garden." Undoubtedly, efforts to recycle images and ascribe new meanings to sites are not always successful, at least while people remember a location's previous "incarnation."

The Navy Mechanics School, popularly known as ESMA (Escuela de Mecánica de la Armada), is one of the major "landmarks" of the repression, a symbol of state terrorism and a site with which most participants were familiar. I personally find it hard to pass by the building without remembering the atrocities committed there. And I am not the only one who literally "gets the chills." During the trial of the military juntas, Mercedes was a child but used to read the details in the newspaper. She talked about the day when she actually saw the building she had read so much about:

> I remember that we were once driving around in the car along Libertador Avenue. My father told me, "Look, look, that's the Navy Mechanics School." I must have been ten years old. I then associated the acronym and said, "The ESMA, yes, the ESMA." There it was; the proof was there. I used to read about those things but, being ten years old, the Navy Mechanics School was Chinese for me; I didn't even know where it was. That day I saw it.

These comments illustrate how these buildings are testimonies of the past, physical evidence of what took place and reference marks in the topography of terror. Therefore, it should not be surprising that attempts had been made to modify what these sites represent in the collective imaginary and to erase the memories imprinted there.

The Monument Project

The ESMA building is a good example for exploring initiatives to erase the past and any connotation of terror through renovation and recycling. Promotion of ESMA's metamorphosis is an implicit recognition of the memories this site embodies and an indication of the memory battles taking place in the country. The first effort to give a new symbolic value to ESMA was its promotion (in the early 1990s) as a sports center for high school and college students. Although several horrified parents opposed it, many young people used the premises for sports training and competitions.[26] This was followed by President Menem's controversial decree (in 1998) to demolish the building and erect a monument to "national unity" there. The proposed demolition took the process of recycling memory one major step further, endeavoring not just to modify it but to cancel it out. Human rights organizations successfully challenged this decree with public demonstrations and legal demands. The courts declared that the building should be preserved as legal evidence of the crimes committed. The monument project is the perfect example of Freud's argument that communities confront common crimes by covering the location of the crimes with monuments that allow them to be forgotten.[27]

Participants' comments on the ESMA controversy revealed how the media had placed the issue in the public sphere and shed light on different opinions about preserving or suppressing those collective referents. Many interviewees argued that behind this change of image of the site was the decision to forget and erase the past. Pablo summarized it well: "This shows how they don't want us to know anything. They keep on covering everything as if they were painting a wall and throwing one coat of paint on top of the other." The paint as a metaphor is quite evocative because laws or decrees do not regulate memory and, in Argentina, the need for truth and justice continues to resurface, like a dark mark on a wall, impossible to blot out even with multiple coats of paint.

Some participants argued that efforts to placate people by building monuments would never succeed because people cannot be easily manipulated. Silvia brought up her indignation and, like many others, questioned what unity the project was promoting:

> They think we're stupid. That's the way it is. They think that they can silence the people with a monument. It's not like that. Maybe some people, a certain number of persons are satisfied when [Menem] speaks or erects a monument recognizing all this. But there are other people who have disappeared children, and grandchildren, and for them, a monument means nothing. They'd throw it at [Menem's] head. What union is he talking about?

The intention to resignify the horror with unity illustrates official discourses of "reconciliation" based on forgetting. Thus, discussions about the meaning of unity questioned these conciliatory pleas. According to Mercedes:

> I completely disagree with this. The [notion of] national unity is ridiculous. It's [Menem's] invention. There are many things that we can have in this country except union, especially regarding this issue. I believe that social condemnation is stronger each day. [Represores] cannot go into the streets without being insulted. I believe that people strongly want a great many things except reconciliation with the torturers and assassins of that epoch.

Mercedes, thus, was very clear in articulating that society was being asked to pardon major criminals. I also heard opinions that monuments often imply an abandonment of the pursuit of justice. Diego suggested other ways to honor the *desaparecidos*:

> Without the will of clarifying things, what's the point of tearing off your vestments and proclaiming "I built a monument to the *desaparecidos*?" Let them put a monolith in each factory and in each shantytown to honor all the guys who were taken away from there. That'd be great. I studied at a school where the first thing that you see when you enter is a plaque, a small one, but with the name of three guys who studied there and disappeared.

Laura was part of this conversation and emphatically endorsed these ideas:

[Let's put a plaque] in each school and university. At the university, at the pavilion 2, where the School of Architecture is, I don't know if it's still there, and it's not a plaque but a giant banner hanging from one floor to the other that has the names of all the architecture students who disappeared during the *proceso*. It's a giant billboard that fulfills the role of a plaque.

These recommendations for honoring the *desaparecidos* at the sites from where they were taken away would undoubtedly add to the map of memories of the terror. Marking urban spaces with the historical events that happened there has been done in many places around the world—in Paris with episodes from the resistance to Nazi occupation.

Laura also had interesting comments regarding the effectiveness of monuments as devices for remembering or forgetting. She pointed out how they usually "blend" with the landscape and that, after a while, few remember what they are about:

ESMA itself is a monument. I think it's much more of a monument than if they put up a monolith with a soldier and a flag, the typical Argentine monument. It seems to me that [ESMA] is much more of a monument because it's a real fact, an eyewit- ness. I believe that there are corpses in ESMA terrain; it seems logical to me. After a while you get used to a monument and pass by without seeing it. Moreover, some years from now we'd end up passing by the site where ESMA stands and looking at the monument, without seeing it. There were two statues at my school. One day, one of them disappeared. It took more than a week for administrators to realize that it was missing, and one year for everybody else in the school. "They stole the statue." "Which statue?" "The one that was there." "Ah, yes, there was a statue there." I sup- pose that's what could happen. People saying: "Whose statue is this?" "Which statue?" "Ah, yes, the statue of the *desaparecidos*."

There were also comments questioning the constant remembrance of what hap- pened there. Nelson's aunt disappeared in Uruguay. He was very critical of the dicta- torship and aware that human rights activists had defeated the monument project. But he had a problem with activists' insistence on preserving the site:

They wanted to demolish [ESMA] and the Mothers of the Plaza de Mayo asked to keep it because it served to remember so that it won't happen again, something like that. I don't know what Menem wanted to do. I don't remember if he wanted a plaza. Those of the Plaza de Mayo, the grandmothers of the Plaza de Mayo, and also HIJOS raised hell. But it's a site where many persons were kept and tortured. Why did they raise hell to keep it? Each time they pass by they remember, "That's where my son was tortured to death."

For Nelson, thus, the pain that the site provokes prevails over its value as historical and legal evidence. As throughout our conversations, remembering and forgetting, what to remember and why, remained constant topics. As for which characteristics a monument should have to preserve memory, the task remains, as Pilar Calveiro, an ESMA survivor, argues, to maintain the presence of this past "in order to allow its re-elaboration, its re-understanding," and in a form that avoids its disappearance.[28] (More than five years after these conversations, and as I write these lines, on March 24, 2004, the twenty-eighth anniversary of the coup, ESMA was officially handed over to human rights organizations to house a Museum of Memory.)

Conclusions

We have explored how memories of the dictatorship were being constructed and shaped by a multiplicity of texts. The voices of the post-dictatorship generation shed light on the broad spectrum of communication media through which the past had made its way into the present, on the different pages that constitute the dictatorship's "textbook." It would not have been possible to research the ways in which young people remember terror without analyzing their interaction with the media. Even if I had focused exclusively on the role played by the family or the school, recurrent references to the media would have forced me to acknowledge their relevance. This is a pervasive presence in the memory construction process, and it is often difficult to disentangle what was witnessed in the streets, discussed with a friend or in the classroom, read in a magazine, seen on television, or heard on the radio. Therefore, knowledge of the dictatorship is, in part, based on participants' consumption, over time, of a variety of media texts and intertwined with other major sources such as family and school.

There are a variety of roles that the media play: sources of historical knowledge, (hi)storytellers, agenda-setters, triggers of talk, constructors of the social imaginary, and creators of public spheres. Media coverage of the dictatorship had definitely disrupted societal silences. Because the media have brought back this past, family members or educators have been forced to answer the questions it prompted in the younger generation.

Many are the historical referents, the realms of memory that codify and symbolize this traumatic past, the little pieces of information on which young people based their knowledge about it. Television programs, rock concerts, a film, or a former torture center are all windows into the past terror. It is hard to define which of them was more important or influential. It is also difficult to categorize precisely which media products are sources for the representation of this past, which are the films or television programs that deal with it. For it seems to be woven into the post-dictatorship's cultural production and embedded in the most diverse and often apparently unrelated messages. Marginal and fleeting mentions of exile, political turmoil, violence, censorship, or its aftermath are signs of the presence of the dictatorship, showing the different ways in which the events touched the whole society and became part of its memories.

Participants' stories also illustrate the problems that they see in the historical accounts to which they had been exposed, the messages that impacted them and why, and how their own way of thinking, and acting, may have been influenced by these messages. Their knowledge of the events, what was discussed or silenced within their social groups, or their families' experiences during the terror usually determined the effects that particular texts had on participants. There was a consistent relationship between participants' ideological and political background and how they interpreted and acted upon the messages to which they were exposed.

Hence, it is problematic for activists to define how to portray this past in order to achieve particular goals, namely, to educate about the years of terror and prevent their repetition in the future. How to influence what is to be forgotten, what is to be remembered, and, most particularly, how it will be remembered are key challenges; another is how to represent the horror in a form that conveys its magnitude and avoids its "disappearance," to use Calveiro's words. These are the issues we explore in our next chapter.

NINE

Conversations about Representing the Horror

Introduction

So the past has made it into the present. The events of the dictatorship have been transmitted and the communication media have been key sources in this process. The dictatorship's "textbook" has several and varied pages, presenting multiple portrayals and explanations of the horror that went on. But how is this traumatic past maintaining its presence in the public sphere? What stories are these representations telling? How are they telling them and in which forms?

This chapter explores the problems of representing, transmitting, and consuming horror. It is about answers to the questions: How should the magnitude of the atrocities committed by the dictatorship be conveyed without "saturating" the public with its details? How graphic should the portrayal of violence be? As we have seen, there is an overwhelming predominance of horror in participants' postmemories of terror. We look here at how particular representations of this violent past have been interpreted. We aim to assess how these portrayals are impacting people, whether particular representations have a greater effect, and, if so, why. In addition, we analyze participants' recommendations on how to transmit the horror.

An estimated 30,000 voices have been silenced forever, but enough people survived the horror to share their memories of the infernos in which they were submerged. Through them, society can have a more direct access to what it meant to be disappeared. However, even they, as Leydesdorff notes of Holocaust survivors, are the "witnesses of other people's suffering" but "can only fantasize about the horrors" of those who didn't survive.[1] But there are no visual images of the brutality that went on inside the centers for torture and extermination and, to my knowledge, the existence of any such documentation is purely speculative—quite different from the many photos or the film footage of Nazi concentration camps.

Hence, accounts of survivors or their victimizers have provided the details that have inspired representations in film or literature. To explore how the portrayal and transmission of horror shape the memory construction process I consider here two distinct perspectives: the unmediated voices of the survivors, or their direct testimonies, and the fictional, or mediated, representations of their stories, taking film as an example.

Unmediated Voices

Victims' denunciations included in the *Nunca Más*—the report of the Commission to Investigate Disappearances (CONADEP)—and video images of victims' testimonies at the trial of the military juntas are two instances that allow us to explore the effects produced by the exposure to the victims' voices through their words and images. Participants' reactions to them were a recurrent topic during our conversations, which suggests that these voices are an important referent of their memories of terror.

Nunca Más

Nunca Más was the first official document to shock Argentine society with descriptions of how state terrorism operated. When it was first published in 1984, it became an overnight best seller and, throughout the years, its many reprints have continued to be sold in bookstores and on newsstands. The report is a collection of survivors' accounts of the horror. Although it provides contextual information, it does not include the names of kidnappers, torturers, and killers. This omission is a very provocative issue and questions the commitment to justice of a report that gives names of victims but not of victimizers. It was a magazine, *El Periodista*, that published the list of the 1,350 names of those involved in the repression compiled by the CONADEP. They included military personnel, journalists, physicians, and even Pio Laghi, the Papal nuncio, whose presence in torture centers, supposedly to check human rights violations, had been documented by ex-prisoners.[2] The Mothers of the Plaza de Mayo are very critical of the *Nunca Más*' emphasis on the graphic portrayal of violence. As one Mother, Graciela de Jeger, summarized it: "The book was paralyzing because they describe all this horror and they don't give a way out. The assumption is that the disappeared are dead and the story is over."[3]

Nonetheless, *Nunca Más* asserts the validity of testimonies in conveying the horror. It also allows us to compare the credibility assigned to both victims and perpetrators. Paradoxically and very sadly, at the early stages of the disclosure of the past, *represores*' credibility when they talked to the press often surpassed that of the victims. When the report was written, there was caution over presenting some findings. For example, the section on the "death flights" where prisoners were thrown into the ocean starts with the words, "It is hard to believe," although it indicates that it is licit to think that this was one of the methods utilized.[4] It would take the perpetrators' confession for society to have no doubts that the "death flights" had happened. In 1995, naval officer Scilingo publicly described his participation in these flights.

The reading of *Nunca Más* had caused many strong emotional reactions, and the value of the direct testimony is what made it so disturbing for many young people. Most participants were familiar with the book. Many had read it, others had skimmed it, and some had avoided it. Their opinions predominantly centered on the details of the atrocities, with barely no mention of other information included, such as how the repressive system was organized or the complicity of certain sectors, including the Catholic hierarchy.

Luis commented on what he had heard about the report:

I haven't read it but I've an idea of what it's about. They say that it's very strong, that after reading fifteen pages you're very sad and crying. Because these are the accounts of those who were there, in the concentration camps and all that.

Mónica speculated on the disturbing effects on those who lived under terror and have good memories of what fear is:

I only read a bit of it. Many people told me: "I started reading it and had to stop." It's very strong, very intense. I think that it must be more disturbing for people who experienced that epoch than for me who didn't. For those who endured it it's like living it again.

Leonardo, who was also part of this conversation and had heard stories of the dictatorship since he was a kid, had a completely different outlook on the book:

I read it very fast. I think I finished it in two or three days. At night, I stay up in bed reading and I swallow up books. I love reading. I read it without interruption. It didn't shock me that much. It may be because I already knew a lot and it didn't surprise me that much. It's horrible; some of the things it tells are horrible but they didn't impact me because I had already heard a lot of things. One loses the capability of being shocked.

Marcelo had discovered another angle of the dictatorship through his girlfriend, who had a disappeared uncle. He had this to say:

I managed to read some paragraphs of *Nunca Más*, a book to which I also had access through my girlfriend. She was reading it and used to tell me things. She thought that the things that had happened were abominations. She told me about the way people were tortured. That touched me. We knew that they'd done really terrible things, but it was much stronger to read the words, the testimonies of those who survived.

Videos

Other major referents in discussing victims' voices were the images of the trials of the military juntas in 1985. At that time, the victims were denied the possibility of having their voices broadcast live. It is not clear who made that decision and why, but this resolution illustrates how politicians and the military imposed the boundaries of media coverage during the transition to civilian rule,[5] therefore determining what the Argentine people would see and listen to and defining the content, scope, and form that society's mediatic participation in the legal proceedings would take.[6] All hearings were taped but news programs showed only a few minutes of images per day and victims' testimonies were edited by a narrator's voice-over. This undoubtedly affected the impact of the victims' voices. It is quite different to see the image of a witness testifying and a narrator explaining what she said than to listen to the witness recount her ordeal, in her own words and tone of voice, describing, for example, how her toenails were pulled out. Society missed the opportunity to see and hear firsthand the voices of victims or to listen to the *represores* denying, minimizing, or ratifying their atrocities—because the *represores'* accounts were also narrated using voice-over, although we should note that the perpetrators were extremely silent during their trials, which were marked by denials rather than confessions. This is quite different from the live broadcast of the South African TRC's proceedings, which allowed society to witness them and resulted in people throughout the country gathering to collectively listen to or watch the painful and emotional confessions. The TRC raised funds for those broadcasts, which were initially not contemplated because of claims that there was no budget for them.[7] Many South Africans were aware that society's participation in this process was extremely important for promoting healing and reconciliation and that the media had an essential role in facilitating it.

Publishing houses and human rights organizations have produced and marketed videos of this footage. These testimonies, thus, have circulated in a variety of spheres and through diverse channels, such as screenings at homes and schools, or broadcasts by cable television. The effects produced by these images were evident in the accounts of participants exposed to them.

Analía described how devastated she had been:

I can't believe it, I can't believe that [the military] have tortured as many people as they did. They terrify me. I'm telling you, this impacted me a lot. In the video of the trials of the military juntas they showed you the witnesses, people who'd nothing to lose, saying, "Your Honor, they tortured my baby with an electric prod." Do you understand me? I couldn't believe it. I can't believe it. I don't know how some people can go on living with that. I don't know. It's terrible.

Pedro had seen the videos at school and shared his and his classmates' reactions to witnessing the dynamics of the courtroom:

I watched the videos of the trials of the *represores*, the ones distributed by Perfil Press, where they told what had happened. I saw them with a teacher. [The videos] described many of the things they did. [While watching] you feel like killing them all. We wanted to kill all those guys. First we were silent. We then discussed how [those guys] could have had the nerve to sit there, looking calm no less, or how it was possible for the victims to face the person who tortured them and restrain themselves from killing him. There were many testimonies. The truth came out. Each person talked about what she'd suffered. We'd watch those on trial and see the truth of who they really were. Because they pretended to be saints. Their lawyers portrayed them as saints, as if they weren't guilty. You couldn't beat them into saints. You've to have some nerve to be the lawyer of those guys.

The videos allowed Pedro and his classmates to metaphorically sit in the courtroom and draw conclusions based on their own observations of the events. They saw the contrast between those describing their ordeals and the manifest indifference of the *represores*, the absurdity of their pretense of innocence. They were able to understand better the situation of the victims who were forced to share social spaces with their tormentors who benefited from amnesties.

One of the best-known testimonies is that by Adriana Calvo de Laborde, an active member of the association of former political prisoners who had appeared on many television programs, in videos, and in articles. She had her baby under subhuman circumstances while being transported to a torture center. Judging from the many references that I heard, her ordeal had produced a strong impression. As Patricia explained:

The other day I watched the trial of the military on a cable channel. Indeed, I wound up quite upset that day seeing a woman telling her story. She was delivering her baby and was forced inside a car. And she had to have the baby there, she was mistreated. They removed her placenta, took away the baby and, after the delivery [at the detention center], she was forced to clean the floor with buckets of water. Honestly, I was absolutely shocked, hearing that from the woman who suffered it.

Silvia described her reactions to this same testimony:

I heard the case of a woman who was kidnapped. I saw it recently on TV, in a video about the trial. She was telling how she'd been giving birth at the time she was being kidnapped, that her baby came out and was lying on the floor. I put myself in her place and thought: "This is not true, I'd die in such a situation." She was handcuffed and when they arrived at the site she soiled the floor and she was forced to pick up the placenta and clean the floor. [The video] helps you to put yourself in her place, to know how she felt.

Mercedes talked about a documentary produced by the Mothers of Plaza de Mayo that was shown at an outdoor screening during a march. She remembered a testimony about torturing children:

I couldn't finish watching it. I only saw a part of it. I think that I was eighteen years old at the time, an age where things could horrify me. Although perhaps I'd read those testimonies when I was younger and less conscious. The segment that made me realize I'd had enough was during the testimony of an ex-prisoner, when he said that, during his torture, they asked a doctor who was present what was the minimum age for torturing a person, applying electric prod. The doctor said that it was OK to torture a person weighing twenty-five kilograms. This is the weight of an eight-year old child. They were talking about a kid. I don't know what they thought the kid knew. I said to myself, "I don't want to find out." I have no idea what happened later but I said, "Enough is enough." I'm shaking as I remember it. Remembering it makes me shiver.

What survivors have to say is so terrible that all interviewees who had seen any footage of these testimonies were still shocked. It was manifest in the emotional way that they described their responses to those images. But the details of horror were also unbearable for many who, like Mercedes, might opt for not wanting to know more. Both effects are important to consider when representing horror. We should be aware, however, that Argentineans were extremely interested in reliable information documenting this period. In August 1998, the same month that I completed my conversations, the documentary "ESMA: The Day of the Trial," which focused on courtroom scenes related to crimes committed in ESMA, was watched by a television audience of three million people. Twenty-two years after the coup, almost 10 percent of the country's population tuned in to learn more about the repression.[8]

Fictional Representations of the Horror

I have already talked about the film *The Night of the Pencils*. Among participants, it was the quintessential representation of the dictatorship's horror, and most of them mentioned it as a key source of information. The film allows us to explore the effects of representations of repression in a horror-style show, marked by high levels of violence and explicit scenes of torture. We could say that the film is like a dramatized

Nunca Más focusing on the ordeals suffered by young people. This discussion on fictional representations of the horror, thus, centers on comments about this film, which all participants had seen and had things to say about. In particular, there is a scene of the main protagonist tied to a metal bed being tortured by an electric prod that was probably the most talked about scene of torture among interviewees. Thus, I pay special attention to participants' reactions to this and other scenes of violence.

Participants' stories of how the film affected them reveal that its portrayal of horror has been a catalyst for emotional reactions. For many, the film had been an eye-opener to what state terrorism was. Mariana's late grandfather was a high-ranking military officer and she had received other accounts of this past. She explained the impact the film had on her: "I don't know if I watched it because I covered my eyes all the time. Horrible, horrible, and I know that this was just one tenth of what may have actually happened."

Participants quoted some recurrent effects of the film, such as sadness, anger, and impotence. Elvira had known about the events of The Night of the Pencils since she was a little girl because the date also marks her birthday. She had seen the film many times and described her response:

I cry every time I watch it. I feel impotent. The brutality angers and hurts me, how [the military] abused and killed everybody. I cry seeing how they killed so many people, who were taken away, disappeared. And people wouldn't say anything, or wouldn't want to do anything, thus allowing it to happen. You feel impotence.

I also heard of the paralyzing effect that the film might have. Diego discussed his reaction when he saw the film in its television premiere:

It has strong scenes. I remember being very traumatized by that scene when they're torturing the guy with the electric prod. It was strong for a twelve-year-old. Moreover, I was left with a very bad impression about the film. I changed my mind later on. But I first had the feeling that the film was produced with the goal to stop us from being activists or demanding anything. Like a warning: "See, this is what follows if you raise your head." That's the vision I had. I was very critical of the film, absolutely against it. It seemed a film made by the enemy. Then, when I saw it again, I interpreted its message differently. But you need to read between the lines. Otherwise, it has a negative message.

There is no doubt that the film conveys terror and can generate fear. Noemí noted how the film makes the remains of fear in society more understandable:

Now I understand why people are so afraid. My mother is always worried that I'd be riding a bus at 1 AM. I never understood why. I'd say, "Fear of what? A guy may look at me and I'd talk to him and that's it. Maybe he touches me but I don't think he'd kill me." Until I saw *The Night of the Pencils* and understood how much fear there is. Even I became fearful.

Some participants mentioned reacting to the film like they would to any action movie as if there was not a clear connection between what the film depicts and recent historical events. For them, the film was a thriller and they were unable to see representations of repression targeted at people who could be their peers. This was true in Nora's case:

> I saw it as another movie. What happens is that my father and brothers love to watch war movies where everybody kills each other and bleeds to death. When I was younger, I also used to watch them with my family. So when I saw this film I didn't associate it with something from here that had recently happened. It was like another movie with everybody killing and being killed. I have flashes, the scene of this kid in the bed [the torture]. But I don't remember much. I don't know if I thought that it was not true.

This association needs to be analyzed more deeply. Research evaluating screen violence's effects suggests that viewers' reactions to a film depend on how real they perceive the portrayal of pain and suffering to be. But much of the high-tech screen violence is "pain free."[9] Its special effects allow viewers to dissociate themselves, resulting in the "killing of dummies" and the disappearance of pain.[10] Thus, we need to assess whether extensive exposure to violence on the screen translates into consumption of horror but desensitization toward it, whether the lack of contextual knowledge shapes these kinds of readings, or even whether this is a sign of denial of what went on during the dictatorship.

Ignorance about the past was a recurrent theme in discussing the impact of the graphical portrayal of violence. This was true in Leo's case. He explained the process by which his indifference turned into fear:

> Honestly, nothing happened to me. It's like another movie. It impacted me later. When I saw it a long time ago I didn't know that it was a film about real events that took place in Argentina. So I first took it lightly. And then, when I learned, when my father told me, I was a bit afraid.

Fernando, the self-defined apolitical participant, was very affected by the film. The violence depicted in it had contributed to his decision to avoid further contacts with this past:

> I felt pity; maybe I'm too sensitive. It made me feel very sad. I pictured myself in that situation, horror, and shivers. Do you understand? Because of my personality, I couldn't endure something like that. I don't like films about this historical period

because I cannot stand it. I reject it because it hurts me. I don't like it at all. Let's say that I'm susceptible to all human suffering, independently of the film's point of view. That feeling that people are scared, that you couldn't go to bed peacefully, that they'll plant a bomb on you, whatever.

One consequence of transmitting horror without contextual background is that horror is consumed but there is no critical elaboration of its reasons—a recurrent pattern among participants. Jorge's comments illustrate how this works:

[The film] gave me knowledge about things that I hadn't seen or experienced, because I'm eighteen and wasn't alive at that time. First, it shocked me how [the military] were, how they took people away. I then tried to understand why it happened and I couldn't. I cannot understand why a guy was taken away because he studied or was in someone's address book. Even today, I still cannot understand this. Guys that didn't do anything and were taken away, were killed, or are disappeared and no one knows what happened to them. I still cannot understand that. This is what I got from watching the film.

Thus, one of the effects on people who are being exposed for the first time to the events of the dictatorship through representations lacking contextual information may be an awareness of the horror but a lack of understanding of its genesis. What happened to Jorge is characteristic of the fragmented knowledge manifest throughout our conversations.

Nunca Más, the videos of the trials, and *The Night of the Pencils* illustrate how the main historical referents for the post-dictatorship generation are texts where horror is graphically depicted. The content that seems to have impacted participants the most is the detailed description of violence. Even in the case of texts (books, films) that have information on the structural nature of the repression, most references were to tortures. Contextual data, although available, had not been paid the same attention as the details of the horror. At times, it seems that interviewees looked for those horrific details in all the materials to which they were exposed or that the personal impact of those accounts did not allow them to see a more comprehensive account. Determining the reasons for this selective use of information and the consequences of exposure to graphic portrayals of violence is not an easy task.

A Note on Representing Horror: How Much Blood?

The focus on consuming horror needs to be further explored to understand better why there seems to be an attraction toward, even a fascination with, macabre representations. This is why the question of how to represent horror is so timely and relevant for exploring the reconstruction of memories of a violent past. Participants' comments suggest that there are two main concerns in analyzing this issue: why people gravitate toward horror and the consequences of consuming horror. The representation of horror raises several issues: What should be shown and what avoided? Does "more blood" guarantee a stronger response? Should the horror of real life be "softened" for public screening? When is a fictional reenactment of torture useful to inform and when does it turn into what Jean Franco calls "torture porn"?[11]

Representations of horror determine the scope of the possible interpretations of the message, as does the background information that each individual has and the particular moment at which the individual interprets those messages. Hence, at the core of the debate on how to represent horror are the considerations of the consequences that this information may have on people. Showing things as they were can frighten and have a paralyzing effect. And it may increase reluctance to learn more. After all, how many times can someone read a description or watch a scene of torture?

The consumption of horror also needs to be analyzed in relation to what may be a morbid attraction to the description of atrocities, probably encouraged by the media's portrayal of them. The global spectacle of horror, misery, and destruction is commonplace on television screens. As Barbie Zelizer puts it: "We live in a minefield of atrocity representations."[12] It seems that people are attracted to media coverage of disasters and can emotionlessly consume overdoses of images of famine, bombings, or massacres. Why would the case of the dictatorship be different?

Furthermore, we should bear in mind the kind of images to which young people had been exposed. We have seen that what had been intergenerationally transmitted also seemed to concentrate on describing atrocities. And we cannot ignore the effects that the yellow journalism style that characterized the beginning of civilian rule may have had on participants' elders and how it may have shaped what they told the younger generation. Witnesses to the terror remember the repression based both on what they experienced and on what they learned through the media once the public disclosures of the horror began.

The market had also tried to co-opt the horrors of the dictatorship for advertising campaigns. There was an ad for Diesel jeans published in *Colors*, Benetton's magazine, showing young people wearing jeans, their hands tied, presumably dead, at the bottom of the ocean. The copy of the ad read: "These are not your first jeans but could be your last ones. At least, you will leave behind a beautiful corpse." This macabre use—as a selling point—of an event so common during the repression where prisoners, brutally tortured and still alive, were thrown into the ocean crystallizes the level of perversion and superficiality with which human rights violations have been treated.[13]

To discuss the representation and consumption of horror, I encouraged participants to recommend how they would transmit the events of the dictatorship, often asking them to position themselves as ministers of communication or education. I specifically encouraged them to advise on the doses of violence that they thought should be incorporated.

Among the advocates of minimizing exposure to torture the main point was the disturbing nature of the topic and the negative impact that descriptions of torture might have. This was Laura's opinion:

> I think that the theme of tortures is counterproductive. Because it's such a tough topic, always shocking. You learn about it reading *Nunca Más*. I was never allowed to read it but I've read parts of it. Not only about tortures here, I've read about tortures in Chile, a book by an Uruguayan journalist who went to Chile during the dictatorship and interviewed someone. For me, reading is more explicit than a film. It's terrible to read how they pull out their nails or how they introduced the electric prod to women. It's not for everybody.

Laura's reference to *Nunca Más* is yet another example of a generalized pattern in reading the report: focusing on the tortures and skipping the rest.

Another concern was the notion that the description of tortures covers other issues, that there are details of horror in lieu of its genesis and structures. This was Marta's worry when she discussed how to teach the dictatorship to children and pointed to the upsetting effects of highlighting torture:

> I don't know if I'd be very meticulous with tortures and all that stuff. Because it might be shocking for kids and it may not be the most important thing to highlight. Sometimes, by highlighting [torture] other things are covered up.

Participants also talked about the saturation with horror produced by over-emphasizing graphic violence. One of its consequences would be that people close their eyes to this information, which would increase ignorance about the dictatorship. Description of atrocities would therefore act as a metaphorical scarecrow.

Eugenia illustrated this effect with her reluctance to read *Nunca Más*:

> My mother was never able to read it because she'd heard comments of those who read it. It tells everything that [the military] did, how they tortured. So my mother told me that she didn't want to read it. I haven't read it yet. Because to think that it was real made me want to . . . not reject it . . . but it's as if I say, "OK, stop it, it's over," not to forget but to say, "It's enough with all this; I know what happened."

Regardless of the concerns about the perceived consequences of representations emphasizing tortures, most participants maintained that young people should learn the details of the violence that characterized state terrorism. They stressed the necessity to show graphically how things really had been in order for people to understand what went on. According to Diego:

> I think that we've to show everything but with an objective. If it were up to me, my goal wouldn't be to provoke terror. I'd show you the tortures with the aim of mobilizing rather than scaring you.

One argument, thus, was that the magnitude of the repression needed to be conveyed without minimizing its quantitative or qualitative features. As Pedro said: "I'd include a lot. I'd show more torture so [people] would know everything that was done, how [prisoners] suffered. You've to include more torture because only one torture [scene] isn't enough." Even participants who were extremely upset by this type of description insisted on the need for young people to be exposed to these portrayals of violence.

Mercedes's opinions were along these lines, suggesting that exposure to the horror is a rite of passage that young Argentineans should go through, in spite of its potential disturbing effects:

It's very painful for me to remember all this. It depresses me, immensely. I notice that this didn't use to happen to me before. I don't know if it was due to the lack of conscience or to the fearlessness of the young. [Young people] have to know this. It devastates me now but I've seen all of these types of testimonies. They've to know it. If not, everything appears light. Doesn't it? Yes, there were *desaparecidos*, there was torture and that's it.

Among participants who stressed that people must see the violence in order to believe it there were references to television, pointing to the credentials of the medium as a certification of reality and to the styles of representation it establishes. This was argued during a discussion with two of the high school students who produced a community radio program. According to Andrés:

Look at the announcements for traffic accidents. Before, they used to say, "Drive slowly," "Don't make a wrong turn." Now, they directly show you the videos. There's that commercial where the little girl says, "Dad, you almost ran over the old lady." Everything is about accidents. They show you the crash and the head flying. Otherwise people don't realize that they've to drive slowly until they see [the effects].

And this is how Víctor complemented these thoughts:

People seem to react when they see the things on television. If not, it's as if they didn't happen. That's a role that television has taken. I don't know. It seems that [people] are half-asleep; there are things that they don't see.

It is hard to assess whether people react as expected to these visual portrayals of violence. Among participants, there was no consensus on how to best convey the horror from a perspective critical of the human rights violations. The perceived potential effects of consuming horror seemed to vary depending on the particular individual. Moreover, participants' answers were indicative of their own reactions to the graphic portrayal of horror and violence. By rationalizing what they would do, they were arguably signaling the impact on them of what they had seen or read.

Conclusions

Throughout our conversations, we have seen how participants' stories reveal that the consumption of horror took priority over the critical analysis of its genesis and structural nature. This is undoubtedly linked to what the different texts about the past had offered. But young people seemed to have consistently focused on the description of atrocities. Whether or not participants looked for horror or its impact did not allow them to see the rest is another unanswered question.

There were concrete signs of the consequences of this apparent saturation with the details of the horror, ranging from paralyzing fear to the refusal to learn more, and including a certain indifference toward it. These patterns of consumption of the horror had added to the legacy of fears and silences that had contributed to shaping a fragmented and decontextualized knowledge of the dictatorship. They help to explain why there is awareness of the atrocities that took place but little understanding of the reasons why they happened.

With regard to the predominance of horror details in participants' accounts or why people look for the horror, it may well be that horror is so powerful that it buries other information. It may also be that they consciously selected these particular accounts, and even that there could be a morbid attraction to the description of atrocities, probably influenced by the media coverage of them.

Hence, the representation of traumatic pasts, from which no "real" images are left, was subject to debate. Participants' arguments regarding the perceived positive and negative consequences of the graphic portrayal of the violence attest to the complexity of this issue. Each of the opinions that I heard was well thought out, sincere, and focused on the best way to educate the next generations about the dictatorship's crimes. Although there seemed to be agreement that people should know how things were, and on the dangers of softening reality, there were disagreements on the doses of this reality that would be appropriate for public transmission. This is still an unresolved problem. How different texts continue to tell and represent the past horror will either reinforce or disrupt these patterns for its consumption. This, in turn, will shape the scope and content of the postmemories of terror.

Conversations about Human Rights Activism

Introduction

Throughout our conversations, it was evident that the relatives of the *desaparecidos* had become "memorial candles" of this past, as Dina Wardi theorized about the descendants of Holocaust survivors.[1] They have been assigned the heavy burden of continuously reminding society of the dictatorship's crimes and of pursuing truth and justice. They cannot afford to forget or give up.

This chapter looks at human rights activism from two angles. One focuses on young people's opinions on the role activists, specifically the mothers and children of *desaparecidos*, play in society as "memory-keepers" and "justice-seekers," their relationship with society at large, and the effectiveness of their struggles. The other includes conversations with children of the disappeared, whose different experiences and memories help to contextualize and compare the content and perspectives of the "gray zoners" postmemories, including the ever present line between active participants and passive spectators in the process of accountability. Recurrent themes such as fear, silences, knowledge, historical explanations, impunity, indifference, and the media emerge here through the voices of the activist children of the *desaparecidos*.

Participants discussed the goals and tactics of the Mothers of the Plaza de Mayo, HIJOS,[2] and the Grandmothers of the Plaza de Mayo. They talked about mothers seeking their vanished children, children seeking missing parents, and grandmothers seeking stolen babies. Talk about the Grandmothers' activism was in general limited to the discussion of what to do with these children, most of them born in captivity. But when talking about memory issues, the Mothers and HIJOS were the two organizations symbolizing human rights activism within the witness and post-dictatorship generations respectively. These activists have undoubtedly defined a model of activism and comparable groups have emerged in other countries. There are, for instance, Widows in Guatemala (CONAVIGUA, Comisión Nacional de Viudas Guatemaltecas), COMADRES, (the Committee of Mothers and Relatives of Political Prisoners, Disappeared, and Assassinated of El Salvador), and groups of children of victims of the repression in Chile and Guatemala.[3]

The Mothers of the Plaza de Mayo have been marching since April 1977. Every Thursday, from 3:30 to 4:30 PM, their presence in the Plaza de Mayo brings back the *desaparecidos* and reminds society of the dictatorship's unpunished crimes. This weekly public ritual has become a landmark of human rights activism, a *lieu de mémoire* that codifies memories of this past. As Eduardo Galeano notes, "future history professors will explain the 20th Century through its symbols" and "to explain dignity, they will show the white scarf of the [Mothers'] marches in the Plaza de Mayo."[4] HIJOS has also developed a powerful strategy of public condemnation: the *escraches*, which are demonstrations that aim to expose the identities of hundreds of torturers and assassins benefiting from impunity laws. (The word *escrachar* is an Argentine slang term meaning "to uncover").[5] Marchers invade the neighborhoods where the *represores* live and inform the community of the atrocities they committed, giving out facts such as photographs, names, addresses, and details of what they did during the dictatorship, cases of human rights violations in which they are implicated, and their current occupation and place of work.[6]

Many interviewees highlighted how these two groups prevent the closing of the book on the past. As Lucía summarized:

> If the Mothers give up, if HIJOS stops doing *escraches*, and we go on while torturers and assassins are treated as ordinary people, we will really forget what happened. Maybe all those who pass by the Thursday marches see [the Mothers] and remember. [This] maintains the memory. If the Mothers and the HIJOS are no longer there, everything would disappear, [as if] nothing ever happened.

Opinions about Human Rights Activists

How do young people see the Mothers of the Plaza de Mayo? Not surprisingly, participants had different, often contradictory, opinions about the group, ranging from praise to accusations of political manipulation, and including doubts about their achievements.

Supporters of the Mothers see them as the embodiment of the battle against impunity and as indefatigable memory keepers. Mercedes expressed well an understanding of the collective character of their activism and the awareness of society's relationship to the *desaparecidos*—that is, she talked of "our dead" rather than "their children":

> I deeply admire their determination and strength. It's a blessing that they exist because they're the ones who keep the memory alive so people can remember what happened. I think that the wounds left in society by the dictatorship are very deep. I don't think people could forget. But I believe that the fact the Mothers are there is like a red light reminding us: These are the Mothers of our dead. [The Mothers] obtain the reopening of legal causes, so that many military officers and civilians implicated [in the repression] are brought back to trial. I don't know if that would happen without them.

There was also mention of the Mothers' marches as crucial referents of the repression. Omar, a fifteen-year-old high school student, spoke of them as hard-to-avoid reminders:

> If there's anything that's powerful, that's it, that everybody is there on a determined day, week after week. More than anything, they show a lot of resolution, at least to those who go. I don't think it's easy to walk by and see the Mothers of youths who were disappeared or killed. I think you need a lot of courage to pass by and ignore them. I don't think it's possible.

I also heard about the Mothers' talks at schools. Elvira shared her experience:

> We were very interested when we talked with the Mothers of the Plaza de Mayo, because they're Mothers who look for a way to struggle through their suffering. In spite of the many years that went by, they keep on struggling and fighting. You could say that they're resigned because they know that their children are dead and they won't find them. But what they want is that the assassins appear, because there are people who are responsible, who gave orders, who killed.

Víctor was part of this conversation and reinforced these views by pointing to the larger framework of the Mothers' struggle:

> It's important what she says. For example, the Mothers initiated a fight to look for their children. That was all. But they ended up fighting for what everybody should be fighting for, which is social justice, what we need here.

Some participants talked about their admiration for the Mothers' ethics, which is an exception within a social environment of corruption and lies, and of their being among the few in society who speak with the truth. Pablo praised Hebe de Bonafini, president of the *Asociación Madres de Plaza de Mayo*:

I wanted to buy that [book] from Hebe de Bonafini that's all about what happened. But there's no money. She's the one that pushes forward to clean this all up. I think [the book] tells the truth, like when she goes on television programs. She talked the other day with Grondona [conservative host of political debate program]. She challenged him [to his face]: "In the past, you sided with the military, what now?" I was riveted. I had seen her in other programs but that day I listened to her more carefully and gave her more credit. She goes head on.

However, recognition of the Mothers' moral superiority or understanding of their suffering didn't always match perceptions of their achievements. Comments such as those of Beatriz—claiming that their search has no sense at this point in time, based on the impossibility of finding the *desaparecidos*—failed to consider the relevance of pursuing justice:

I think these ladies must be very hurt by what happened. It's logical; it's not easy to lose a child. But the current government isn't responsible for what happened twenty years ago and can't do anything. Even with investigations. If your daughter was thrown into the ocean, she's already eaten by creatures. Nothing can be done now. They can't empty the ocean to look for your daughter. It's over. I mean, it's not over, the suffering will continue for as long as you live. But the current government can't do anything, except bring to trial those involved.

Antonio answered my question as to whether or not he knew the Mothers of the Plaza de Mayo by reflecting on the futility of their activism:

They're the mothers of the kids disappeared during the proceso that are constantly protesting, always struggling to find out what happened to their children. What they're doing is the same as nothing. There's nothing they can do. Tell me what they've achieved? They have no possibilities. Why? Because the military are free, because of all that's going on. They can't stay at home without knowing what happened to their children. That's why they've been doing this for twenty years.

There were other comments denouncing the politicization of the Mothers. According to Fabiana, a fifteen-year-old student:

I think it's pure politics. Because I think that if a mother wants justice she won't go on a TV program to say, "I want my son to appear." Obviously, there are different ways of thinking but I think they're more interested in politics than anything else.

I also heard opinions that human rights activists have a political agenda aimed at manipulating the younger generation. Guillermo was emphatic in accusing supporters of the Mothers and insisting on another "version" of the events:

> I think that all those surrounding the Mothers have no idea of how [the dictatorship] was. These are the people who brainwash their grandchildren and others and then the latter say, "If my grandma says so, she must have a reason." They have no opinions, nor the character to say "No, I'll investigate and find out [what happened]." [They] always resort to what's easy, to what grandma teaches. And maybe we should look at it from a different angle, analyze the point of view of [the Mothers of] the Plaza de Mayo through what the coup really was.

Attacks on the Human Rights Movement's Credibility

Accusations of political manipulation are not the only way of discrediting the human rights movement. Some comments showed the transmission of discourses very critical of activists, specifically of the main leaders, who are women. The criticisms center on the credibility and mental health of those activists, mirroring the criticisms made during the dictatorship. At that time, the Mothers of the Plaza de Mayo did what none in society dared to do: demonstrate publicly for the return of their children. Not surprisingly, they were called the *locas* (crazy ladies).[7] The first time that the dictatorship's Minister of the Interior General Harguindeguy received a group of anguished Mothers, he insulted them, suggesting that their sons may have run off with a woman or that their daughters may have been working as prostitutes somewhere.[8]

Discredit of those who struggle for human rights (and indirectly of the *desaparecidos*) had been handed on to the next generation. Twenty years later, and in spite of the irrefutable documentation on disappearances, I heard rumors that the children of some of the Mothers might be living in another country.

Carmen commented on doubts cast over the Mothers:

> They say that there's one, Hebe de Bonafini, whose children are in Spain, not disappeared. They say that some [Mothers] know where their children are, that they're really alive, that they fight for money, politics, this and that. They're [comments] from the TV and from people who, for instance, belong to Catholic groups. My mother and I live in the house of a lady who belongs to Catholic groups. A lady from Caritas [Catholic welfare organization] told her that, yes, she knows from reliable sources that Hebe de Bonafini's sons are in Spain.

It seems that these bad faith arguments circulate in various spheres, not only within Church circles—where this should not be surprising given the Catholic hierarchy's collaboration with the dictatorship. But as Graciela said, "I don't think that [the son] is in Spain. It's just popular folklore." However, despite the fact that no participant actually believed this rumor, rumors do instill doubts. Putting aside the possibility of survivors who changed identities or left the country (something very difficult to verify because of the difficulty of documenting every case) these statements reveal that, for some, it is more convenient to believe that people left rather than that they disappeared.

Worries about the mental health of the women who fight for human rights was another concept transmitted. At the time of this study, Graciela Fernandez Meijide was a potential presidential candidate for La Alianza, the main opposition party for the October 1999 elections.[9] Her teenage son disappeared and, although she did not belong to the Mothers of the Plaza de Mayo, the idea that mothers of *desaparecidos* are *locas* may for some constitute grounds to doubt her capacity to hold office.[10] Mónica had this story:

> Meijide has a disappeared son and I heard people saying, "She must be crazy because she has a disappeared son and she can do anything once in power." As if having a disappeared son would make her want to implement things that don't benefit the people. I don't know if she's crazy because of that. I don't think that's the issue. She lived a reality shared by many people and it may be good if people who went through that were in power.

Paradoxically, many voters did not question the qualifications of torturers and assassins to be governors or mayors. It seems that some people were more concerned about the public actions of someone who had suffered than of those who had tortured and killed. They did not seem to care about the level of monstrosity of the *represores* and how this condition may affect their performance. Or, as Mónica suggested, they failed to consider that it may be beneficial for society to elect those who were directly affected by the repression to office.

Conversations with Human Rights Activists: HIJOS

Most of the young people with whom I talked sympathized with HIJOS, the organization of the activist children of *desaparecidos*, assassinated militants, political prisoners, and exiles, and many of whose members belonged to participants' generational cohort. (At the time of these interviews, 1998, the average age of the members of HIJOS was mid-twenties to late twenties). HIJOS thus emerged as the bearers of memory with whom participants could strongly identify and relate. In general, there were no conflicts in understanding their experiences and their quest for justice.[11]

Mercedes, who also had great respect for the Mothers, voiced a generalized opinion:

> It's their own history; so they have to be involved in this kind of activism. If it hurts all of us it must hurt them much more. It's logical that they demand justice. They

were deprived of the possibility of knowing their parents, living with them, having a normal life.

Even Jorge, who was critical of most human rights groups' activities, had only words of praise for HIJOS:

> You see, I do agree with them, yes. These guys are not the same as the Mothers of the Plaza de Mayo. You can say whatever you want but it's not the same. These guys are OK. Maybe they can find their parents in the future. And they're struggling so they'll tell them who did it, where their parents are, obtain the lists. The guys from HIJOS struggle because they know that there are lists with their parents' names.

Talking with members of HIJOS provides a marked contrast with the participants of this study—the activists as compared to the "gray zoners." Their postmemories are shaped by their particular stories and experiences, all of them marked by tragedy and suffering. There are significant differences in knowledge and points of view about the dictatorship. Moreover, their activism is fueled by powerful feelings and unyielding commitment that drive them to demand justice with an intensity that differs greatly from the vast majority of the young people with whom I talked.

I conducted interviews and had several informal conversations with members of HIJOS. I also attended lectures they organized and participated in a couple of their *escraches*. I share here comments made by HIJOS about recurrent themes addressed throughout my conversations with "gray zoners" and presented in this book. They have much to say about fears, silences, knowledge and ignorance of the dictatorship, impunity, society's indifference, and prospects for accountability. I transcribe here the voices of four members of HIJOS. With Martín and Juan, I conducted in-depth interviews. Florencia and Eduardo were panelists at an event held on July 14, 1998, at the Teatro Del Pueblo, a theater in downtown Buenos Aires. Their statements are responses to questions from the panel moderator and the public, which addressed similar issues to the ones I discussed during my interviews. This is what the HIJOS had to say: their personal stories and feelings, their demands and strategies of struggle, their interaction with the media and society at large, and their advice to the post-dictatorship generation.[12]

Personal Stories and Feelings

The personal stories and feelings of members of HIJOS help us to understand their pain and suffering, their fears, their anger, and the reasons why they got together and organized.

> At an individual level, I believe that many of us got together because of the pain and then realized that there are many things that you can do with that pain. At the beginning, the feeling may be, "Why is my dad disappeared?" Of course we are afraid. We undergo all these things, as anybody does. (Florencia)

Most of us witnessed the kidnapping of our parents. Some of our *compañeros* were born in captivity, others, after being kidnapped, were left at an orphanage. Let's say that we're well aware of how each operative went. I think that the pain doesn't diminish, doesn't stop. What can be done is to share it. We share it and that's what strengthens us the most. A recurrent question posed to us, especially from the younger people, is if we're afraid. Maybe yes, we're afraid and that's why we get together. We, daughters and sons, get together and share our pain, not only over our relatives but also for 30,000 *desaparecidos*. Let's assume it, they were not only our relatives, they were militants in the popular arena, they were the best of society at that time in the 70s and their struggle was the struggle of everybody, for everybody. (Eduardo)

Both my mom and dad [disappeared]. I was one-month old. My dad was kidnapped at a meeting place that was given away. They went for my mother at the house where we lived and left me with a neighbor. At dawn, heavily armed police surrounded the house of my aunt and uncle. They told them to go pick me up and gave them the address where I was. (Martín)

I belong to the generation of children of exiles. I don't have disappeared parents, I've exiled parents. It's not only the 30,000 *desaparecidos*, which is the most relevant event because it's the most aberrant. But there are also two million exiles, 10,000 political prisoners, and thousands of assassinations. And there are also exiles within the country, *compañeros* of my parents who were forced to move around the country with their families to avoid being killed. This is another form; it's internal exile. Exile is a tough topic. We were born abroad but I wanted to come and meet my grandparents, to know this country. I always felt Argentinean. I had a lot of resentment. To be the child of a *desaparecido* generates a lot of resentment, to be born in exile generates a lot of resentment, to know that your parents were tortured and raped generates a lot of anger. (Juan)

Demands, Strategies, and Styles of Struggle

HIJOS's demands reflect their well-defined categorization of who the culprits are. Theirs was an all-inclusive list, beyond military personnel, and with careful assessment of different levels of responsibility. They were very clear on what the just punishment for culprits should be and had no doubts that the dictatorship's crimes must be punished.

We're going to demand prison for the *genocidas* and their accomplices from anybody, from whoever is in power. The only place for an assassin is jail and there's no democracy without justice. When we talk of trial and punishment for all the guilty and their accomplices we don't exclusively refer to low range military officers. We talk of the business groups that benefited, the priests who blessed the tortures, the political parties that delivered their men to participate in the municipal governments, embassies, whatever. They're also accomplices of the dictatorship, the repression, the assassinations, the kidnappings. (Eduardo)

While the demands of HIJOS are comparable to those of other human rights organizations, the creativity and style of their strategies—in particular the *escraches*—had made the group very visible and well known. Moreover, their campaigns paid special attention to targeting the post-dictatorship generation.

The way of reaching people is through talks at school, through *escraches*. With *escraches* we go directly to inform the neighbors: "Here lives so and so who did such and such." We have a newspaper. Talks at schools are to preserve the memory. At the same time, we're telling [students], "We have to act, we have to fight for our rights." HIJOS doesn't trust this justice, doesn't trust this government. We only bet on the struggle in the streets. Whenever we do something, we always do it for the whole society. Although older people may already have a view you cannot change, we can reach young people, who may have an opinion, or who don't know, but pay more attention to us. (Martín)

Thus, talks at school are a key component of HIJOS's activism. They explained the dynamics of these presentations:

Talks happen through schools that are interested and contact us, via a teacher or principal who's more open-minded than the rest and invites us. Also via the student center or students who know quite a lot about the issues, not because they were directly affected but because their parents told them much more than those of other kids and they want to do something about it. So we go and talk briefly about our personal stories and then focus on explaining what we do and why we do it. (Martín)

HIJOS also discussed the goal of their *escraches*, their landmark communication strategy:

[We aim] for repudiation by the people, so assassins cannot walk calmly in the streets knowing that people, neighbors, will repudiate them. That's why we organize *escraches*, to tell the neighbors, "Look, you have an assassin next door." This is the idea, that people condemn them, so they don't feel comfortable in their homes, or streets, nor when they go to a bar, or to Church, or any place. (Juan)

Interaction between HIJOS and Society at Large

HIJOS's interaction with society at large, in particular with the post-dictatorship generation, highlights the differences between activists and larger sectors of society. Be it through their friends, classmates, and coworkers, or through talks at schools and at other public events, HIJOS activists find that the societal fears, silences, ignorance, and apparent apathy that we discussed in previous chapters, usually emerge in these realms.

This is what HIJOS had to say regarding difficulties in communicating with "non-HIJOS":

> What happened to all of us, when we talked to people who were not directly affected by the dictatorship, is that it wasn't easy. Some [people] got interested and some didn't. With those who were interested but didn't understand, it was difficult to explain or have a conversation about it. This doesn't happen among us. You say something and it's understood [by all]. At times, some get hooked. In general, my friends didn't hook into my stuff. I'd say, "I'm going to a march, would you like to come?" And, no, they wouldn't come. (Martín)

HIJOS also spoke about the lack of knowledge about the repression, making specific links between fear and ignorance. And, in discussing the historical explanations given to the younger generation on why it happened, HIJOS blamed the "Two Devils" theory for the misconceptions. Moreover, they elaborated on the reasons for the gap between what activists and nonactivists know.

> What happens is that kids don't know or know very little. Then, there's the fear their parents kept. Because the dictatorship terrorized everybody and fear remained. So parents transmit it; they're afraid that something will happen [to their children]. In reality, what parents have is fear. [At school], they don't address the topic. It's not included in the study plans, or only certain things are included. But it's not covered in the schools because the dynamic doesn't allow it and anyway education is so bad that programs are often abandoned. For sure, [students] bring up the theory of the Two Devils. They say, "But they [desaparecidos] also planted bombs, killed people." It's also a matter of education. Beyond the fear, we have this economic model that obviously won't allow discussion of these issues. OK, there's talk, but only from the perspective of Two Devils, not about the desaparecidos as revolutionaries who wanted social change. (Martín)

> We've been very active with talks at schools and there have been some surprises, good and bad ones. For example, one day a girl asked if it was true that Luis Miguel [contemporary singer] was banned during the dictatorship. Those things are quite upsetting. Like that survey published a couple of years ago in the magazine La Maga, an important cultural publication, where they asked high school kids who was Che [Guevara] and one kid said, "A leader from the 19th century." It generates anger among activists, that there's so much ignorance, that they don't want to learn, that only a few of us are constantly concerned with these issues. But we also understand that they aren't solely responsible for this situation. We know that this was a goal of the dictatorship, and it worked. To disappear 30,000 people and implement a plan

of total extermination that's related to people's ignorance. To keep people ignorant so they cannot defend their rights, so they won't take to the streets and fight, so they won't demand what's theirs. (Juan)

HIJOS were extremely critical of educational plans and how they were affecting young people's attitudes. But they noted that, in spite of the attempts to paralyze society and erase history, young people showed interest in the past.

The invitations to participate in talks, debates at high school student centers, or when some teachers from primary school invite us to share our testimonies with their students, are, somehow, very interesting starting points. When these high school students ask us, "What can we do to help you?" we answer them, "Organize yourselves." So the response of young people is quite positive, in spite of all the cultural restraints for any debate. (Eduardo)

I don't believe that there's no consciousness. What I do believe is that there was the imposition of a strong fear, at the general level, in all areas, in all places of society. It's difficult to connect. It's very difficult to reorganize, reunite. It's a very slow process. As time goes by, many young people are approaching us. They may be kids who are just finishing high school, without any concrete background about the coup, without having received good history lessons. Because the history taught in both primary and high school is a history amputated of a series of historical events and social subjects. In spite of this, there's a certain common sense that says, "There's something weak here, something that's not right." And, slowly, people approach us, get together, and reunite again. We at HIJOS perceive this. (Florencia)

Two Devils was necessarily linked to the historical explanations young people had received, to the reasons why people disappeared, and to the generalized ignorance about the political activism of most of the *desaparecidos*.

Many [people] think that, even if there are, more or less, 30,000 [disappeared], they're all people involved in something rare, something ugly. What's even worse, is when they say that they disappeared for being [involved] in something rare. We define this something rare, as solidarity, commitment, and a project for a more just society. The foreword of the *Nunca Más* opens with the theory of the Two Devils. It sucks that issues are presented in such a way. When they tell me that our parents planted bombs and killed, I discuss this from a legal perspective. I believe that, if there was justice, what you do to the guerrillas who did that, is to allow their right to lawyers, send them to prisons without torturing them, because torture is illegal and, above all, they shouldn't disappear. Moreover, from my personal story, my parents, neither my mom nor my dad killed anybody, tortured anybody, raped anybody. And, yes, they were forced to leave the country. So? (Juan)

There was constant mention of fear, either in connection with ignorance or as a catalyst for learning and acting. HIJOS pointed to contemporary forms of repression adding new fears and reinforcing old fears:

> Repression has many forms. Young people aren't repressed only for one reason. They're repressed when they go to concerts, to a demonstration. Going to a concert implies being careful of the police, drinking in the streets, and not necessarily a beer, implies being careful of the police. And to participate in many activities where there are gatherings, including going to a soccer match, implies being careful of the police. In the last five or seven years there's a growing awareness that in all these places, supposedly recreational, the police represses. This also generates consciousness, in spite of the fear instilled for such a long time. (Florencia)

The Communication Media

HIJOS shared observations about the communications media. They discussed some experiences and strategies to deal with journalists and invitations to participate in television programs, such as the ones of Mirta Legrand (who has been inviting people to lunch five days a week for over three decades) and of yellow journalist Mauro Viale.

> Mirta Legrand invited us, but many shitty people have sat around that table. So we discussed going and how. We voted to go but to talk to the producers so it's a table convenient for us, without any assassin. A table where we can talk calmly without entering into an argument that would probably be based on the theory of the Two Devils. Because it's very upsetting when they start saying "But your father planted bombs." This generates an argument on a program that's not political, because one day you have an actor, another a movie star and a musician, and another day there's [President] Menem. There are programs like the one of Mauro Viale where you can go without invitation. One day there was Turco Julián [the infamous torturer] and some children of *desaparecidos* who weren't from HIJOS And they confronted that guy, who's sinister. Producers and audience encouraged them, "Well, you want to punch him, go and hit him," things like that, very clownish that don't serve any purpose, bread and circus. People thinking, "Let's see if he beats him or not," and the kid cries, "You're an assassin, you're an assassin, my dad." You can't go to that type of program. (Martín)
>
> When you lose the political angle of the situation and it becomes a personal matter, that the kid who lost his father has in front of him the guy who killed him. It turns into that. And it's not that way. It's a political matter. These programs don't give us a space to say that our parents disappeared for a concrete reason, because they had a project for a more solidary and just country. (Juan)

I also heard comments about media representations of the dictatorship, in particular the problems with graphic portrayals of violence.

If we see the book *Nunca Más*, a lot of blood comes from it. You squeeze it and blood pours from it. The issue with *The Night of the Pencils* is that it shows what happened to a particular group of students who struggled for a student bus fare and were kidnapped and disappeared for that. In addition to struggling for that, the kids were organized and, being younger and high school students, did the same things that my parents did. It's not that they struggled only for that bus fare, they wanted other things as well. But the film doesn't show it. So the kids watch the film and think, "They struggled for a bus fare and were killed." And it's paralyzing. It paralyzes some, others feel bad, and others don't care and do things. But, in general, it generates fear. It's the same with parents when they talk about this topic and the student centers. They say "Leave the center, focus on studying." (Martín)

HIJOS's Advice to Young People

In spite of their disappointment at the ignorance and apparent apathy of the postdictatorship generation, HIJOS were, as we have seen, optimists for what they saw as an awakening of young people, an undeniable sign of the overcoming of fear and apathy. Thus, their advice to them was a call for active participation, for switching from bystanders to actors.

We want to stress the importance of uniting, of being able to overcome the role of spectator and access that other place, the realm of action, of playing an active role in something. Something that has to do with your own identity, with the identity that each one assumes and considers her own. Get organized, assemble, unite, resist. It's possible to change things. We wouldn't be here if it weren't the case, and you wouldn't be here, nor people that have been struggling throughout many years, not only for the last 20 years, but throughout our history. This is important. Maybe in simple ways, without many complications, organizing in a neighborhood for community activities or at the university to discuss the budget. There are many ways. The important thing is to rescue [activism], to switch from being a passive spectator into being an active subject, a subject that resists and doesn't need to tolerate all the repressions that we experience in this model. (Florencia)

Conclusions

These conversations about human rights activism and with HIJOS illustrate well the marked gap between two very different memory communities within the postdictatorship generation: the activists and the "gray zoners." Relatives of the disappeared have indeed became "memorial candles." This is manifest both in what participants said about activists and in the way that the HIJOS have assumed their mission to challenge amnesia, educate about the past, and struggle against impunity.

Among "gray zoners," there was a trend toward evaluating the relatives' activism in emotional terms. Stressing the pain inflicted on the victims' families often prevented a deeper analysis of the relationship between society at large and the direct victims of the repression. The result is a concern for "their" suffering, rather than "our" suffering, or an admiration for what "they" do, rather than what "we" do, which may create distances rather than build bridges.

HIJOS, on the other hand, does not center its activism on personal stories. Its members share experiences that brought them together. But they minimize their individual stories and suffering by focusing on the political goals and strategies of their organization. They have a good understanding of the genesis of and support for state terrorism and vindicate their parents' political activism. They do not want people to feel sorry for them but rather to understand what happened, why it happened, how the events affected the whole social body, and the need for everybody to participate in the pursuit of truth and justice.

Except for a few exceptions, the wide gap between activists and participants was evident. When comparing my conversations with these two groups, I felt that I was listening to young people living in two different worlds although within the same city. The interaction or isolation between these two groups will either close or widen this gap. This will, in turn, shape the "gray zoners'" postmemories of terror and influence their positions as either passive spectators or active subjects in processes of memory-keeping and justice-seeking. The HIJOS were working hard to build bridges with their peers, aware of the reasons for the generalized ignorance among the younger generation, conscious of the challenges they faced, energized by their achievements, and convinced that young people do care about this past and that the paralyzing remains of fear were gradually fading.

Afterword

This has been a journey into young Argentineans' postmemories of terror, an exploration into how the events of the dictatorship were being constructed, transmitted, and reconstructed. Participants' voices have shed light on young people's understanding of what happened and why it happened, the sources on which they base their knowledge, what their attitudes toward this historical period and its aftermath were, and how particular ways of remembering shape opinions and actions.

The information gathered is rich, varied, complex and, most important, indicative of an ongoing dynamic process of which this research has grasped a specific moment, in a specific place, at a particular point in time. What I have shared in this study are a series of snapshots of how a group of young Argentineans from Buenos Aires were thinking and feeling about the events of the dictatorship in the year 1998, a vital period of renewed contestation of events the elite considered were safely buried in public amnesia. These conversations, thus, do not aim to present "the definitive truth" about how this past was being incorporated into Argentineans' memories; rather they identify patterns of memory transmission through what young people knew about this period, how they learned what they knew, and how they were processing this information.

We can say that participants perceived the long-term effects of the dictatorship on society as engraved for current and future generations and that the post-dictatorship generation "remembered" the horror experienced by the witness generation. People had not forgotten what happened and current fears were proof of how strong and deep postmemories of terror are. It is worth noting the dictatorship's capacity to extend its silencing and paralyzing effects for over two decades translated into a lack of talk about the past, a lack of political participation, and the encouragement of amnesia—"don't talk, don't remember, don't participate, don't demand justice." And I am concerned about the potential consequences for young people extremely critical of the atrocities committed but somehow resigned to live under a culture of impunity. I am disturbed by the social ramifications of a new apolitical generation that adopts a bystander position.

Processes of memory construction work through exposure over time to a series of sources of transmission, including the family, the school, and the media. This combination of sources and multiplicity of texts were shaping young people's postmemories. Each memory community to which participants belonged had contributed to shape representations of the past. What was discussed or silenced at home had been re-elaborated by stories heard through peers, teachers, or the media. I found that participants who had been, over the years or simultaneously, part of several memory communities, were, at the time of this fieldwork, elaborating varied, and often contradictory, representations of the dictatorship. Most of them seemed to be in the middle of an ongoing process, still in need of organizing and digesting information to fill an incomplete puzzle and finally understand what happened during the terror.

It is difficult to assess how belonging to a specific group determines a particular way of remembering. For instance, what prevails in the memory of the daughter of a police officer? Is it what she heard at home or what she was told by a woman with a disappeared sister whom she met at Church? What is more influential on a teenager, his family's insistence on how terrible this period was or his peers' encouragement to be apolitical and stop thinking about what happened? Thus, the particular experiences of participants' families during the dictatorship do shape ways of remembering but do not determine them.

Fear and silences have been highly effective in determining how the dictatorship has been explained and how these accounts have been endorsed or challenged. Terror emerged as a vivid memory but, overall, young people were not clear on why the horror had taken place, and this was affecting how they incorporated this past into the present. Many participants lacked the information for a deeper analysis and a critical elaboration of this past. There was limited awareness of its complexity, ranging from ignorance about the genesis of state terrorism or its supporters to a narrow awareness of how society at large was affected by the terror—well summarized by comments such as "The military didn't do anything to me." There was an absence of knowledge about society's role during the repression and of how fear, ignorance, indifference, or collaboration may explain its passive spectator position during and after the dictatorship.

But, at the time of this fieldwork, there were ongoing battles for the control of the past, and institutional forgetting was challenged by a memory "from below." In spite of the official plans to regulate memory with legislation that would encourage political amnesia, the dictatorship continued to resurface. This suggests that society was undergoing a process whereby the importance and presence that this past had in the present could be altered. This could be triggered by an array of factors, such as new friends, coworkers, a professor, a book, a film, or a television program. Postmemories, thus, were in constant transformation.

In 1998, the culture of fear had been replaced by a culture of impunity. Current events suggest that sectors of the generation that witnessed the terror are rewriting its history through actions aimed at proving that justice is possible and that it is never too late for it. Since President Kirchner took office in May 2003, major events have been unfolding in Argentina that might set historical precedents in matters of justice for crimes against humanity.[1] The events of the dictatorship keep coming back to build and meet the political will to settle accounts with the past. Twenty years later, and for the first time since the commencement of civilian rule, there are concrete prospects for canceling the cycle of impunity.[2] Most important, there has been an annulment of a decree denying requests for extradition from Argentina so *represores* can be judged in other countries,[3] and Congress annulled the impunity laws "Due Obedience" and "Full Stop," which now allows for the initiating of trials against all *represores*, even those benefiting from amnesties. And, as already mentioned, the sinister ESMA was taken away from the navy and the former center of torture and extermination will house the Museum of Memory.

These developments attest both to the strength and stubbornness of the witness generation's memories as well as to the younger generation's postmemories. I often wonder whether the young people with whom I spoke more than six years ago, most of whom wanted punishment for the culprits, are participating in Argentina's overwhelming majority that celebrates the new prospects for justice.[4] The post-dictatorship generation's attitudes toward human rights abuses and its perpetrators will be crucial for obtaining justice. These young people are the millions of voters who will support particular political agendas based on what they know, on what they remember. This is why memories are so relevant.

In this fieldwork, there were signs suggesting that, in spite of fears, silences, ignorance, legalized impunity, and apparent indifference, many young people might be truly committed to "never again." Many were aware of society's tolerance or responsibilities for what happened and were truly convinced that society's participation is key to making sure that history will not be repeated. So I would like to close on an optimistic note, sharing a comment by Antonio, the law school student who was quite skeptical and neither very much interested in knowing more about this past, nor in participating in campaigns for accountability. His contradictory statement certainly challenged my perceptions of what a generalized apathy really means, for right beneath his apathy is the admission of the injustice that took place, of the pain, guilt, and anger it still produces. And in this apparent apathy, I see a ray of light, a call to action, from those who claim not to care.

> If it ever happens again, and people let it happen, we deserve that they beat the shit out of us, that we all go to jail, that we're thrown into the river with stones tied to our neck. That's what I think. . . .

Appendix A: Chronology of Events

1816	Declaration of independence from Spain.
1930	Military coup overthrows Hipólito Irigoyen from the Radical Party and starts series of coups in the twentieth century.
1946	Juan Domingo Perón is elected president.
1952	Eva Perón (Evita) dies.
1955	Military coup overthrows Perón before ending his second term. The Peronist Party is proscribed for eighteen years.
1973	Perón returns to Argentina and is elected president for a third term with his wife Isabel Martinez de Perón (Isabelita) as vice-president.
1974	Perón dies. Isabelita becomes president.
1975	Isabel Perón's government issues decree to eliminate subversion.
1976	On March 24, a military coup overthrows Isabel Perón and establishes seven years of dictatorship.
1982	Argentina declares, fights, and loses a war against Great Britain over the Malvinas (Falkland) Islands.
1983	End of the dictatorship. The military issue a "self-amnesty." Raúl Alfonsín, from the Radical Party, wins the elections and takes power in December.
1984	The *Comisión Nacional para la Desaparición de Personas* (CONADEP), appointed to investigate disappearances, issues its report *Nunca Más*.
1985	Trials to the Military Juntas. Top commanders sentenced to life terms.
1986	First uprising of mid-rank officers (*Carapintadas*).
1986	Sanctioning of the first impunity law, "Full Stop," which applies the statute of limitations to the prosecution of torturers and assassins.
1987	Sanctioning of "Due Obedience," second impunity law, acquitting *represores*, on the basis that they obeyed orders.
1989–1999	Carlos Saúl Menem, from the Peronist Party, is president for two terms.
1989–1990	Menem's Decrees of Pardon order the end to proceedings against officers not covered by the impunity laws and pardon *represores* and guerrilla leaders serving time.
1999–2001	Presidency of Fernando De la Rúa from the Radical Party. He was forced to resign after massive popular protests in December 2001. In the twelve days that follow Argentina has five provisional presidents.
2002	Eduardo Duhalde, from the Peronist Party, remains interim president until the 2003 elections.
2003	Néstor Kirchner, from the Peronist party, becomes president. Beginning of a period with major developments toward ending the cycle of impunity—for example, the nullification of impunity laws.

Appendix B: Glossary of Terms and Individuals

Astiz, Alfredo: Navy officer known as the "Angel [of Death]." Infiltrated human rights groups, accused of several crimes, condemned, in absentia, to life term in France for the disappearance of French nuns.`

Cavallo, Domingo: Minister of economy of Menem and De la Rúa. Continued with the major restructuring of the economy initiated during the dictatorship.

Desaparecidos: People who had disappeared.

ERP (Ejército Revolucionario del Pueblo, People's Revolutionary Army): Guerrilla organization.

Escrache: Demonstrations against *represores* organized by HIJOS.

ESMA (Escuela de Mecánica de la Armada, Navy Mechanics School): One of the most infamous centers of torture and extermination.

Firmenich, Mario Eduardo ("Pepe"): Leader of Montoneros.

Galtieri, Leopoldo Fortunato: General and de facto president when Argentina declared war on England.

Grandmothers of the Plaza de Mayo: Organization of grandmothers of disappeared children, most of them babies born in the torture chambers.

HIJOS: Organization formed by the adult daughters and sons of either *desaparecidos*, murdered political activists, or activists forced into exile.

Martinez de Hoz, José Alfredo: Minister of economy of the dictatorship. Advocate of neoliberal policies. Initiated major structural economic reforms.

Massera, Eduardo Emilio: Admiral and member of the first military junta. Key in orchestrating the repression and its methodology.

Menem, Carlos Saúl: From the Peronist party, served two terms as president.

Montoneros: Guerrilla organization aligned with the Peronist Left.

Mothers of the Plaza de Mayo: Organization of mothers of *desaparecidos*.

Mugica, Carlos: Catholic priest, activist, aligned with the Peronist Left. Assassinated in 1974.

Nunca Más: Name of the CONADEP's report.

Olimpo: Center for torture and extermination.

Peronist Party: Party founded by Juan Perón.

Proceso: Term defining the dictatorship, which called itself "Proceso de Reconstrucción Nacional."

Radical Party: Party founded by Hipólito Yrigoyen.

Represores: Generic term for torturers, assassins, "disappearers" [of people] and their accomplices.

Santucho, Mario Roberto ("Robi"): Leader of ERP. Assassinated in 1976.

Scilingo, Adolfo: Retired navy officer who participated in the death flights and came public to provide details about them.

Turco Julián: Code name of "renowned" torturer Julio Simón.

Videla, Jorge Rafael: General and de facto president of the first military junta after the 1976 coup. Most disappearances occurred while he was "president."

Appendix C: Questions Topics

Interviews and group discussions were organized to follow an agenda around specific topics but I remained receptive to new information that participants offered, being flexible in modifying my approach to certain issues. I triggered talk through open-ended questions and stimulated conversation within the discussion groups. Certain questions were posed to all respondents but in-depth interviews or longer sessions allowed deeper exploration of the same issues or additional topics tangential to this study that enriched my understanding of what it was to be a young person in contemporary Argentina (e.g., police harassment). Since I was not using a standard written questionnaire, the words and phrasing varied. The main questions asked are included in what follows.

Regarding Knowledge about the Dictatorship

I never started an interview asking about the dictatorship, terror, or human rights violations, because I wanted participants to define the period in their *own* words and not be constrained by a terminology openly critical of it. Except for one answer that first linked the 1970s with cultural issues—specifically with "flower power" and the fashion of those times, even mentioning bell-bottom pants—most participants immediately mentioned "military coup," "dictatorship," or *desaparecidos*. From this point on, I acknowledged that this was the topic I was interested in discussing and questions were aimed at finding out the information that had been transmitted to them.

– What do you know about everyday life during those years?
– What did your family tell you about that period?
– What was your family's experience during the dictatorship?
– Has anybody told you about the fears during those times?
– Do you know what was done to people, what happened to them?
– Why [was there] such repression?
– What were you told about the reasons for the [dictatorship] to do what it did?
– Do you think that people knew or didn't know [what was going on]?
– What do you think that people thought about [what was going on]?
– In general, when there is talk about [the dictatorship], who are the "bad guys?"
– Do young people talk about the many torturers who are free, walking around the streets?
– Who do you think supported the military [dictatorship]?
– Do you think that there are people who benefited from [what happened] or lived well during that period?
– Does your family (or you) know someone who disappeared?
– Do you know any human rights organization?
– Do you know about their activities?

Since defending the dictatorship does not seem to be very popular, I always asked for the good things that they had heard. This was intended to overcome any reticence in sharing with me or in front of classmates or friends any comments in support of the dictatorship.

– Has anybody told you good things about those times?
– Do you know people who defend and justify what was done?
– If someone is criticizing the [military dictatorship] and there is a young person who supports it, do you think that she will say something or that she will remain silent?

Regarding Sources of This Knowledge

While talking about what they knew, participants revealed many sources of knowledge (i.e., "I talked about it for the first time with my mother when I saw a film on television"). To complement this, I made sure to gather information on the different circles in which the dictatorship had been discussed and on the main referents or texts about it.

– Do you remember the first time that you heard something about what happened in the 1970s? How old were you?
– Who are the [older] people who have told you anything about that epoch?
– Have you discussed this topic with your family?
– Did you talk about [the dictatorship] in primary school? In high school?
– Has this topic been discussed at the university? Have there been lectures or other related events?
– Have you ever discussed [the dictatorship] with your classmates?
– Have you read books or seen films or television programs about [this past]? Which ones?
– When you were in primary school, if teachers ever discussed [these issues], did you feel that the kids had talked [about them] with their parents?
– Lately, have you talked to anybody [about this past]? Have you heard or read anything?

Regarding how They Were Processing Their Knowledge

I posed questions addressing their opinions, attitudes, or recommendations of how this past should be approached by them and by society. I was interested in assessing how the information they had received had shaped their thoughts and actions, in finding out what they thought about remembering and forgetting, or about issues of truth, impunity, accountability, and punishment.

– Are you interested in knowing more about this period?
– Do you think young people are interested and want to know more?
– Do you think there should be more talk about what happened?
– Would you like to be taught more about it in school?
– Whenever a professor opens a space to talk about [the dictatorship], are students interested?
– What do people your age think about [the dictatorship]?
– What do young people think about continuing with demands for justice?
– Are you active in any group or organization (i.e., school, Church, cultural, political)?
– Have you participated in human rights demonstrations or political gatherings?
– Do you think that people should go to [human rights] marches?
– Do you think that the Grandmothers have to continue [searching for their grandchildren]?
– What role do you think society should play in this process?

I usually told participants to imagine that they were government advisers or ministers in three areas—justice, education, and communication. Then, I asked them to recommend what to do with this past.

– What would be your recommendation regarding justice for what happened during [the dictatorship]? What will be best for the country?
– If you would have to design a plan, what would you do?
– If we talk about justice now, at this time, who do you think is responsible?
– Who should be tried, if any?
– Should those responsible be punished? How?
– What do you think should be done with all those who tortured, killed, and are free?
– Would you include this historical period in the educational plans?
– How would you teach small kids about it?
– What would you do in the area of communication?
– Suppose that you are in charge of a ministry where you can do what you want regarding media campaigns or educational plans. You have the structure and the resources to tell society this history. What would you do?
– What kind of information would you include, what kind of details?
– You have the budget to produce films or print books. Considering the way that [this period] was transmitted to you, what would you include and exclude from it, what would you add? Why?

Notes

Introduction

1. Almost three decades after her disappearance, I received the first information about my friend. It was through a denunciation made in 2004 by the sister of another *desaparecida* to the Spanish Judge Baltasar Garzón: Marta Ofelia Borrero, a.k.a. "Violeta," was seized on January 21, 1977 and taken to the ESMA where witnesses saw her corpse that same day.
2. Miguel Angel Giovanetti's artwork.
3. Marianne Hirsch, "Projected Memory: Holocaust Photographs in Personal and Public Fantasy," in *Acts of Memory: Cultural Recall in the Present*, ed. Mieke Bal, Jonathan Crewe, and Leo Spitzer (Hanover: University Press of New England, 1999), 3–23, p. 8.
4. Luisa Passerini, "Introduction," in *Memory and Totalitarianism*, ed. Luisa Passerini (New York: Oxford University Press, 1992), 1–17, p. 2, and "Between Silence and Oblivion," lecture at the Regional Oral History Office, University of California, Berkeley, November 7, 2001.
5. This book is based on data collected and analyzed for my doctoral dissertation. See Susana Kaiser, "*De Eso No Se Habla* (We Don't Talk About That): Transmission of Silences and Fragmented [Hi]stories in Young Argentineans' Memories of Terror" (Ph.D. diss., University of Texas at Austin, 2000).
6. The Social Science Research Council developed a research project exploring memories of the repression, coordinated by Elizabeth Jelin, and focusing on the Southern Cone (Argentina, Brazil, Chile, Paraguay, Perú, and Uruguay). Siglo Veintiuno (Spain/Argentina) is publishing a series of books documenting these studies.
7. Main human rights organizations estimate 30,000 people. Figures vary considerably. The official figure of the commission to investigate disappearances (CONADEP) is 8,961 but the commission made it clear that it estimated many more victims.
8. Pigna argues that the colonial period is crucial to understand Argentina's present, including the conformation of a corrupted State. Felipe Pigna, *Los mitos de la historia argentina* (Buenos Aires: Grupo Editorial Norma, 2004), 101.
9. For a summary of the pre and post coup violence see Horacio Verbitsky, "Foreword," in *Las Cifras de la Guerra Sucia* (Buenos Aires: Asamblea Permanente por Los Derechos Humanos, 1988).
10. For an analysis of these issues, see Alicia García, *La Doctrina de Seguridad Nacional* (Buenos Aires: Centro Editor de America Latina, 1991).

11. For a comprehensive study of this institution, see Lesley Gill, *School of the Americas: Military Training and Political Violence* (Durham, NC: Duke University Press, 2004).

12. See *Nunca Más: Informe de la Comisión Nacional Sobre la Desaparición de Personas* (Buenos Aires: EUDEBA, 1984); Alipio Paoletti, *Como los Nazis, como en Vietnam* (Buenos Aires: Editorial Contrapunto, 1987).

13. Marie-Monique Robin's documentary *Death Squadrons: The French School* (2003), focusing on Algiers, offers amazing footage of interviews with the French military's "students" from the United States and Argentina, including this candid statement, about the decision to make political prisoners disappear, by Argentine General (R) Díaz Bessone: "Do you think we could have (publicly) executed 7,000? Look at the mess the pope started for (Spanish dictator) Franco when he merely executed three. The world would have fallen in on us."

14. See Verbitsky, "Foreword."

15. The CONADEP did not have subpoena powers and investigations were carried on based on voluntary testimonies of victims and military personnel. For an analysis of Alfonsín's human rights policies see the work of one of the legal architects, Jaime Malamud-Goti, *Game Without End: State Terror and the Politics of Justice* (Norman: University of Oklahoma Press, 1996).

16. For a study of Truth Commissions, see Priscilla Hayner, *Unspeakable Truths* (New York: Routledge, 2000).

17. Alex Boraine, "Truth and Reconciliation in South Africa: The Third Way," in *Truth v. Justice: The Morality of Truth Commissions*, ed. Robert I. Rotberg and Dennis Thompson (Princeton: Princeton University Press, 2000), 141–157, p. 143. Boraine further discussed how South Africans studied the case of Argentina during a personal conversation with the author at the University of Texas at Austin in October 1998, the month that the TRC issued its report.

18. "Full Stop" is Law No. 23493 (December 23, 1986) and "Due Obedience" is Law No. 23521 (June 4, 1987).

19. The uprising was in April 1987. Aldo Rico led the "*carapintadas*" (officers who used black camouflage painting on their faces and wore commando fatigues).

20. Menem's Decrees of pardon Nos. 1002–05 (October 7, 1989) ordered the end to proceedings against officers not covered by the impunity laws; Decrees Nos. 2741–43 (December 30, 1990) pardoned those *represores* serving time. The December 1990 decrees also pardoned some guerrilla leaders, including Mario Firmenich from Montoneros.

21. See Benedict Anderson, *Imagined Communities: Reflections on the Origin and Spread of Nationalism* (New York: Verso, 1983); James Fentress and Chris Wickham, *Social Memory* (Oxford: Blackwell, 1992); Eric Hobsbawm and Terence Ranger, eds., *The Invention of Tradition* (New York: Cambridge University Press, 1983); Nicolas Shumway, *The Invention of Argentina* (Berkeley: University of California Press, 1991).

22. Quoted in Anderson, *Imagined Communities*, 199.

23. See Lupicinio Iñiguez, Jose Valencia, and Félix Vázquez, "The Construction of Remembering and Forgetfulness: Memories and Histories of the Spanish Civil War" and Jose Marques, Darío Páez, and Alexandra Serra, "Social Sharing, Emotional Climate and the Transgenerational Transmission of Memories," in *Collective Memory of Political Events: Social Psychological Perspectives* ed. James Pennebaker, Darío Páez, and Bernard Rimé (New Jersey: Lawrence Erlbaum Associates, 1997), 237–252; 253–276.

24. Popular Memory Group, "Popular Memory: Theory, Politics, Method," in *Making Histories. Studies in History-Writing and Politics*, ed. Richard Johnson et al. (London: Hutchinson, 1982), 205–252, p. 211.

25. Ibid., 219.

26. See Fentress and Wickham, *Social Memory*, 74, 125; Maurice Halbwachs, *On Collective Memory*, trans. and ed. Lewis A. Coser (Chicago: The University of Chicago Press, 1992), 38–41; Eviatar Zerubavel, "Social Memories: Steps to a Sociology of the Past," *Qualitative Sociology* 19:3 (Fall 1996); 283–299.

27. Peter Burke, "History as Social Memory," in *Memory, History, Culture and the Mind*, ed. Thomas E. Butler (Oxford, UK: Basil Blackwell, 1989), 97–113, p. 107.

28. Sergio Ciancaglini and Martín Granowsky, *Nada más que la verdad* (Buenos Aires: Planeta, 1995), 359, cite Emilio Mignone's estimate that out of the CONADEP's figure of *desaparecidos* (8,961) between 5% and 10% (i.e., 450–896) may have been guerrillas; they give an estimate of 1,300 members of guerrilla organizations. Prudencio García, *El Drama de la Autonomía Militar* (Madrid: Alianza Editorial, 1995), 405, estimates 800–1,000 armed combatants.

29. For the dictatorship's explanations and denials during the terror and the transition, see Martin E. Andersen, *Dossier Secreto: Argentina's "Desaparecidos" and the Myth of the "Dirty War"* (Boulder: Westview Press, 1993); Eduardo Luis Duhalde, *El Estado Terrorista Argentino* (Buenos Aires: El Caballito, 1983); Jo Fisher, *Mothers of the Disappeared* (Boston: South End Press, 1989); *Nunca Más*; Paoletti, *Como los Nazis*.

30. Victoria Ginzberg, "La soberanía de matar y robar bebés," *Página 12*, November 4, 1999; Juan Gelman, "Epidemias," *Página 12*, November 11, 1999.

31. This is different from the public support to dictator Pinochet by the crowds that took to the streets to protest his 1998 detention in London.

32. Although I use this expression, I make sure that it is always within quotes.

33. For the genesis of the theory see Ernesto Jauretche, *Violencia y Política en los 70: No dejés que te la cuenten* (Buenos Aires: Colihue, 1997), 23–24. See also Carina Perelli, "Setting Accounts with Blood Memory: The Case of Argentina," *Social Research* 59:2 (Summer 1992). Perelli argues that blaming both sides was aimed at facilitating the reprocessing of memory without widening the gaps separating society. González Bombal and Landi note that the theory is a diagnosis, successfully established by the Alfonsín government, which dominated the "cultural trial" of the dictatorship, meaning the one that takes place outside the courts, in public political discussion. Inés González Bombal and Oscar Landi, "Los Derechos en la Cultura Política," in *Juicio, Castigos y Memorias: derechos humanos y justicia en la política argentina*, ed. Carlos Acuña (Buenos Aires: Nueva Visión, 1995), 189.

34. *Escraches* are demonstrations whose goal is to uncover the identities of hundreds of *represores* benefiting from amnesties. For an analysis of this communication strategy, see Susana Kaiser, "*Escraches*: Demonstrations, Communication and Political Memory in Post-Dictatorial Argentina," *Media, Culture and Society* 24:4 (2002): 499–516.

35. Witness must tell the truth (can be prosecuted for lying) but cannot be prosecuted for the crimes under national law. Other countries may initiate proceedings invoking international jurisdiction for crimes against humanity.

36. In 1998, "Full Stop" and "Due Obedience" laws were revoked, a step shorter than nullified, which meant that those already benefiting from them could not be put on trial.

37. Naval officer Astiz was condemned in absentia in France for the disappearance of two French nuns. In Spain, Judge Garzón was prosecuting those responsible for the

disappearance of Spanish citizens. Italy and Germany had also initiated legal proceedings.

38. Alessandro Portelli, *The Death of Luigi Trastulli and Other Stories* (Albany, NY: State University of New York Press, 1991), 52.

39. For key works on memory, see, among others, Mieke Bal, Jonathan Crewe, and Leo Spitzter, eds., *Acts of Memory: Cultural Recall in the Present* (Hanover: University Press of New England, 1999); Thomas Butler, "Memory: A Mixed Blessing," in *Memory, History, Culture and the Mind*, ed. Thomas E. Butler (Oxford, UK: Basil Blackwell, 1989), 1–31; Paul Connerton, *How Societies Remember* (New York: Cambridge University Press, 1989); Fentress and Wickham, *Social Memory*; Maurice Halbwachs, *The Collective Memory* (New York: Harper & Row, 1980) and *On Collective Memory*; Andreas Huyssen, *Twilight Memories: Marking Time in a Culture of Amnesia* (New York: Routledge, 1995); Jun Jing, *The Temple of Memories. History, Power, and Morality in a Chinese Village* (Stanford, CA: Stanford University Press, 1996); Pierre Nora, "Between Memory and History: Les Lieux de Mémoire," *Representations* 26 (Spring 1989): 7–24; James Pennebaker, Darío Páez, and Bernard Rimé, eds., *Collective Memory of Political Events: Social Psychological Perspectives* (New Jersey: Lawrence Erlbaum Associates, 1997); Popular Memory Group, "Popular Memory"; Joanne Rappaport, *The Politics of Memory: Native Historical Interpretation in the Colombian Andes* (New York: Cambridge University Press, 1990); Marita Sturken, *Tangled Memories: The Vietnam War, the AIDS Epidemic, and the Politics of Remembering* (Berkeley: University of California Press, 1997).

40. Burke, "History," 107.

41. Iñiguez, Valencia, and Várquez, "The Construction of Remembering," 239; Popular Memory Group, "Popular Memory," 223.

42. Huyssen, *Twilight Memories*, 5.

43. For the need to insist on the diversity and plurality of memory, see Passerini, "Introduction," 18.

44. As research on uses and effects of the media shows, there are many interpretations to the same text. For a seminal work on the content of texts and their possible diverse readings, see Stuart Hall, "Encoding/Decoding," in *Media and Cultural Studies: KeyWorks*, ed. Gigi Durham and Douglas Kellner (Malden, MA: Blackwell, 2000).

45. See, e.g., Jing's study of a community's reconstruction of a temple destroyed during the Chinese Cultural Revolution. Jing, *The Temple*.

46. Tzvetan Todorov, *Les Abus de la Mémoire* (Paris: Arléa, 1995).

47. Judith Herman, "Trauma and Recovery: The Aftermath of Violence—From Domestic Abuse to Political Terror," in *Violence in War and Peace*, ed. Nancy Scheper-Hughes and Philippe Bourgois (Oxford, UK: Blackwell, 2004), 368–371.

48. Martín-Baró, a Jesuit, psychologist, theologian, and human rights advocate, was assassinated by government soldiers on November 1989, at the Universidad Centroamericana in El Salvador, together with five other Jesuits, the housekeeper, and her daughter. See chapters 6 and 7 in Ignacio Martín-Baró, *Writings for a Liberation Psychology*, ed. Adrianne Aron and Shawn Corne (Cambridge, MA: Harvard University Press, 1994), 114, 122, 124, 133.

49. For seminal studies on the culture of fear in the Southern Cone, see Juan Corradi, Patricia Weiss Fagen, and Manuel Antonio Garretón, eds. *Fear at the Edge: State Terror and Resistance in Latin America* (Berkeley, CA: University of California Press, 1992), 3.

50. Nora illustrates it with the generation of 1968, which was still defining and redefining itself years later. Pierre Nora, "Generations," in *Realms of Memory: Rethinking the French Past Vol I*, ed. Pierre Nora (New York: Columbia University Press, 1996), 499–531.

51. According to Nora, *lieux de mémoire* are those sites that codify memory and have a capacity for an endless recycling of their meaning. They include geographical places, buildings, historical figures, archives, popular literature, commemorations—all suggesting that communities' memories are located in a variety of cultural artifacts and media products. See Pierre Nora, "Preface," in *Realms of Memory: Rethinking the French Past Vol. I*, ed. Pierre Nora (New York: Columbia University Press, 1996), xv–xxiv.

52. Nora, "Generations," 531.

53. For a study of political activism in Argentina in the period previous to and immediately following the 1976 coup, see Eduardo Anguita and Martín Caparrós, *La Voluntad: Una historia de la militancia revolucionaria en la Argentina, Vols. I, II, III* (Buenos Aires: Grupo Editorial Norma, 1997 and 1998). For an analysis of the generation of 1968 in Italy, see Luisa Passerini's *Autobiography of a Generation* (Hanover: Wesleyan University Press, 1996).

54. Nora, "Generations," 531.

55. Ibid., 527.

56. Alessandro Portelli, *The Order Has Been Carried Out* (New York: Palgrave Macmillan, 2003), 286.

57. Gabriel García Márquez, *Vivir Para Contarla* (Bogotá: Editorial Norma, 2002).

58. My use of the term "gray zone" is different to Auschwitz survivor Primo Levi's use of the concept to define that space of privilege and collaboration where concentration camps inmates cooperated with the enemy in exchange for small benefits and the possibility of survival. Primo Levi, "The Gray Zone," in *Violence in War and Peace*, ed. Nancy Scheper-Hughes and Philippe Bourgois (Oxford, UK: Blackwell, 2004), 83–90.

59. Pierre Bourdieu, "Comprendre," in *La Misère du Monde*, ed. Pierre Bourdieu (Paris: Seuil, 1993), 920.

60. I relied on "Preparing Interview Transcripts for Documentary Publication: A Line-by-Line Illustration of the Editing Process," in Michael Frisch, *A Shared Authority: Essays on the Craft and Meaning of Oral and Public History* (Albany: State University of New York Press, 1990).

61. Juan Gelman, "Del Silencio," *Página 12*, August 13, 1998, Contratapa.

One: Conversations about Knowledge: Why Did It Happen?

1. Documents found range from detention orders of people now disappeared to instructions for counterinsurgency operatives. See José Maggi, "El Jefe de Policía Anunció que Encontró Miles de Fojas," *Página 12*, November 14, 1999.

2. According to García, three of these victims were wives and five were children of military officers. García, *El Drama*, 53–54. See chapter 1 for estimates of members of guerrilla organizations.

3. On December 1, 1983, the Alfonsín administration issued decrees Nos. 157 and 158 to prosecute guerrilla leaders and military juntas respectively.

4. Menem's Decree of Pardons in December 1990.

5. They took place during Bernardo Neustadt's television program in April and May 1995.

6. Ciancaglini and Granowsky, *Nada más*, 340–341.

7. Retired captain D'Andrea Mohr documented 129 cases of murder and disappearance of military personnel. José Luis D'Andrea Mohr, *El Escuadrón Perdido* (Buenos Aires: Planeta, 1998).

8. Printed by the *International Herald Tribune*, Paris, May 26, 1977.

9. *Nunca Más: The Report of the Argentine National Commission on the Disappeared People* (New York: Farrar, Strauss, and Giroux, 1986), 333.

10. Martín-Baró, *Writings*, 155.

11. Ibid., 163.

12. In his study of the memories of a 1944 Nazi massacre in Rome in retaliation to a bomb planted by partisans, Portelli noted that a dominant explanation blamed the partisans rather than the Nazis. Portelli, *The Order*. In China, Jing found people saying that they had been erroneously targeted during the Cultural Revolution rather than questioning persecution by the authorities. Jing, *The Temple*, 56.

13. The Mothers of the Plaza de Mayo have consistently vindicated the political activism of their daughters and sons. According to Hebe Bonafini, its president, "No other organization or political party makes the vindication [as political activists] that we do of our daughters and sons." See Susana Kaiser, "The 'Madwomen' Memory Mothers of the Plaza de Mayo: A case of Counter-Hegemonic Communications Developed by A Unique Group: Mothers of Disappeared People from Argentina." (MA Thesis, Communications, Hunter College of the City University of New York, 1993).

14. González Bombal and Landi argue that the trials of the military juntas impeded the political recuperation of the actions of the *desaparecidos*, who are seen only as victims. González Bombal and Landi, "Los Derechos," 164.

15. Irma, Víctor, Elvira, and Andrés.

16. "Super Minister" Cavallo also held an official position during the dictatorship and was minister of economy in the government of president De la Rúa, who was forced to resign in 2001.

17. Words of Pavlovsky (1999) to define the many Argentineans who collaborated by indifference. Eduardo Pavlovsky, "Sobre la Complicidad Civil con el Terrorismo de Estado," *Página 12*, June 24, 1999. For an overview of sectors whose support was crucial for the dictatorship, see Horacio Verbitsky, "Militares, Civiles y el Miedo," in *Ni el Flaco Perdón de Dios: Hijos de Desaparecidos*, ed. Juan Gelman and Mara La Madrid (Buenos Aires: Planeta), 124–135.

18. Calveiro has written a compelling account of life during terror from inside the inferno of the camps. It is a disturbing analysis of the relationship between concentration camps and society and the role played by society in relation to the "disappearing power" of the dictatorship. Pilar Calveiro, *Poder y Desaparición: Los Campos de Concentración en la Argentina* (Buenos Aires: Colihue, 1998).

19. Jurgen Habermas and Adam Michnik, "Overcoming the Past," *New Left Review* 203 (1994): 3–16, p. 7.

20. The other three were Nevares, Novack, and Husayne. *Nunca Más*, 357–360.

21. Emilio Mignone, *Witness to the Truth: The Complicity of the Church and Dictatorship in Argentina* (New York: Orbis, 1988.) Mignone, whose daughter disappeared, wrote a detailed account of the Catholic hierarchy's collaboration with the dictatorship, including the bishops' calls for reconciliation. See also *Nunca Más*; Paoletti, *Como los Nazis*.

22. In Chile, under the *Vicaría de la Solidaridad*, the Catholic hierarchy helped persecuted people, offering asylum and means to leave the country. See Hugo Fruhling, "Resistance to Fear in Chile: The Experience of the Vicaría de las Solidaridad," in *Fear at the Edge: State Terror and Resistance in Latin America*, ed. Juan Corradi, Patricia Weiss Fagen, and Manuel Antonio Garretón (Berkeley, CA: University of California Press, 1992), 121–141.

23. In July 1998, I participated in a demonstration against Graselli organized by the Mothers of the Plaza de Mayo. The Mothers painted the walls of the school with slogans such as "Graselli assassin" in an effort to inform current students of their confessor's dirty past.

24. Verbitsky, "Militares," 124.

25. For an analysis of the diverse social forces that supported the dictatorship, see Garcia, *El Drama*, 329–332.

26. Dictator Massera has claimed that society was a chameleon, that people were now silent and horrified but at the time encouraged the destruction of the enemy, that he was told: "Admiral, go and kill them all. Hunt them in their hideouts and kill them." Cited in Ciancaglini and Granowsky, *Nada más*, 354. A good friend of torturer/assassin Astiz tells of witnessing how a man approached Astiz in the street and thanked him for everything he had done for the country. Cited in Uki Goñi, *Judas: la verdadera historia de Alfredo Astiz el infiltrado* (Buenos Aires: Sudamericana, 1996), 208.

27. See Valeria Dabenigno et al. "Entre el recuerdo y el olvido: interpretaciones de una historia compartida," (paper presented at the Latin American Studies Association Conference, Chicago, September 24–26, 1998).

28. Declaration of General Martín Balza on April 25, 1995, http://www.redesweb.com/memoriadebida/index.htm (Accessed April 20, 2000).

29. Rico, leader of the 1987 uprising and participant of the 1988 rebellion against the first civilian government, was eventually elected mayor of the town of San Miguel (province of Buenos Aires).

30. For example, Bussi, leader of the repression in Tucumán, served as a democratically elected governor of this province. For information about torturer Patti who was elected by 73% of voters as mayor of Escobar (province of Buenos Aires) and in 1999 run for governor of Buenos Aires see "La Historia del Candidato que figura en la CONADEP," *Página12*, April 9, 1999.

31. For a detailed account of Nazi criminals' "migration" to Argentina with Perón's support and the complicity of the Vatican and the Argentine Catholic Church, see Uki Goñi, *The Real Odessa: Smuggling the Nazis to Peron's Argentina* (New York: Granta, 2002).

32. For the Nazism of the *represores* see *Nunca Más*; Leonardo Senkman and Mario Szanjder, *El Legado del Autoritarismo; Derechos Humanos y Antisemitismo en la Argentina Contemporánea* (Buenos Aires: Grupo Editor Latinoamericano, 1995); Jacobo Timmerman, *Prisoner without a Name, Cell without a Number* (New York: Random House, 1981).

Two: Conversations about Fear

1. A good example is the description of the hunting and killing of Mario Santucho, leader of the ERP, at an apartment in the outskirts of Buenos Aires. See Maria Seoane, *Todo o Nada* (Buenos Aires: Planeta, 1991).
2. *Webster's New Universal Unabridged Dictionary*, 2nd edition, 1983.
3. For the short- and long-term effects of living under terror in Argentina, see Diana Kordon and Lucila Edelman, eds., *Psychological Effects of Political Repression* (Buenos Aires: Sudamericana/Planeta, 1988); See also, Sofía Salimovich, Elizabeth Lira, and Eugenia Weinstein, "Victims of Fear: The Social Psychology of Repression," in *Fear at the Edge: State Terror and Resistance in Latin America*, ed. Juan Corradi, Patricia Weiss Fagen, and Manuel Antonio Garretón (Berkeley, CA: University of California Press, 1992), 72–89.
4. Manuel Antonio Garretón, "Fear in Military Regimes," in *Fear at the Edge: State Terror and Resistance in Latin America*, ed. Juan Corradi, Patricia Weiss Fagen, and Manuel Antonio Garretón (Berkeley, CA: University of California Press, 1992), 13–25, p. 14.
5. Survivors have argued that this was a way of informing society. See Calveiro, *Poder y Desaparición*. See also María Seoane, *Argentina: El siglo del progreso y la oscuridad (1900–2003)* (Buenos Aires: Crítica, 2004), 139.
6. I was told that, after the return to civilian rule, the institution published a booklet about its employees who had disappeared.
7. The concept of "flashbulb" memories has been applied for the study of collective memories of political events; e.g., Kennedy's assassination, Challenger's explosion. (We may now include the events of September 11, 2001). See Martin Comway, *Flashbulb Memories* (Hove, UK: Lawrence Erlbaum, 1995).
8. "The Night of the Long Sticks" was when the Infantry Guard entered the university in the city of La Plata in 1966, under a previous military dictatorship. Reference to this night sheds light on how old some memories of fear are.
9. The 1999 U.S. State Department Human Rights Report pointed to the repression of demonstrators in Argentina. http://www.state.gov/www/global/human_rights/99hrp_index.html (Accessed March 3, 2000).
10. See the Introduction to *Fear at the Edge: State Terror and Resistance in Latin America*, ed. Juan Corradi, Patricia Weiss Fagen, and Manuel Antonio Garretón (Berkeley, CA: University of California Press, 1992), 1–10, p. 2.
11. There is widespread belief in this torture "technique." The case of a medical doctor who performed an autopsy and found a rat inside the corpse of her daughter (who had been kidnapped, killed, and her corpse returned to the family by military authorities) is quoted in Afredo Martin's *Les Meres "folles" de la Place de Mai* (Paris: Renaudot, 1989), 60.
12. See *Nunca Más*.

Three: Conversations about Silences

1. He observed this regarding cases as diverse as the Putumayo, Congo, and Argentina. Michael Taussig, "Culture of Terror—Space of Death: Roger Casement's Putumayo Report and the Explanation of Torture," in *Violence in War and Peace*, ed. Nancy Scheper-Hughes and Philippe Bourgois (Oxford, UK: Blackwell, 2004), 39–53, p. 40.

2. For an analysis of social silences during the dictatorship and the creation of alternative public spheres to counter official misinformation see Susana Kaiser, "The 'Madwomen' Memory Mothers."

3. Horacio Verbitsky, *Civiles y Militares: Memoria Secreta de la Transición* (Buenos Aires: Editorial Contrapunto, 1987), 114. For information on this clandestine press experience, see Horacio Verbitsky, *Rodolfo Walsh y la Prensa Clandestina* (Buenos Aires: Ediciones La Urraca, 1985).

4. See, among others, Fentress and Wickham, *Social Memory*, ix; James Pennebaker and Becky Banasik, "On the Creation and Maintenance of Collective Memories: History as Social Psychology," in *Collective Memory of Political Events: Social Psychological Perspectives*, ed. James Pennebaker, Darío Páez, and Bernard Rimé (New Jersey: Lawrence Erlbaum Associates, New Jersey, 1997), 3–19, p. 17; Popular Memory Group, "Popular Memory," 210.

5. Juan Rial, "Makers and Guardians of Fear," in *Fear at the Edge: State Terror and Resistance in Latin America*, ed. Juan Corradi, Patricia Weiss Fagen, and Manuel Antonio Garretón (Berkeley, CA: University of California Press, 1992), 90–103, p. 101.

6. Passerini, "Between Silence and Oblivion."

7. Passerini, "Introduction," 13–15; Luisa Passerini, "Work Ideology and Consensus under Italian Fascism," in *The Oral History Reader*, ed. Robert Perks and Alistair Thomson (New York: Routledge, 1998) 53–62, pp. 58–59.

8. Passerini, "Between Silence and Oblivion."

9. Jing, *The Temple*, 56.

10. Selma Leydesdorff, "A Shattered Silence," in *Memory and Totalitarianism*, ed. Luisa Passerini (New York: Oxford University Press, 1992), 145–163, quotes in pp. 148, 159.

11. "Red diaper babies" is the name given to the children of members of the U.S. Communist Party.

12. In 2003, Néstor Kirchner, a Peronist, was elected president of Argentina.

13. Daniela, Anabella, Natalia, Noemí, and Alejandra.

14. See Inés Dussel, Silvia Finocchio, and Silvia Gojman, *Haciendo memoria en el país del Nunca Más* (Buenos Aires: Eudeba, 1997). The book, developed by educators, is a tool for teaching about the dictatorship and suggests activities for a critical reading of the "*Nunca Más.*" For instance, watching Kurasawa's *Rhapsody in August* (about the American grandson visiting relatives in Japan and the family's conversations remembering the atomic bomb) and draw comparisons with what happened in Argentina.

15. Oral history is a resourceful tool to teach across generations. The Bay Area Holocaust Oral History Project has programs to teach high school students. I use it for historical experiences not necessarily connected with terror in the course I teach on Latinos in the United States at the University of San Francisco.

16. See studies about the Spanish Civil War and Chile in Darío Páez, Nekan Besabe, and José Luis Gonzalez, "Social Processes and Collective Memory: A Cross-Cultural Approach to Remembering Political Events," in *Collective Memory of Political Events: Social Psychological Perspectives*, ed. James Pennebaker, Darío Páez, and Bernard Rimé (New Jersey: Lawrence Erlbaum Associates, New Jersey, 1997), 147–173, p. 159.

17. See study on China in Jing, *The Temple*, 168; see also Páez, Besabe, and Gonzalez, "Social Processes," 147.

18. Márques, Páez, and Serra, "Social Sharing," pp. 255–257; Pennebaker and Banasik, "On the Creation," 17.

19. Márques, Páez, and Serra, "Social Sharing," 255.

Four: Conversations about Awareness and Denial

1. Roy F. Baumeister and Stephen Hastings, "Distortions of Collective Memory: How Groups Flatter and Deceive Themselves," in *Collective Memory of Political Events: Social Psychological Perspectives*, ed. James Pennebaker, Darío Páez, and Bernard Rimé (New Jersey: Lawrence Erlbaum Associates, New Jersey, 1997), 277–293; Páez, Besabe, and Gonzalez, "Social Processes."
2. Alessandro Portelli, "Las peculiaridades de la historia oral," in *Historia oral e historias de vida* (Costa Rica: FLACSO, Cuaderno de Ciencias Sociales No. 18, 1988), 23.
3. Baumeister and Hastings, "Distortions," 279–280.
4. There were many initiatives to improve the dictatorship's image. The government hired a U.S. public relations agency (Burson-Marsteller) and created the Centro Piloto at the Argentine Embassy in Paris, this latter to counter the growing international networks of solidarity with human rights activists. See Kaiser, "The 'Madwomen' Memory Mothers," for an analysis of media corporations' collaboration with the dictatorship.
5. Patricia Derian (Human Rights Secretary for the Carter Administration) visited the country in 1977 and the Inter American Commission on Human Rights of OEA (Organización de Estados Americanos) in September 1979. Both visits generated reports incriminating the dictatorship.
6. Figures by the CONADEP classify their 8,961 *desaparecidos* as follows: Sex: Males 70%, Women 30%. Age: 10.61% (16–20), 32.62% (21–25), 25.90% (26–30), 12.26% (31–35), 19.61% (less than 16 and more than 36). Occupation: Workers 30.2%, Students 21%, Employees17.8%, Professionals 10.7%.
7. See "Introduction" of this book for different estimates on the number of *desaparecidos*. After issuing its 1984 report, many new continue to be added to the original list.
8. For a detailed description of the operations and effects of state terrorism, see Duhalde, *El Estado Terrorista*.
9. Portelli, *The Death of Luigi Trastulli*, 1–26.
10. See chapter five of this book for a discussion of the systematic stealing of political prisoners' babies.
11. This is very different from Chile, where there were fewer killings and disappearances but thousands of Chileans were victims of, and survived, torture.
12. This was in reference to his film *Hombres Armados (Men with Guns)*, where a Central American medical doctor suddenly discovers the genocide taking place in his country. Interview in *The New York Times*, March 5, 1997, Arts Section.
13. Passerini points to these effects of guilt and attitudes of victimization. "Introduction," 11.

Five: Conversations about Impunity

1. See "Introduction" of this book for information on impunity laws and presidential pardons.
2. A national poll conducted when Videla was jailed in 1998 found that 75% thought that Videla should be in prison and 63% that the investigations for the dictatorship's crimes should continue. *Página 12*, July 20, 1998, pp. 6–7.

3. In Ciancaglini and Granowsky, *Nada Más*, 348.

4. For presence of *represores* in television programs, see Claudia Feld, "El relato del horror en la televisión: los represores tienen la palabra," in *La Cultura en la Argentina de fin de siglo, ensayos sobre la dimensión cultural*, ed. Mario Margulis and Marcelo Urresti (Buenos Aires: UBA, 1997), 339–345; Marguerite Feitlowitz, *A Lexicon of Terror* (New York: Oxford, 1998), 193–256.

5. This was on yellow-journalism icon Mauro Viale's program. Ciancaglini and Granowsky, *Nada Más*, 339–340.

6. Interview by journalist Gabriela Cerruti published in the magazine *3 Puntos* in January 14, 1998.

7. Declarations by former prisoner Mercedes Carazo. *Página 12*, November 16, 1998.

8. Tina Rosenberg, *Children of Caín: Violence and the Violent in Latin America* (New York: Morrow, 1991), 89.

9. Alvaro Alsogaray, a conservative politician, justified the seizing of babies with these arguments in a documentary broadcast by the television program *Todo Noticias* on October 21, 1998. See Adriana Meyer, "Apropiación indebida de los hijos de desaparecidos," *Página 12*, October 28, 1998.

10. For a detailed account of the stealing of babies, and the ongoing struggles of the Grandmothers of the Plaza de Mayo to recuperate them, see Rita Arditti, *Searching for Life* (Berkeley, University of California Press, 1999).

11. Conversation with author, June 18, 1998.

12. During 1996–1997, I collaborated with Derechos/Human Rights (www.derechos.org) by coordinating posting of information from the Mothers of the Plaza de Mayo's publication. I received a large quantity of e-mails addressed to them.

13. Raúl Kollman, "Los querían blanquitos y recién nacidos," *Página 12* online http://www.pagina12.com.ar/2000/00–01/00–01–09/pag03.htm (Accessed February 2, 2004).

14. Arditti, *Searching for Life*, 125.

15. Pro Búsqueda (In Favour of Searching), an organization looking for Salvadoran children, has almost 600 cases on its books. See Tom Gibb, "Missing Children Haunt El Salvador," *Guardian Weekly*, October 19–25, 2000, p. 26. The organization ¿Dónde Están los Niños y las Niñas? (Where are the children?) is searching for children in Guatemala.

Six: Conversations about Indifference

1. This is the title of the pertinent book by Ricardo Sidícaro and Emilio Tenti Fanfani, eds., *La Argentina de los jóvenes; entre la indiferencia y la indignación* (Buenos Aires: Losada, 1998).

2. Landi and González Bombal cite some surveys conducted when most participants of this study were children, which are indicative of Argentineans' opinions on the need for memory and justice. A poll conducted in 1983, end of the dictatorship, found that 53% of respondents disagreed with turning the page and forgetting the *desaparecidos*. In a 1987 poll, after the sanctioning of the impunity law "Due Obedience," 73% said that all military personnel involved in the repression, whatever their rank, violated

human rights. In a poll conducted in 1989, year of the first presidential pardons, 72% said that military officers and 83% that Firmenich (guerrilla leader) should remain in jail. González Bombal and Landi, "Los Derechos," 153, 169–170, 174.

3. I borrowed this expression from John Downing.
4. See Ronald L. Cohen, "Silencing Objections: Social Constructions of Indifference," *Journal of Human Rights* 1:2 (June 2002): 187–206.
5. See Kaiser, "The 'Madwomen' Memory Mothers."

Seven: Conversations about Justice

1. Mahmood Mamdani, "From Conquest to Consent as the Basis of State Formation: Reflections on Rwanda," *New Left Review* 216 (March/April, 1996): 3–36, p. 22.
2. A Hugo Haime y Asociados poll at the time of this fieldwork, July of 1998, found that opinions of the armed forces were: 35.5% bad, 27.6% regular, 24.5% good, and 12.4% did not know. *Página 12*, July 20, 1998, pp. 6–7.
3. Portelli, *The Order*, 147.
4. Paoletti, *Como los Nazis*, 382–384.
5. García, *El Drama*, 53–54.
6. Hugo Haime y Asociados poll in July 1998.
7. This was in reference to Priebke, who was judged in Italy for his responsibility in the 1944 Fosse Ardeatine massacre in Rome. See Portelli, *The Order*.
8. Hannah Arendt, "From Eichman in Jerusalem: A Report on the Banality of Evil," in *Violence in War and Peace*, ed. Nancy Scheper-Hughes and Philippe Bourgois (Oxford, UK: Blackwell, 2004), 91–100.
9. A famous "confession" is that of navy officer Adolfo Scilingo who participated in the death flights where prisoners were thrown into the ocean. He confessed because he had trouble sleeping and was abusing alcohol, not for denouncing that he was *forced* to commit crimes. See Horacio Verbitsky, *The Flight: Confessions of an Argentine Dirty Warrior* (New York: The New Press, 1996).
10. Calveiro, *Poder y Desaparición*. Similarly, Portelli reminds us that Nazi criminal Priebke was not a beast but a human being like us. Portelli, *The Order*, 272.

Eight: Conversations about the Communication Media

1. John Downing's work has been invaluable for my research on issues regarding alternative media, communication under totalitarian regimes, and media as a tool of resistance. See John Downing, *Radical Media: Rebellious Communication and Social Movements* (Thousand Oaks, CA: Sage Publications, 2001).
2. See, among others, Bal, Crewe, and Spitzter, *Acts of Memory*; Fentress and Wickham, *Social Memory*; Popular Memory Group, "Popular Memory."
3. Halbwachs, *The Collective Memory*, 70.
4. Cited in Sturken, *Tangled Memories*, 121.
5. See Anderson, *Imagined Communities*; Daniel Dayan and Elihu Katz, "Defining Media Events: High Holidays of Mass Communication," in *Television: The Critical*

View, ed. Horace Newcomb (New York: Oxford University Press, 1994, 5th edition), 332–351.

6. See Juanjo Igartúa and Darío Páez, "Art and Remembering Traumatic Collective Events: The Case of the Spanish Civil War," in *Collective Memory of Political Events: Social Psychological Perspectives*, ed. James W. Pennebaker, Darío Páez, and Bernard Rimé (New Jersey: Lawrence Erlbaum Associates, 1997), 79–101.

7. Ibid.

8. Sturken, *Tangled Memories*.

9. Yosefa Loshitsky, "Fantastic Realism: *Schindler's List* as Docudrama," in *Why Docudrama? Fact Fiction on Film and TV*, ed. Alan Rosenthal (Carbondale: Southern Illinois University Press, 1999), 357–369; Miriam Bratu Hansen, "*Schindler's List* Is Not *Shoah*: The Second Commandment, Popular Modernism, and Public Memory," in *The Historical Film: History and Memory in Media*, ed. Marcia Landy (New Brunswick, NJ: Rutgers University Press, 2000), 201–217.

10. For journalists' collaboration with the dictatorship and reproductions from articles in magazines and newspapers during those years see Eduardo Cid Varela, *Los Sofistas y la Prensa Canalla* (Córdoba: El Cid Editor, 1984); Eduardo Cid Varela, *La Imbecilización de la Mujer* (Córdoba: El Cid Editor, 1984).

11. For an analysis of magazines' coverage of the horror during 1983–1985 see Silvia Tabachnik, "Primeras Transcripciones del Archivo. Los medios y la construcción narrativa del pasado en la inmediata post-dictadura," (paper presented at the Latin American Studies Association Conference, Miami, March 16–18, 2000).

12. In an editorial of the Buenos Aires newspaper *La Nación* cited by Ciancaglini and Granowsky, *Nada Más*, 355.

13. Payne has analyzed the purpose of these confessions. Leigh Payne, "The Politics of Memory, the Politics of Silence: Confessions of Torturers," (paper presented at the Latin American Studies Association Conference, Chicago, September 24–26, 1998). Feld talks about a new arena for venting crimes without any legal consequence. Feld, "El relato del horror."

14. "*Cola*" means being the last one and also "derriere."

15. The popular U.S. television series *Hogan's Heroes* faced similar criticism for portraying a Nazi POW's camp that avoided connections with the Holocaust.

16. See, among others, Mark C. Carnes, ed., *Past Imperfect: History According to the Movies* (New York: Henry Holt and Company, 1995); Marc Ferro and Jean Planchais, *Les Médias et L'histoire: Le Poids du Passé Dans le Chaos de L'actualité* (Paris: CFPJ, 1997); Marcia Landy, ed., *The Historical Film: History and Memory in Media* (New Brunswick, NJ: Rutgers University Press, 2000); Donald D. Stevens, ed., *Based on a True Story: Latin American History at the Movies* (Wilmington: Scholarly Resources, 1997).

17. Alan Rosenthal, ed., *Why Docudrama? Fact Fiction on Film and TV* (Carbondale: Southern Illinois University Press, 1999), xvii.

18. Ferro and Planchais, *Les Médias et L'histoire*, 12.

19. For a detailed account of the ordeal, see Maria Seoane and Héctor Ruiz Nuñez, *La Noche de los Lápices* (Buenos Aires: Editorial Contrapunto, 1986).

20. See Mario Ranalletti, "La construcción del relato de la historia argentina en el cine, 1983–1989," *Film-Historia* IX.1 (1999): 3–15, 14.

21. See Pablo Vila, "Rock nacional, crónicas de la resistencia juvenil," in *Los Nuevos Movimientos Sociales: Mujeres, Rock Nacional*, ed. Elizabeth Jelin (Buenos Aires: Centro

Editor de America Latina, 1985), 83–148; Susana Kaiser, "Singing, Dancing, and Remembering: The Links Between Music and Memory," (paper presented at the International Communication Association Conference, San Diego, May 23–26, 2003).

22. See, e.g., Waleska Pino-Ojeda, "A Detour to the Past: Memory and Mourning in Chilean Post-Authoritarian Rock," in *Rockin' Las Américas*, ed. Deborah Pacini Hernandez, Héctor Fernández L'Hoeste, and Eric Zolov (Pittsburgh: University of Pittsburgh Press, 2004), 290–311; Oren Meyers and Eyal Zandberg, "The Sound-Track of Memory: *Ashes and Dust* and the Commemoration of the Holocaust in Israeli Popular Culture," *Media, Culture and Society*, 24:3 (2002): 389–408.

23. See Rappaport, *The Politics of Memory*, 11; Fentress & Wickham, *Social Memory*, 94, 121.

24. CONADEP's figures in relation to their total of 8,961.

25. CONADEP's terminology and figures. See *Nunca Más*.

26. For details of the sports teams that used the ESMA and the related controversies, see Margaret Feitlowitz, "The House of the Blind, Spatial Discourse in Argentina's *Dirty War*," (paper presented at the Latin American Studies Association Conference, Chicago, September 24–26, 1998).

27. Cited in Marques, Páez, and Serra, "Social Sharing," 255.

28. Interview to Pilar Calveiro by María Moreno, "Fisuras del poder," *Página 12*, January 21, 2000.

Nine: Conversations about Representing the Horror

1. Leydesdorff, "A Shattered Silence," 146.

2. Verbitsky, *Civiles y Militares*.

3. Fisher, *Mothers*, 131.

4. *Nunca Más*, 235.

5. For an analysis of how these images have circulated see Claudia Feld, *Del estrado a la pantalla: Las imágenes del juicio a los ex comandantes en Argentina* (Madrid: Siglo Veintiuno de España, 2002).

6. There are a total of 530 hours of video, a copy of which has been deposited in Oslo, under the custody of the Norwegian Parliament.

7. Alex Boraine discussed these broadcasts at a talk at the University of Texas Law School in October 1998.

8. The documentary was coproduced by journalist Magdalena Ruiz Guiñazú (a member of the CONADEP) and its television broadcast was on August 24, 1998. See Freedom Forum's website http://www.freedomforum.org/international/1998/9/22esma.asp (Accessed November 10, 1998).

9. Stephen Prince, ed., *Screening Violence* (New Brunswick, NJ: Routledge, 2000), 22, 28.

10. Vivian C. Sobchack, "The Violent Dance: A Personal Memoir of Death in the Movies," in *Screening Violence*, ed. Stephen Prince (New Brunswick, NJ: Routledge, 2000), 110–124, p. 124.

11. Jean Franco discussed "torture porn" in contemporary Latin American literature dealing with recent dictatorships at a lecture at the University of Texas at Austin, March 16, 2000.

12. Barbie Zelizer, *Remembering to Forget; Holocaust Memory through the Camera's eye* (Chicago: University of Chicago Press, 1998), 213.

13. The ad is reproduced in an article analyzing this type of marketing. Anibal Ford and Carolina Vinelli, "El marketing de lo cruel," *Clarín*, July 19, 1998, pp. 14–15.

Ten: Conversations about Human Rights Activism

1. Dina Wardi, *Memorial Candles: Children of the Holocaust* (New York: Routledge, 1992).
2. For interviews with children of *desaparecidos* conducted in the first two years of the creation of the group, which are invaluable to understand their origins, motivations, and goals better, see Juan Gelman and Mara La Madrid, *Ni el Flaco Perdón de Dios: Hijos de Desaparecidos* (Buenes Aires: Planeta, 1997).
3. In 1994, the French support group of the Mothers of the Plaza de Mayo organized a conference in Paris of "Mothers who struggle," with participation of groups from various countries, including Palestine, Italy, Brazil, Israel, and Spain.
4. On the back cover of Alejandro Diago, *Hebe Bonafini Memoria y Esperanza* (Buenos Aires: Dialectica, 1988), my translation.
5. The Chilean group has comparable demonstrations called "*funas.*"
6. For my analysis of this communication strategy see Kaiser, *Escraches*.
7. For information on how the Mothers were treated by the authorities, both the military and the civilian ones during the process of democratic transition, see Kaiser, "The 'Madwomen' Memory Mothers."
8. Fisher, *Mothers*, 29.
9. Eventually, the Alianza, a coalition of several parties, won the 1999 elections with Fernando De la Rúa, from the Radical party, as presidential candidate.
10. She emerged into politics after being active at the Asamblea Permanente de los Derechos Humanos.
11. Although there were participants critical of their *escraches*, which they considered an aggressive communication strategy. See Kaiser, *Escraches*.
12. Throughout this section, I use the acronym HIJOS in two ways: to mean "the daughters and sons" or the members of the group (plural) and as the name of the organization (singular).

Afterword

1. The election of Kirchner was the end of a process initiated in December 2001 where major political turmoil and massive public demonstrations forced the resignation of President De la Rúa.
2. There are a variety of factors contributing to this political momentum, ranging from the passage of time to the pressure exercised by legal proceedings initiated in other countries.
3. Decree 1581/01 was President De la Rúa's contribution to block international justice and perpetuate impunity.
4. A July 2003 poll found that 85% of Argentineans approved Kirchner's policies about the military, including lifting restrictions for trials and punishment of *represores*, either in Argentina or foreign countries. See Maria Noailles, "Derogar la impunidad o juzgarlos en el exterior." *Página 12*, July 13, 2003.

Bibliography

Andersen, Martin E. *Dossier Secreto: Argentina's "Desaparecidos" and the Myth of the "Dirty War."* Boulder: Westview Press, 1993.

Anderson, Benedict. *Imagined Communities: Reflections on the Origin and Spread of Nationalism*. New York: Verso, 1983.

Anguita Eduardo, and Martín Caparrós. *La Voluntad: Una historia de la militancia revolucionaria en la Argentina, Vols. I, II, III*. Buenos Aires: Grupo Editorial Norma, 1997 and 1998.

Arditti, Rita. *Searching for Life*. Berkeley: University of California Press, 1999.

Arendt, Hannah. "From Eichman in Jerusalem: A Report on the Banality of Evil." In *Violence in War and Peace*, edited by Nancy Scheper-Hughes and Philippe Bourgois. Oxford, UK: Blackwell, 2004.

Bal, Mieke, Jonathan Crewe, and Leo Spitzter, eds. *Acts of Memory: Cultural Recall in the Present*. Hanover: University Press of New England, 1999.

Baumister, Roy F., and Stephen Hastings. "Distortions of Collective Memory: How Groups Flatter and Deceive Themselves." In *Collective Memory of Political Events: Social Psychological Perspectives*, edited by James W. Pennebaker, Darío Páez, and Bernard Rimé. New Jersey: Lawrence Erlbaum Associates, 1997.

Boraine, Alex. "Truth and Reconciliation in South Africa: The Third Way." In *Truth v. Justice: The Morality of Truth Commissions*, edited by Robert I. Rotberg and Dennis Thompson. Princeton: Princeton University Press, 2000.

Bourdieu, Pierre. "Comprendre." In *La Misère du Monde*, edited by Pierre Bourdieu. Paris: Seuil, 1993.

Bratu Hansen, Miriam. "*Schindler's List* Is Not *Shoah:* The Second Commandment, Popular Modernism, and Public Memory." In *The Historical Film: History and Memory in Media*, edited by Marcia Landy. New Brunswick, NJ: Rutgers University Press, 2000.

Burke, Peter. "History as Social Memory." In *Memory, History, Culture and the Mind*, edited by Thomas E. Butler. Oxford, UK: Basil Blackwell, 1989.

Butler, Thomas. "Memory: A Mixed Blessing." In *Memory, History, Culture and the Mind*, edited by Thomas E. Butler. Oxford, UK: Basil Blackwell, 1989.

Calveiro, Pilar. *Poder y Desaparición: Los Campos de Concentración en la Argentina*. Buenos Aires: Colihue, 1998.

Carnes, Mark C., ed. *Past Imperfect: History According to the Movies*. New York: Henry Holt and Company, 1995.

Ciancaglini, Sergio, and Martín Granowsky. *Nada más que la verdad*. Buenos Aires: Planeta, 1995.

Cid Varela, Eduardo, ed. *Los Sofistas y la Prensa Canalla*. Córdoba: El Cid Editor, 1984.

——— *La Imbecilización de la Mujer*. Córdoba: El Cid Editor, 1984.

Cohen, Ronald L. "Silencing Objections: Social Constructions of Indifference." *Journal of Human Rights* 1:2 (June 2002): 187–206.

Comway, Martin. *Flashbulb Memories*. Hove, UK: Lawerence Erlbaum, 1995.

Connerton, Paul. *How Societies Remember*. New York: Cambridge University Press, 1989.

Corradi, Juan, Patricia Weiss Fagen, and Manuel Antonio Garretón, eds. *Fear at the Edge: State Terror and Resistance in Latin America*. Berkeley, CA: University of California Press, 1992.

D'Andrea Mohr, José Luis. *El Escuadrón Perdido*. Buenos Aires: Planeta, 1998.

Dabenigno, Valeria, et al. "Entre el recuerdo y el olvido: interpretaciones de una historia compartida." Paper presented at the Latin American Studies Association Conference, Chicago, September 24–26, 1998.

Dayan, Daniel and Elihu Katz. "Defining Media Events: High Holidays of Mass Communication." In *Television: The Critical View*, edited by Horace Newcomb. New York: Oxford University Press, 1994, 5th edition.

Diago, Alejandro. *Hebe Bonafini Memoria y Esperanza*. Buenos Aires: Dialectica, 1988.

Downing, John. *Radical Media: Rebellious Communication and Social Movements*. Thousand Oaks, CA: Sage Publications, 2001.

Duhalde, Eduardo Luis. *El Estado Terrorista Argentino*. Buenos Aires: El Caballito, 1983.

Dussel, Inés, Silvia Finocchio, and Silvia Gojman. *Haciendo Memoria en el País del Nunca Más*. Buenos Aires: Eudeba, 1997.

Feitlowitz, Marguerite. *A Lexicon of Terror*. New York: Oxford University Press, 1998.

———. "The House of the Blind, Spatial Discourse in Argentina's *Dirty War*." Paper presented at the Latin American Studies Association Conference, Chicago, September 24–26, 1998.

Feld, Claudia. "El relato del horror en la televisión: los represores tienen la palabra." In *La Cultura en la Argentina de fin de siglo, ensayos sobre la dimensión cultural*, edited by Mario Margulis and Marcelo Urresti. Buenos Aires: UBA, 1997.

———. *Del estrado a la pantalla: Las imágenes del juicio a los ex comandantes en Argentina*. Madrid: Siglo Veintiuno de España, 2002.

Fentress, James and Chris Wickham. *Social Memory*. Oxford: Blackwell, 1992.

Ferro, Marc and Jean Planchais. *Les Médias et L'histoire; Le poids du passé dans le chaos de l'actualité*. Paris: CFPJ, 1997.

Fisher, Jo. *Mothers of the Disappeared*. Boston: South End Press, 1989.

Ford, Anibal and Carolina Vinelli. "El marketing de lo cruel," *Clarín*, July 19, 1998, pp. 14–15.

Frisch, Michael. *A Shared Authority: Essays on the Craft and Meaning of Oral and Public History*. Albany: State University of New York Press, 1990.

Fruhling, Hugo. "Resistance to Fear in Chile: The Experience of the Vicaría de las Solidaridad." In *Fear at the Edge: State Terror and Resistance in Latin America*, edited by Juan Corradi, Patricia Weiss Fagen, and Manuel Antonio Garretón. Berkeley: University of California Press, 1992.

García, Alicia. *La Doctrina de Seguridad Nacional*. Buenos Aires: Centro Editor de America Latina, 1991.

García, Prudencio. *El Drama de la Autonomía Militar*. Madrid: Alianza Editorial, 1995.

García Márquez, Gabriel. *Vivir Para Contarla*. Bogotá: Editorial Norma, 2002.

Garretón, Manuel Antonio. "Fear in Military Regimes." In *Fear at the Edge: State Terror and Resistance in Latin America*, edited by Juan Corradi, Patricia Weiss Fagen, and Manuel Antonio Garretón. Berkeley: University of California Press, 1992.

Gelman, Juan. "Epidemias," *Página 12*, November 11, 1999.

——— "Del Silencio," *Página 12*, August 13, 1998, Contratapa.

Gelman, Juan and Mara La Madrid. *Ni el Flaco Perdón de Dios: Hijos de Desaparecidos*. Buenos Aires: Planeta, 1997.

Gibb, Tom. "Missing Children Haunt El Salvador," *Guardian Weekly*, October 19–25, 2000.

Gill, Lesley. *School of the Americas: Military Training and Political Violence*. Durham, NC: Duke, 2004.

Ginzberg, Victoria. "La soberanía de matar y robar bebés," *Página 12*, November 4, 1999.

González Bombal, Inés and Oscar Landi. "Los Derechos en la Cultura Política." In *Juicio, Castigos y Memorias: Derechos Humanos y Justicia en la Política Argentina*, edited by Carlos Acuña. Buenos Aires: Nueva Visión, 1995.

Goñi, Uki. *Judas: la verdadera historia de Alfredo Astiz el infiltrado*. Buenos Aires: Sudamericana, 1996.

——— *The Real Odessa: Smuggling the Nazis to Peron's Argentina*. New York: Granta, 2002.

Habermas, Jurgen, and Adam Michnik. "Overcoming the Past." *New Left Review* 203 (Jan./Feb. 1994): 3–16.

Halbwachs, Maurice. *The Collective Memory*. New York: Harper & Row, 1980.

——— *On Collective Memory*, translated and edited by Lewis A. Coser. Chicago: The University of Chicago Press, 1992.

Hall, Stuart. "Encoding/Decoding." In *Media and Cultural Studies: KeyWorks*, edited by Gigi Durham and Douglas Kellner. Malden, MA: Blackwell, 2000.

Hayner, Priscilla. *Unspeakable Truths*. New York: Routledge, 2000.

Herman, Judith. "Trauma and Recovery: The Aftermath of Violence—From Domestic Abuse to Political Terror." In *Violence in War and Peace*, edited by Nancy Scheper-Hughes and Philippe Bourgois. Oxford, UK: Blackwell, 2004.

Hirsch, Marianne. "Projected Memory: Holocaust Photographs in Personal and Public Fantasy." In *Acts of Memory: Cultural Recall in the Present*, edited by Mieke Bal, Jonathan Crewe, and Leo Spitzer. Hanover: University Press of New England, 1999.

Hobsbawm, Eric and Terence Ranger, eds. *The Invention of Tradition*. New York: Cambridge University Press, 1983.

Huyssen, Andreas. *Twilight Memories: Marking Time in a Culture of Amnesia*. New York: Routledge, 1995.

Igartúa, Juanjo and Darío Páez. "Art and Remembering Traumatic Collective Events: The Case of the Spanish Civil War." In *Collective Memory of Political Events: Social Psychological Perspectives*, edited by James W. Pennebaker, Darío Páez, and Bernard Rimé. New Jersey: Lawrence Erlbaum Associates, 1997.

Iñiguez, Lupicinio, Jose Valencia, and Félix Vázquez. "The Construction of Remembering and Forgetfulness: Memories and Histories of the Spanish Civil War." In *Collective Memory of Political Events: Social Psychological Perspectives*, edited by James W. Pennebaker, Darío Páez, and Bernard Rimé. New Jersey: Lawrence Erlbaum Associates, 1997.

Jauretche, Ernesto. *Violencia y Política en los 70: No dejés que te la cuenten*. Buenos Aires: Colihue, 1997.

Jing, Jun. *The Temple of Memories: History, Power, and Morality in a Chinese Village*. Stanford, CA: Stanford University Press, 1996.

Kaiser, Susana. "The 'Madwomen' Memory Mothers of the Plaza de Mayo; A Case of Counter-hegemonic Communications Developed by a Unique Group: Mothers of Disappeared People from Argentina." MA thesis, Hunter College of the City University of New York, 1993.

———— "*De Eso No Se Habla* (We Don't Talk About That): Transmission of Silences and Fragmented [Hi]stories in Young Argentineans' Memories of Terror." Ph.D. diss., University of Texas at Austin, 2000.

———— "*Escraches*: Demonstrations, Communication and Political Memory in Post-Dictatorial Argentina." *Media, Culture and Society* 24:4 (2002): 499–516.

———— "Singing, Dancing, and Remembering: The Links Between Music and Memory," Paper presented at the International Communication Association Conference, San Diego, May 23–26, 2003.

Kollman, Raúl. "Los querían blanquitos y recién nacidos," *Página 12* online http://www.pagina12.com.ar/2000/00-01/00-01-09/pag03.htm (Accessed February 2, 2004).

Kordon, Diana and Lucía Edelman, eds. *Psychological Effects of Political Repression*. Buenos Aires: Sudamericana/Planeta, 1988.

Landy, Marcia, ed. *The Historical Film: History and Memory in Media*. New Brunswick, NJ: Rutgers University Press, 2000.

Levi, Primo. "The Gray Zone." In *Violence in War and Peace*, edited by Nancy Scheper-Hughes and Philippe Bourgois. Oxford, UK: Blackwell, 2004.

Leydesdorff, Selma. "A Shattered Silence." In *Memory and Totalitarianism*, edited by Luisa Passerini. New York: Oxford University Press, 1992.

Loshitsky, Yosefa. "Fantastic Realism: *Schindler's List* as Docudrama." In *Why Docudrama? Fact Fiction on Film and TV*, edited by Alan Rosenthal. Carbondale: Southern Illinois University Press, 1999.

Maggi, José. "El jefe de policía anunció que encontró miles de fojas." *Página 12*, November 14, 1999.

Malamud-Goti, Jaime. *Game Without End: State Terror and the Politics of Justice*. Norman: University of Oklahoma Press, 1996.

Mamdani, Mahmood. "From Conquest to Consent as the Basis of State Formation: Reflections on Rwanda," *New Left Review* 216 (March/April 1996): 3–36.

Marques, José, Darío Páez, and Alexandra Serra. "Social Sharing, Emotional Climate and the Transgenerational Transmission of Memories: the Portuguese Colonial War." In *Collective Memory of Political Events: Social Psychological Perspectives*, edited by James W. Pennebaker, Darío Páez, and Bernard Rimé. New Jersey: Lawrence Erlbaum Associates, 1997.

Martin, Afredo. *Les Meres "folles" de la Place de Mai*. Paris: Renaudot, 1989.

Martín-Baró, Ignacio. *Writings for a Liberation Psychology*, edited by Adrianne Aron and Shawn Corne. Cambridge, MA: Harvard University Press, 1994.

Meyer, Adriana. "Apropiación indebida de los hijos de desaparecidos," *Página 12*, October 28, 1998.

Meyers, Oren and Eyal Zandberg. "The Sound-Track of Memory: *Ashes and Dust* and the Commemoration of the Holocaust in Israeli Popular Culture." *Media, Culture and Society* 24:3 (2002): 389–408.

Mignone, Emilio. *Witness to the Truth: The Complicity of Church and Dictatorship in Argentina, 1976–1983*. New York: Orbis, 1988.

Noailles, Maria. "Derogar la impunidad o juzgarlos en el exterior," *Página 12*, July 13, 2003.

Nora, Pierre. "Between Memory and History: *Les Lieux de Mémoire*." *Representations* 26 (Spring 1989): 7–24.

———— "Generations," in *Realms of Memory: Rethinking the French Past Vol. I*. Edited by Pierre Nora. New York: Columbia University Press, 1996.

———— "Preface," in *Realms of Memory: Rethinking the French Past Vol. I.* Edited by Pierre Nora. New York: Columbia University Press, 1996.

Nunca Más. Informe de la Comisión Nacional Sobre la Desaparición de Personas. Buenos Aires: EUDEBA, 1984.

Nunca Más: The Report of the Argentine National Commission on the Disappeared People. New York: Farrar, Strauss, and Giroux, 1986.

Páez, Darío, Nekan Besabe, and José Luis Gonzalez. "Social Processes and Collective Memory: A Cross-Cultural Approach to Remembering Political Events." In *Collective Memory of Political Events: Social Psychological Perspectives*, edited by James W. Pennebaker, Darío Páez, and Bernard Rimé. New Jersey: Lawrence Erlbaum Associates, 1997.

Paoletti, Alipio. *Como los Nazis, como en Vietnam.* Buenos Aires: Editorial Contrapunto, 1987.

Passerini, Luisa. "Introduction." In *Memory and Totalitarianism*, edited by Luisa Passerini. New York: Oxford University Press, 1992.

———— *Autobiography of a Generation.* Hanover: Wesleyan University Press, 1996.

———— "Work Ideology and Consensus under Italian Fascism." In *The Oral History Reader*, edited by Robert Perks and Alistair Thomson. New York: Routledge, 1998.

———— "Between Silence and Oblivion." Lecture at the Regional Oral History Office, University of California, Berkeley, November 7, 2001.

Payne, Leigh. "The Politics of Memory, the Politics of Silence: Confessions of Torturers." Paper presented at the Latin American Studies Association Conference, Chicago, September 24–26, 1998.

Pavlovsky, Eduardo. "Sobre la Complicidad Civil con el Terrorismo de Estado," *Página 12*, June 24, 1999.

Pennebaker, James, Darío Páez, and Bernard Rimé, eds. *Collective Memory of Political Events: Social Psychological Perspectives.* New Jersey: Lawrence Erlbaum Associates, 1997.

Pennebaker, James and Becky Banasik. "On the Creation and Maintenance of Collective Memories: History as Social Psychology." In *Collective Memory of Political Events: Social Psychological Perspectives*, edited by James W. Pennebaker, Darío Páez, and Bernard Rimé. New Jersey: Lawrence Erlbaum Associates, 1997.

Perelli, Carina. "Setting Accounts with Blood Memory: The Case of Argentina." *Social Research* 59:2 (Summer 1992).

Pigna, Felipe. *Los mitos de la historia argentina.* Buenos Aires: Grupo Editorial Norma, 2004.

Pino-Ojeda, Walescka. "A Detour to the Past: Memory and Mourning in Chilean Post-Authoritarian Rock." In *Rockin' Las Américas*, edited by Deborah Pacini Hernandez, Héctor Fernández L'Hoeste, and Eric Zolov. Pittsburgh: University of Pittsburgh Press, 2004.

Popular Memory Group. "Popular Memory: Theory, Politics, Method." In *Making Histories: Studies in History-Writing and Politics*, edited by Richard Johnson, Gregor McLennan, Bill Schwartz, and David Sutton. London: Hutchinson, 1982.

Portelli, Alessandro. "Las peculiaridades de la historia oral." In *Historia oral e historias de vida*. Cuaderno de Ciencias Sociales No. 18, Costa Rica: FLACSO, 1988.

———— *The Death of Luigi Trastulli and Other Stories.* Albany, NY: State University of New York Press, 1991.

———— *The Order Has Been Carried Out.* New York: Palgrave Macmillan, 2003.

Prince, Stephen, ed. *Screening Violence.* New Brunswick, NJ: Routledge, 2000.

Ranalletti, Mario. "La construcción del relato de la historia argentina en el cine, 1983–1989." *Film-Historia* IX.1 (1999): 3–15.

Rappaport, Joanne. *The Politics of Memory: Native Historical Interpretation in the Colombian Andes*. New York: Cambridge University Press, 1990.

Rial, Juan. "Makers and Guardians of Fear." In *Fear at the Edge: State Terror and Resistance in Latin America*, edited by Juan Corradi, Patricia Weiss Fagen, and Manuel Antonio Garretón. Berkeley: University of California Press, 1992.

Rosenberg, Tina. *Children of Caín: Violence and the Violent in Latin America*. New York: Morrow, 1991.

Rosenthal, Alan, ed. *Why Docudrama? Fact Fiction on Film and TV*. Carbondale: Southern Illinois University Press, 1999.

Salimovich, Sofía, Elizabeth Lira, and Eugenia Weinstein. "Victims of Fear: The Social Psychology of Repression." In *Fear at the Edge: State Terror and Resistance in Latin America*, edited by Juan Corradi, Patricia Weiss Fagen, and Manuel Antonio Garretón. Berkeley: University of California Press, 1992.

Senkman, Leonardo and Mario Szanjder. *El Legado del Autoritarismo: Derechos Humanos y Antisemitismo en la Argentina Contemporánea*. Buenos Aires: Grupo Editor Latinoamericano, 1995.

Seoane, María. *Todo o Nada*. Buenos Aires: Planeta, 1991.

——— *Argentina: El siglo del progreso y la oscuridad (1900–2003)*. Buenos Aires: Crítica, 2004.

Seoane, Maria and Héctor Ruiz Nuñez. *La Noche de los Lápices*. Buenos Aires: Editorial Contrapunto, 1986.

Shumway, Nicolas. *The Invention of Argentina*. Berkeley: University of California Press, 1991.

Sidícaro, Ricardo and Emilio Tenti Fanfani, eds. *La Argentina de los jóvenes: entre la indiferencia y la indignación*. Buenos Aires: Losada, 1998.

Sobchack, Vivian C. "The Violent Dance: A Personal Memoir of Death in the Movies." In *Screening Violence*, edited by Stephen Prince. New Brunswick, NJ: Routledge, 2000.

Stevens, Donald D., ed. *Based on a True Story: Latin American History at the Movies*. Wilmington: Scholarly Resources, 1997.

Sturken, Marita. *Tangled Memories: The Vietnam War, the AIDS Epidemic, and the Politics of Remembering*. Berkeley: University of California Press, 1997.

Tabachnik, Silvia. "Primeras Transcripciones del Archivo. Los medios y la construcción narrativa del pasado en la inmediata post-dictadura." Paper presented at the Latin American Studies Association Conference, Miami, March 16–18, 2000.

Taussig, Michael. "Culture of Terror—Space of Death: Roger Casement's Putumayo Report and the Explanation of Torture." In *Violence in War and Peace*, edited by Nancy Scheper-Hughes and Philippe Bourgois, Oxford, UK: Blackwell, 2004.

Timerman, Jacobo. *Prisoner without a Name, Cell without a Number*. New York: Random House, 1981.

Todorov, Tzvetan. *Les Abus de la Mémoire*. Paris: Arléa, 1995.

Verbitsky, Horacio. *Rodolfo Walsh y la Prensa Clandestina*. Buenos Aires: Ediciones de la Urraca, 1985.

——— *La Posguerra Sucia*. Buenos Aires: Legasa, 1985.

——— *Civiles y Militares: Memoria Secreta de la Transición*. Buenos Aires: Editorial Contrapunto, 1987.

——— "Foreword." In *Las Cifras de la Guerra Sucia*. Buenos Aires: Asamblea Permanente por Los Derechos Humanos, 1988.

——— "Militares, Civiles y el Miedo." In *Ni el Flaco Perdón de Dios: Hijos de Desaparecidos*, edited by Juan Gelman and Mara La Madrid. Buenos Aires: Planeta, 1997.

————— *The Flight: Confessions of an Argentine Dirty Warrior*. New York: The New Press, 1996.

Vila, Pablo. "Rock nacional, crónicas de la resistencia juvenil." In *Los Nuevos Movimientos Sociales: Mujeres, Rock Nacional*, edited by Elizabeth Jelin. Buenos Aires: Centro Editor de America Latina, 1985.

Wardi, Dina. *Memorial Candles: Children of the Holocaust*. New York: Routledge, 1992.

Zelizer, Barbie. *Remembering to Forget: Holocaust Memory Through the Camera's Eye*. Chicago: University of Chicago Press, 1998.

Zerubavel, Eviatar. "Social Memories: Steps to a Sociology of the Past." *Qualitative Sociology* 19:3 (Fall 1996).

Index